D0065450

Other Books by Daniel R. White

The Official Lawyer's Handbook
White's Law Dictionary
What Lawyers Do...

TRIALS & TRIBULATIONS

Appealing Legal Humor

A Collection Edited By
DANIEL R. WHITE

CATBIRD PRESS

No part of this book may be used or reproduced in any manner
without written permission, except in the context of reviews.
CATBIRD PRESS, 44 North Sixth Avenue, Highland Park, NJ
08904 201-572-0816. Our books are distributed to the trade by
Independent Publishers Group.

Special thanks to Pat Lesnefsky for typing the manuscript
of this book into a computer.

Library of Congress Cataloging in Publication Data
Trials and tribulations : appealing legal humor : a collection /
  edited by Daniel R. White.
   p.   cm.
   Bibliography: p.
   Includes index.
   ISBN 0-945774-05-2 : $19.95
   1. Lawyers—Humor. 2. Practice of law—Humor. 3. Lawyers-
-Caricatures and cartoons. I. White, D. Robert (Daniel Robert)
PN6231.L4T75 1989
818'.540208035234—dc20   89-15865
                                                         CIP

To Taylor and Alexander

CONTENTS

INTRODUCTION

I T IS NOT THE WAY OF LAWYERS to write from scratch. They'll write *for* scratch—or bread, dough, jack, flaps, clams, whipout, long green, simoleons, or what some have been known to call "cash." For that matter, if you tickle their pecuniary glands (gloves are probably a good idea), they'll not only write, but draft, draw, engrave, inscribe, scribble, doodle, underline, highlight, street light, Miller Lite, and lighten up. Many will even transliterate and redact, so long as everyone in the room is a consenting adult.

But that's another issue.

Call it laziness, call it respect for precedent, call it long distance (collect)—the invariable first step of a lawyer undertaking to produce anything in writing is to track down everything that has ever been written along similar lines ... and then rip it off.

Thus did I, true to my training and familial roots in the law, commence work on the present introduction by looking at, and in more than a few instances reading, the introduction to literally every other humor anthology I could find. My search for anthological precedent, constrained only by the limits of my physical and emotional stamina, carried me on a journey, Marco Polo-like, to the farthest reaches of my apartment.

It was a gripping odyssey—from the dust-streaked mounds of books on my night table, to the wobbly, dust-covered stacks against the back wall of my closet (held up by the ironing board), to the dust-filled nooks and crannies of my study, to the strangely dusty but otherwise suitable-for-display hardbacks on the end tables in my living room. I even checked—call me compulsive, but thoroughness is the hallmark of legal excellence—a box of books in my car trunk that I had been meaning to drop off at the Salvation Army, many of them inexplicably caked with dust.

My search turned up four anthologies, the introductions to virtually all of which I read in full, for the most part. The exertion was not without the anticipated rewards.

I learned that the introduction to a humor anthology has, by tradition, two functions. The first is to justify the editor's selections. This justification typically consists of a spiffed-up version of "It's my list, and if you don't like it, come up with your own. Thppft."

The second function is to explain humor, or at least cut into it and peek in, as if checking to see if it's done—and then, after concluding that humor doesn't admit of explanation, and only marginally tolerates being tested for redness on the inside, to say something about just who you are, anyway, to be compiling a humor anthology. I mean, who appointed you the expert on funny? Comments in fulfillment of this function should not only answer this question, but also demonstrate such cleverness as to leave no doubt that it is only because of your extraordinary and winning modesty that the book contains as little of your own material as it does—not one syllable more than you were absolutely compelled to include for the sake of literary posterity.

What follows is an attempt to fulfill these two functions.

*   *   *

The method by which I decided what to include in this collection is as simple as it is scientific, although history makes clear how difficult it is for the originator of any new concept to escape charges of obscurantism and complexity for complexity's sake. In this respect, among others, the parallels between my anthological method and Einstein's theory of relativity are hard to overlook.

I call it the gather-everything-and-then-weed-out-the-weak-stuff approach—derived largely from the Darwinian methods employed by New York law firms toward their associates. As utilized in preparing the present volume, it consisted of assembling everything I could find that (a) pertained to the law and (b) contained a modicum of humor—and then, because the pile was, in publishing jargon, "too big," weeding out the weak stuff. As complex as this may seem at first blush, I submit that it will eventually become clear to anyone whose ancestors were not extremely closely related.

By what standard did I decide which items constituted the "weak stuff"? I applied Justice Potter Stewart's rigorous "I know it when I see it" test, originally propounded in the pornography context but clearly capable—such was Stewart's genius—of broader application.

No doubt in applying this test I was guilty to some extent of projecting my personal tastes onto the world at large. I made a good-faith effort to avoid doing so, however, and not (only) out of concern for sales. There was also a self-protection motive.

Everyone's sense of humor comes equipped with more than a

few wrinkles or quirks, enabling one—happily, for the most part—to find humor in places where few others find it. But some of these places are very private, perhaps even on one's own body, and thus inappropriate for public viewing, at least when small children are likely to be awake and watching. In other words, shamelessly indulging my own taste in humor would have left me shamefully overexposed—to the detriment, possibly the disgust, of everyone concerned.

*   *   *

As for the second purpose of an introduction, shedding light on the nature of humor, let us start with E. B. White's oft-quoted if inappropriate-for-the-dinner-table simile: "Humor can be dissected, as a frog can, but the thing dies in the process and the innards are discouraging to any but the pure scientific mind." Elsewhere, presumably recognizing that innards can be not only discouraging but unilluminating, E. B. opines, "Essentially, [humor] is a complete mystery."

No doubt this seems particularly true in the context of the present book, law and humor reputedly having only a passing acquaintance with one another, if, indeed, they have ever been properly introduced at all. Psychologists employing word-association tests have established that "humor" is among the very last words in the English language to spring to the average primate's mind upon hearing the word "lawyer." (Other contenders for the last-place slot include "sexual prowess" and "omelet.")

Why this perception of law as incompatible with humor? Why the saying, "There are no funny lawyers, only funny people who made career mistakes"?

Ernest Hemingway wrote, "They say the seeds of what we will do are in all of us, but it always seemed to me that in those who make jokes in life the seeds are covered with better soil and a higher grade of manure." This passage seems relevant here, not only because it constitutes an authoritative pronouncement on the value of humor in all areas of human endeavor, but also because of the frequency with which references to "manure" and its variants creep into conversations about lawyers. Assuming people are only minimally attracted to manure—and I'm going out on a limb here with respect to farmers and politicians—one is forced to conclude that people are only minimally attracted to lawyers.

Again, why? Do lawyers make too few jokes in life? Do they lack the capacity for amiable jest about themselves or their work?

Nothing could be further from the truth. Or virtually nothing. Not a lot of things, anyway. Because lawyers *wallow* in humor—up to their armpits.

Not only do they stimulate jokes in others—with their *de rigeur* pinstripes, their leather lunchboxes ("briefcases"), the hair coming out of their ears—but they love *telling* jokes—on clients, fellow lawyers, poor people. And as for *appreciating* jokes, well, just wander down to the nearest courthouse and watch them roar and howl at the barest hint of humor from a judge. (Hence, judges' perception of themselves as world-class comedians, and their well-known propensity to torture their friends, families, yard workers, and dogs with the japes and musings with which they've caused such seeming hilarity in court).

Words are lawyers' stock-in-trade—which, to be sure, means they suffer from an excess of inventory, but it also means that they are endowed with one of the essential tools of humor. Most lawyers also come equipped with an acute sense of the absurd—a natural response to being paid loads of lucre right out of law school for proofreading documents. These factors combine to produce a potentially limitless capacity for levity.

*

This leaves unresolved—indeed, it raises all the more compellingly—the question of why lawyers are so commonly thought of as humorless. Do people not *get* lawyers' jokes? Certainly they understand precious little that lawyers say or write when trying to be straight. In this regard, one can hardly be faulted for speculating on whether lawyers as a group suffer from what Hemingway called "the slight distortion of vision that unrelieved turgidness presents." To persons in "that portentous state," said Papa, "all objects look different ... slightly larger, more mysterious, and vaguely blurred."

Perhaps—a simpler explanation—people in general are humorless. And lawyers having become so numerous in recent years, they're being confused with people.

My own view is that the answer lies elsewhere.

Assume for a moment that you're a non-lawyer—inert, uncomprehending, turnip-like. (If you really are a non-lawyer, assume anything you want—it doesn't matter.) Now, consider the kinds of circumstances that might lead you to set up an appointment with a lawyer. It's time for your periodic check-up? We're not talking about your gynecologist here, or your car mechanic—who, by the way, should be two different people. Invariably something has happened—and not the kind of something any normal person wishes for when blowing out the candles on a birthday cake. More often it's a marital collapse, or a car wreck, or a business deal gone sour (that new stud bull you paid so much for has turned out to be a little light in his loafers). Such events do not put the typical person in the mood for mirth.

True, most encounters with doctors and car mechanics are not exactly happy occasions either. But at least a doctor who takes out your appendix (or bibliography) leaves you a scar to show for your trouble, and the mechanic who charges you $400 for letting your car sit in his parking lot leaves cigarette butts in your ashtray and grease on your steering wheel to remember him by.

What does a layperson get from his lawyer?

A bill.

This isn't to say lawyers are necessarily to blame. *They* can't help it if nobody ever stops by their offices just to chat, reminisce about young love, and swap lies about fish that got away. Still, though it may not be their fault, it is their problem.

Hence this book, which I hereby submit to the court of public opinion as tangible proof of the existence of "legal humor," a distinct, identifiable, *sizeable* body of funny stuff written about—and sometimes *by*, as well as about—lawyers.

To be sure, the need for such proof should not be overstated. Generations of American law students bred on the wit as well as wisdom of William "Mr. Torts" Prosser cannot doubt that the law was for many years blessed with its own Mark Twain. In Britain, readers of the magazine *Punch* learned from the "Case of the Negotiable Cow," as well as countless other contributions by the legendary A. P. Herbert to England's "Uncommon Law," that those called to the bar do not necessarily hold it in reverence and awe.

Still, within the law and without, skeptics abound. It is to these in particular that I would commend the writings of which the present collection necessarily constitutes but a sampling. Read them, smile at them, laugh out loud at them—and appreciate the heart and humanity of the law.

D.R.W.

"Not America. Think of the lawsuits."

THE LAW

William L. Prosser
MY PHILOSOPHY OF LAW*

Myself, when young, did eagerly frequent
Doctor and Saint, and heard great argument
About it and about, but evermore
Came out by the same door where in I went.
—*The Rubaiyat*

WHEN I FIRST HEARD that this book was going to be published, I expected of course to be invited to do a piece for it about my philosophy of law. I knew that there must be thousands of people, myself included, who would be anxious to know what my philosophy of law is, and I stood ready to yield to popular demand. I must confess that I was distinctly miffed, in a nice kind of way, when it turned out that I wasn't asked. I had all the feelings of the boy who brought his harp to the party and wasn't asked to play. I even considered writing a polite sort of letter about it to the Julius Rosenthal Foundation, which was getting out the book. Now that I see the list of those who were invited to contribute, of course I can understand it. The list includes Joseph Walter Bingham, Morris R. Cohen, Walter Wheeler Cook, John Dewey, John Dickinson, Lon L. Fuller, Leon Green, Walter B. Kennedy, Albert Kocourek, Karl N. Llewellyn, Underhill Moore, Edwin W. Patterson, Roscoe Pound, Thomas Reed Powell, Max Radin, and John H. Wigmore. When it comes to these gentlemen, I can see that I am just not in their class. Now that I come to think of it, I can't recall that any one ever came to me and asked me that direct question, "What is your philosophy of law?" I suppose that that must happen to these gentlemen all the time. I imagine that some of them are so pestered with inquiries that they haven't time to eat lunch. It must have been a positive relief to

---

* This piece, a review of *My Philosophy of Law—Credos of Sixteen American Scholars*, Boston Law Book Co., was reprinted from 27 *Cornell Law Quarterly* 292-95 (1942). © Copyright 1942 by Cornell University. All rights reserved. By permission of Cornell Law Review and Fred B. Rothman & Co.

them to have the opportunity to put it all down in print where people can go and read it. And besides that, there are even a couple of deans on that list. Obviously I don't belong there at all.

Now that I have been invited to review the book, I am of course very glad of the chance. For one thing, I have been given a free copy, which is the way that law reviews get books reviewed. It is a very nice looking book indeed, all bound in some kind of brown leather-looking stuff, with cream-tinted pages and the kind of rough edges that really high-class publishers put in their really high-class books to show that they are really high-class. The type is very nice and legible, and the whole thing just radiates elegance. There are even photographs of all the sixteen contributors, each of them occupying a full page in glossy print, with a blank page on the back; and one or two of them are certainly very handsome and distinguished-looking men. The book is going to improve greatly the general tone of my bookshelves, which are all cluttered up with broken-backed copies of Ames and Smith's *Cases on Torts* and Mr. Roughead's *Enjoyment of Murder*, and things like that. I have been badly in need of something pretty to point out to visitors, and this book is just the thing. And besides that, the invitation to review it gives me the opportunity to satisfy popular demand, and give the public what it has been clamoring for, my own philosophy of law. Book reviewers always write about their own ideas while they are reviewing the book. I know, because I have just published a book and had it reviewed.

Before starting this review, I read the book. I know that some reviewers don't believe in doing that, but in this case I thought it would be rather a decent thing to do, since the book was such an expensive one and I got it free. For my purposes, however, it turned out to be a mistake. These gentlemen have got me all mixed up, and now that I come to write about my philosophy of law, I don't know what it is.

It isn't as if I didn't know something about philosophy. Back in 1914, when I was a freshman at Harvard, I had a course in it under Professor William Ernest Hocking, who was supposed to know a great deal about it. I don't remember that course very well, the way I remember the formula for nitroglycerine and the date of the Congress of Vienna and a lot of other useful things that I learned in college. As I recall it, I was pretty well mixed up even then. The philosophy people all used a lot of words like theological and categorical imperative, and they all disagreed with one another most hideously. I can see from this book that they still do. I remember that there was a fellow named Bishop Berkeley who had the idea that when a bell rang it would make no sound unless there was somebody around to hear it, and that if you feel a pain in your toe you have no assurance that there is any pain, or any toe. I suppose the equivalent of that for present purposes would be the current notion that the opinions of courts are optical illusions and don't mean what they say. Then there was a Frenchman named Descartes, who started out with the proposition that "I think, therefore I am," and proceeded to build up a philosophy from there. I remember that I was finally willing to concede his major premise, and even his initial conclusion, but that some of his ensuing syllogisms got a bit obscure. Then there was William James, who was the brother of Henry, *not* Jesse, and was driven to the conclusion that any philosophy that works well enough to let you get away with it is all right. I know some lawyers who seem to me to be proceeding on that theory. There were also a couple of men named Spencer and Hume, who spent their time proving that you can't prove anything, and ended by proving, to me at least, that you can't prove that you can't prove anything, because, you see, they proved it to me; and there were also Kant and Hegel, who, I recall, were extremely hard to read in German and harder still in English, so that I finally read them, for examination purposes, in the Encyclopedia Britannica, and got an A, which proved that the Encyclopedia was right, and thus cast further doubt upon Spencer and Hume.

Then by way of extra-curricular research, I discovered for myself a philosopher who wasn't in the course. He was a Persian named Omar, who made tents for a living, and took up philosophy as a sideline, probably because there wasn't enough money in it as a regular job. His philosophy was simple, and easy to comprehend and apply, which may have been one reason that it appealed to me. His theory was that you couldn't possibly figure it out anyway and it was a waste of time to try, and that the thing to do was to forget it and go out and get drunk. This seemed to me to be a very sound idea at the time—although of course I have attained years of discretion since.

The principal thing that I remember about philosophy, however, is the definition of a philosopher. I am sure that everyone knows it: a philosopher is a blind man in a dark cellar at midnight looking for a black cat that isn't there. He is distinguished from a theologian, in that the theologian finds the cat. He is also distinguished from a lawyer, who smuggles in a cat in his overcoat pocket, and emerges to produce it in triumph. This is a very helpful definition, which throws a flood of light on the whole situation.

Now each of these learned gentlemen in this beautiful book, except one, reports that he has found the cat. According to definition, that makes them all theologians, and not philosophers at all. I wouldn't want to go further and say that it makes them lawyers, because I have too much respect for that intellectual integrity of every one of them to suppose that he would smuggle anything in. Most of them, I realize, are in fact lawyers by profession, but I don't want to suggest that they are writing *as* lawyers at all; I think it is perfectly clear that they are writing in a purely non-professional capacity, and I should be the first to maintain it. Well, that leaves theology, which is something that I am not qualified to talk about because it was not in Professor Hocking's course. Even then, what perplexes me most is that they have found fifteen different cats. They are not even the same breed of cats. Some of them are not even black. I can recognize four or five Maltese, several Angoras, at least a couple of Siamese, an Alley or two, and one Manx, which is a cat without a tail. I am rather modest about my qualifications as a cat-fancier, so I will not attempt to specify, but I am sure that the reader will be able to pick them out for himself. Each learned author, of course, insists that his is the original and only genuine Cat. Without wanting to cast any reflections or aspersions or doubts upon anything or anybody, and in the best spirit in the world, all that I can say is that there seems to have been an astonishing amount of feline miscegenation going on in that coal cellar.

So, as I said, now I am all mixed up. I have always supposed that law was the product of a lot of pulling and hauling in society, a set of rather inadequate compromises brought about by very headstrong mules all going in different directions, and that the reason that it is in a mess is that society is in the same kind of mess. I had thought that our law was merely a facet of our civilization, about as multifarious, scrambled and altogether unsatisfactory as our civilization itself, and about as difficult to do anything effective about. The lawyers and the judges and even the legislators seemed to me to be a group of struggling opportunists trying to get along and doing their best in the face of specific jobs from day to day; and if they had no particular idea or plan or philosophy about it, and no very sensible pattern was discernible, it was not at all surprising, because look at the rest of the world. In particular, look at it just now. I never have seen any reason why law should make any more sense than the rest of life; and I think that the attitude of those of us who have anything to do with it should be that of the familiar sign in the western dance hall, "Don't shoot the piano player, he's doing the best he can."

None of the learned authors in this nice book says anything like that at all, with the single exception of Professor Thomas Reed Powell, who, if I understand him aright, says it and says it very well.

So when I come to write about my philosophy of law, I find that I haven't any, and that overwhelming popular demand will just have to be disappointed. About all that I can say, with great humility, is that I can't discover even one cat in that cellar, let alone fifteen. The whole thing has revived my old appreciation of the philosophy of Omar the Tentmaker, who may have had something like the right idea about a philosophy of law after all. There seems to me to be more than a vague hint of a similar point of view in the piece written by Professor Thomas Reed Powell.

> Oh, many a Cup of this forbidden Wine
> Must drown the memory of that insolence!

Are you with me, Tom?

Anonymous
THE DYING LAWYER

> Old Quillit, his race upon earth almost run,
> Thus sagely advised his too diffident son:
> "Like a true limb of law, would you live at your ease
> Ne'er boggle on any side, lad, to take fees;
> Keep clear of a noose, though you merit to swing,
> And be sure to sell justice for what it will bring."—
> "*Sell* justice!" Retorted his wondering heir,
> "A thing of such value, so precious, so rare,
> The cement of society, honour's best band—
> *Sell* justice?"—"Ay, *sell* it, and that out of hand,
> You extravagant rascal! If 'tis as you say,
> A thing of such price, would you give it away?"

A. P. Herbert
THE NEGOTIABLE COW*
Board of Inland Revenue *v.* Haddock; Rex *v.* Haddock

"WAS THE COW crossed?"

"No, your worship, it was an open cow."

These and similar passages provoked laughter at Bow Street to-day when the Negotiable Cow case was concluded.

Sir Joshua Hoot, K.C. (appearing for the Public Prosecutor): Sir Basil, these summonses, by leave of the Court, are being heard together, an unusual but convenient arrangement.

The defendant, Mr. Albert Haddock, has for many months, in spite of earnest endeavours on both sides, been unable to establish harmonious relations between himself and the Collector of Taxes. The Collector maintains that Mr. Haddock should make over a large part of his earnings to the Government. Mr. Haddock replies that the proportion demanded is excessive, in view of the inadequate services or consideration which he himself has received from that Government. After an exchange of endearing letters, telephone calls, and even cheques, the sum demanded was reduced to fifty-seven pounds; and about this sum the exchange of opinions continued.

On the 31st of May the Collector was diverted from his respectable labours by the apparition of a noisy crowd outside his windows. The crowd, Sir Basil, had been attracted by Mr. Haddock, who was leading a large white cow of malevolent aspect. On the back and sides of the cow were clearly stencilled in red ink the following words:

---

* The author of this piece, besides being a frequent contributor to *Punch*, was a long-time Member of Parliament for Oxford University. He was knighted in 1945. Reprinted from A. P. Herbert, *Uncommon Law*, 1935, by permission of A P Watt Limited on behalf of Crystal Hale and Jocelyn Herbert.

```
To the London and Literary Bank, Ltd.
     Pay the Collector of Taxes, who is
no gentleman, or Order, the sum of fifty-
seven pounds (and may he rot!).
     £57/0/0
```

                                    Albert Haddock

Mr. Haddock conducted the cow into the Collector's office, tendered it to the Collector in payment of income-tax and demanded a receipt.

Sir Basil String: Did the cow bear the statutory stamp?

Sir Joshua: Yes, a twopenny stamp was affixed to the dexter horn. The Collector declined to accept the cow, objecting that it would be difficult or even impossible to pay the cow into the bank. Mr. Haddock, throughout the interview, maintained the friendliest demeanour;* and he now remarked that the Collector could endorse the cow to any third party to whom he owed money, adding that there must be many persons in that position. The Collector then endeavoured to endorse the cheque—

Sir Basil String: Where?

Sir Joshua: On the back of the cheque, Sir Basil, that is to say, on the abdomen of the cow. The cow, however, appeared to resent endorsement and adopted a menacing posture. The Collector, abandoning the attempt, declined finally to take the cheque. Mr. Haddock led the cow away and was arrested in Trafalgar Square for causing an obstruction. He has also been summoned by the Board of Inland Revenue for nonpayment of income-tax.

Mr. Haddock, in the witness-box, said that he had tendered a cheque in payment of income-tax, and if the Commissioners did not like his cheque they could do the other thing. A cheque was only an order to a bank to pay money to the person in possession of the cheque or a person named on the cheque. There was nothing in statute or customary law to say that that order must be written on a piece of paper of specified dimensions. A cheque, it was well known, could be written on a piece of notepaper. He himself had drawn cheques on the backs of menus, on napkins, on handkerchiefs, on the labels of wine-bottles; all these cheques had been duly

---

* *'Mars est celare martem.'* (Selden, *Mare Clausum,* lib. I, c. 21)

honoured by his bank and passed through the Bankers' Clearing House. He could see no distinction in law between a cheque written on a napkin and a cheque written on a cow. The essence of each document was a written order to pay money, made in the customary form and in accordance with statutory requirements as to stamps, etc. A cheque was admittedly not legal tender in the sense that it could not lawfully be refused; but it was accepted by custom as a legitimate form of payment. There were funds in his bank sufficient to meet the cow; the Commissioners might not like the cow, but, the cow having been tendered, they were estopped from charging him with failure to pay. (Mr. Haddock here cited *Spowers* v. *The Strand Magazine, Lucas* v. *Finck*, and *Wadsworth* v. *The Metropolitan Water Board*.)

As to the action of the police, Mr. Haddock said it was a nice thing if in the heart of the commercial capital of the world a man could not convey a negotiable instrument down the street without being arrested. He had instituted proceedings against Constable Boot for false imprisonment.

Cross-examined as to motive, witness said that he had no cheque-forms available and, being anxious to meet his obligations promptly, had made use of the only material to hand. Later he admitted that there might have been present in his mind a desire to make the Collector of Taxes ridiculous. But why not? There was no law against deriding the income-tax.*

Sir Basil String (after the hearing of further evidence): This case has at least brought to the notice of the Court a citizen who is unusual both in his clarity of mind and integrity of behaviour. No thinking man can regard those parts of the Finance Acts which govern the income-tax with anything but contempt. There may be something to be said—not much—for taking from those who have inherited wealth a certain proportion of that wealth for the service of the State and the benefit of the poor and needy; and those who by their own ability, brains, industry, and exertion have earned money may reasonably be invited to surrender a small portion of it towards the maintenance of those public services by which they benefit, to wit, the Police, the Navy, the Army, the public sewers, and so forth. But to compel such individuals to bestow a large part

---

* Cf. Magna Carta: '*Jus ridendi nulli negabimus.*'

of their earnings upon other individuals, whether by way of pensions, unemployment grants, or education allowances, is manifestly barbarous and indefensible. Yet this is the law. The original and only official basis of taxation was that individual citizens, in return for their money, received collectively some services from the State, the defence of their property and persons, the care of their health or the education of their children. All that has now gone. Citizen A, who has earned money, is commanded simply to give it to Citizens B, C, and D, who have not, and by force of habit this has come to be regarded as a normal and proper proceeding, whatever the comparative industry or merits of Citizens A, B, C, and D. To be alive has become a virtue, and the mere capacity to inflate the lungs entitles Citizen B to a substantial share in the laborious earnings of Citizen A. The defendant, Mr. Haddock, repels and resents this doctrine, but, since it has received the sanction of Parliament, he dutifully complies with it. Hampered by practical difficulties, he took the first steps he could to discharge his legal obligations to the state. Paper was not available, so he employed instead a favourite

*"I enjoy practicing law ... but inside me
there's an accountant struggling to get out."*

Reprinted by permission of Leo Cullum.

cow. Now, there can be nothing obscene, offensive, or derogatory in the presentation of a cow by one man to another. Indeed, in certain parts of our Empire the cow is venerated as a sacred animal. Payment in kind is the oldest form of payment, and payment in kind more often than not meant payment in cattle. Indeed, during the Saxon period, Mr. Haddock tells us, cattle were described as *viva pecunia*, or 'living money', from their being received as payment on most occasions, at certain regulated prices.* So that, whether the cheque was valid or not, it was impossible to doubt the validity of the cow; and whatever the Collector's distrust of the former it was at least his duty to accept the latter and credit Mr. Haddock's account with its value. But, as Mr. Haddock protested in his able argument, an order to pay is an order to pay, whether it is made on the back of an envelope or on the back of a cow. The evidence of the bank is that Mr. Haddock's account was in funds. From every point of view, therefore, the Collector of Taxes did wrong, by custom if not by law, in refusing to take the proffered animal, and the summons issued at his instance will be discharged.

As for the second charge, I hold again that Constable Boot did wrong. It cannot be unlawful to conduct a cow through the London streets. The horse, at the present time a much less useful animal, constantly appears in those streets without protest, and the motor-car, more unnatural and unattractive still, is more numerous than either animal. Much less can the cow be regarded as an improper or unlawful companion when it is invested (as I have shown) with all the dignity of a bill of exchange.

If people choose to congregate in one place upon the apparition of Mr. Haddock with a promissory cow, then Constable Boot should arrest the people, not Mr. Haddock. Possibly, if Mr. Haddock had paraded Cockspur Street with a paper cheque for one million pounds made payable to bearer, the crowd would have been as great, but that is not to say that Mr. Haddock would have broken the law. In my judgment Mr. Haddock has behaved throughout in the manner of a perfect knight, citizen, and taxpayer. The charge brought by the Crown is dismissed; and I hope with all my heart that in his action against Constable Boot Mr. Haddock will be successful. What is the next case, please?

---

* Mandeville uses *Catele* for 'price'. (Wharton's Law Lexicon)

Gilbert Abbot à Becket
OF TRESPASS*

ANY UNLAWFUL ACT of one man, by which another is dam-
nified, is a trespass; and, indeed, the word has so large a sense
that every one is more or less addicted to trespassing. If A comes
and tells me a long story, he trespasses on my time; but if he will
not go away when my dinner is announced, he trespasses on my
patience, and I am compelled to get rid of him by ouster, or by
ringing the bell, which is equivalent to an action of ejectment.

But trespass, in the sense we are about to use it, is merely an
unlawful entry on another man's ground; as if A gets over my wall
into my yard, where my clothes may be hanging to dry, he breaks
my close, and perhaps also breaks my clothes-line.

A man is answerable for the trespass of his cattle; and I am
liable if my horse treads on my neighbour's corn, or my donkey
dances among his chickens; or if my bull rushes into my
neighbour's china shop, he need not take the bull by the horns, but
may proceed against me personally for the damage.

Entry on another's land, without the owner's leave, is not
always trespass; for any one may go uninvited into a public house;
but if he begins alleging that he

> Won't go home till morning,
> Till daylight does appear,

and seems inclined to act upon this anti-domestic sentiment, the
landlord may at once treat him as a trespasser. By the common law,
any one may go on another's grounds to hunt the fox and other
ravenous beasts of prey; but a bill-discounting bailiff is not a
ravenous beast of prey, within the meaning of the common law
privilege which allows the hunting of such animals.

As in an action for trespass, not wilful and malicious, the
plaintiff gets no costs unless he recovers more than forty shillings
damages, we do not recommend the article for general use to legal
customers.

---

* Reprinted from Gilbert Abbot à Becket, *The Comic Blackstone of Punch*, Collector
Publishing Co., 1897. Originally published in *Punch* in the 1840s.

Veronica Geng
SUPREME COURT ROUNDUP*

WASHINGTON, May 8—The Supreme Court took the following actions today:

First Amendment

In a landmark decision, the Court ruled unanimously in favor of a twelve-year-old plaintiff who sought damages on account of being denied the chance to audition for the Clint Eastwood role in the motion picture *Maddened Rustlers*. The Court's opinion, written by Chief Justice Happ, argued that exclusion of the little girl was "tactless." The case was not decided, as had been expected, on the ground of sex discrimination; rather, the Justices invoked the First Amendment's guarantee of freedom of expression. The Court thus affirmed for the first time the constitutional right to a screen test.

Search and Seizure

Overturning the "dog's breakfast" doctrine of search and seizure, the Court held unconstitutional the Drug Enforcement Administration's system of obtaining search warrants, under which a judge who issues a warrant receives a warm, wet kiss on the mouth, while a judge who refuses a warrant is reclassified as a Controlled Substance. Justice Happsberger, writing for the majority, said that such procedures "lean upon the delicately coiffed maiden of the Fourth Amendment with the great ugly brutish heavily muscled shoulder of procedural error," and cited Judge Cheerful Hand's famous dictum "I shall keep at it with these metaphors till I'm old and it's unbecoming."

Taxes

Without hearing arguments on the issue, the Court ordered the Internal Revenue Service to desist at once from collecting personal income taxes—a practice that Justice Hapenny defined in his

---

* Excerpt from "Supreme Court Roundup" from *Partners* by Veronica Geng. Copyright © 1984 Veronica Geng. Reprinted by permission of Harper & Row, Publishers, Inc.

opinion as "a crying shame" and "the product of diseased minds." He pointed out that the government could easily collect the same amount of money by manufacturing and selling wall plaques that say UNCLE SAM LOVES YOUR FIRST NAME HERE.

Controversy

In one of their occasional "Piggyback" decisions, the Justices resolved some of the long-standing issues that clog the Court calendar. They ruled that nurture is more influential than nature, that men make history, that Iago is driven by motiveless malignancy, that one isn't too many and a thousand is enough, that there is an earthly paradise, and that Don Bucknell's nephew Ed doesn't look anything like Richard Gere. Justice Hapworth dissented but was too polite to say so.

Moral Blight

Citing "want of attractiveness" as a reason, the Court declined, 7-2, to hear an appeal by the publisher of two so-called men's magazines, *Rude Practices* and *Men's Magazine*. In the majority opinion, Chief Justice Happ explained that appellant's arguments were "unprepossessing and—let's be frank about it—just incredibly disingenuous." Dissenting, Justices Happer and Happner said they wanted to pretend to hear the case and then "fix appellant's wagon" for "putting out such a typographically unappetizing publication." In a related decision, the Justices unanimously refused to hear a song written by a Kleagle of the Ku Klux Klan.

Criminal

By a 9-0 vote, the Court held unconstitutional a New York City statute that would have mandated criminal convictions for suspects who fail to take policemen aside and "read them their duties." The statute had required that suspects deliver these "Caliban warnings" to policemen in order to remind them of their power of life and death, their obligation to attend to personal hygiene, etc. The Court, in an opinion by Justice Happell, contended, "Who can doubt that this would be the first step toward compelling suspects to serve their arresting officers creamed chicken on toast points?"

UNITED STATES SUPREME COURT

© 1937 Al Hirschfeld. Drawing reproduced by special arrangEment with
Hirschfeld's exclusive representative, The Margo Feiden Galleries, NY.

Gibberish

The Court voted unanimously not to review a case in which a
court of appeals struck down a lower federal court's decision to
vacate an even lower court's refusal to uphold a ruling that it is not
unconstitutional to practice "reverse discrimination." Chief Justice
Happ, who wrote the opinion, said that the Court "is not, nor will
it consent to be, a body of foolosophers easily drawn into jive
baloney-shooting." The Modern Language Association filed a brief
of *amicus curiae* ("friendly curiosity").

Greed

Splitting 8-1, the Court upheld the constitutionality of a
federal program for the redistribution of wealth. Under the program, which is known as "horizontal divestiture," rich people are
asked to lie down, and poor people then divest them of their money.
Justice Happold, dissenting, said that the program would diminish
the impact of a standing court order requiring that income in excess
of $15,000 a year be bused across state lines to achieve bank-account
balances.

As is their custom, the Justices closed the session with an
informal musicale, playing a Corelli *gigg*. Justices Hapgood, Hapworth, Happner, and Happer performed on violin, Justice Happell
on bassoon, Justice Happsberger on harpsichord, Justice Happold

on oboe, Justice Hapenny on flute, and Chief Justice Happ on viola
d'amore.

Mark Twain
FOSTER'S CASE

> William Foster was sentenced to death for murder. His father,
> the murdered man's wife, members of the jury, and many
> prominent persons petitioned the governor of New York to
> commute the sentence of life imprisonment. The New York
> *Tribune* of March 6, 1873, carried a full page of letters concern-
> ing the case.

To the Editor of the "Tribune":
      I have read the Foster petitions in
Thursday's "Tribune." The lawyers'
opinions do not disturb me, because I
know that those same gentlemen could make
as able an argument in favor of Judas Iscariot, which is a great deal for me to
say, for I never can think of Judas Iscariot without losing my temper. To my
mind Judas Iscariot was nothing but a
low, mean, premature Congressman. The attitude of the jury does not unsettle a
body, I must admit; and it seems plain
that they would have modified their verdict to murder in the second degree if
the Judge's charge had permitted it. But
when I come to the petitions of Foster's
friends and find out Foster's true character, the generous tears will flow--I cannot help it. How easy it is to get a
wrong impression of a man. I perceive
that from childhood up this one has been
a sweet, docile thing, full of pretty
ways and gentle impulses, the charm of
the fireside, the admiration of society,
the idol of the Sunday-school. I recognize in him the divinest nature that has
ever glorified any mere human being. I
perceive that the sentiment with which he

regarded temperance was a thing that
amounted to frantic adoration. I freely
confess that it was the most natural
thing in the world for such an organism
as this to get drunk and insult a
stranger, and then beat his brains out
with a car-hook because he did not seem
to admire it. Such is Foster. And to
think that we came so near losing him!
How do we know but that he is the Second
Advent? And yet, after all, if the jury
had not been hampered in their choice of
a verdict I think I could consent to lose
him.

The humorist who invented trial by
jury played a colossal, practical joke
upon the world, but since we have the system we ought to try to respect it. A
thing which is not thoroughly easy to do,
when we reflect that by command of the
law a criminal juror must be an intellectual vacuum, attached to a melting heart
and perfectly macaronian bowels of compas-
sion.

I have had no experience in making
laws or amending them, but still I cannot
understand why, when it takes twelve men
to inflict the death penalty upon a person, it should take any less than 12 more
to undo their work. If I were a legislature, and had just been elected and had
not had time to sell out, I would put the
pardoning and commuting power into the
hands of twelve able men instead of dump-
ing so huge a burden upon the shoulders
of one poor petition-persecuted individual.

Nicholas Boileau
EVEN-HANDED JUSTICE*

Once, says an author, where I need not say,
Two travellers found an oyster on their way.
Both fierce, both hungry, the dispute grew strong,
When scale in hand, Dame Justice passed along.
Before her each with clamor pleads the laws,
Explains the matter, and would win the cause.
Dame Justice, weighing long the doubtful right,
Takes, opens, swallows it before their sight.
The cause of strife removed so rarely well,
"There, take," says Justice, "take you each a shell,
We thrive in courthouses on fools like you.
'Twas a fat oyster; live in peace—Adieu."

John Mortimer
RUMPOLE'S GREAT VICTORY**

'YOU LOOK CHARMING, my dear.' Hilda, resplendent in a long dress, her shoulders dusted with powder, smiled delightedly at Mrs Marigold Featherstone, who was nibbling delicately at an after-dinner mint.

'Really, Rumpole.' Hilda looked at me, gently rebuking. '"She!"'

'She?' Marigold was mystified, but anxious to join in any joke that might be going.

'Oh, "She",' I said casually. 'A woman of fabulous beauty. Written up by H. Rider Haggard.' A waiter passed and I created a diversion by calling his attention to the fact that the tide had gone out in my glass. Around us prominent members of the legal profes-

---

* Nicholas Boileau was a seventeenth-century French satirist known as "the legislator of Parnasse." This poem was translated from the French by the eighteenth-century British satirist Alexander Pope.
**Reprinted from "Rumpole and the Heavy Brigade," in John Mortimer, *Rumpole of the Bailey,* Penguin, 1978.

sion pushed their bulky wives about the parquet like a number of fresh-faced gardeners executing elaborate manoeuvres with wheelbarrows. There were some young persons among them, and I noticed Erskine-Brown, jigging about in solitary rapture somewhere in the vicinity of Miss Phyllida Trant. She saw me and gave a quick smile and then she was off circling Erskine-Brown like an obedient planet, which I didn't consider a fitting occupation for any girl of Miss Trant's undoubted abilities.

'Your husband's had a good win.' Guthrie Featherstone was chatting to Hilda.

'He hasn't had a "good win", Guthrie.' She put the man right. 'He's had a triumph!'

'Entirely thanks ... to my old hat.' I raised my glass. 'Here's to it!'

'What?' Little of what Rumpole said made much sense to Marigold.

'My triumph, indeed, my great opportunity, is to be attributed solely to my hat!' I explained to her, but She couldn't agree.

'Nonsense!'

'What?'

'You're talking nonsense,' She explained to our hosts. 'He does, you know, from time to time. Rumpole won because he knows so much about blood.'

'Really?' Featherstone looked at the dancers, no doubt wondering how soon he could steer his beautiful wife off into the throng. But Hilda fixed him with her glittering eye, and went on, much like the ancient mariner.

'You remember Daddy, of course. He used to be *your* Head of Chambers. Daddy told me. "Rumpole", Daddy told me. In fact, he told me that on the occasion of the Inns of Court summer ball, which is practically the last dance we went to.'

'Hilda!' I tried, unsuccessfully, to stem the flow.

'No. I'm going to say this, Horace. Don't interrupt! "Horace Rumpole", Daddy told me, "knows more about bloodstains than anyone we've got in Chambers."'

I noticed that Marigold had gone a little pale.

'Do stop it, Hilda. You're putting Marigold off.'

'Don't you find it,' Marigold turned to me, 'well, sordid sometimes?'

'What?'

'Crime. Don't you find it terribly sordid?'

There was a silence. The music had stopped, and the legal fraternity on the floor clapped sporadically. I saw Erskine-Brown take Miss Trant's hand.

'Oh, do be careful, Marigold!' I said. 'Don't knock it.'

'I think it must be sordid.' Marigold patted her lips with her table napkin, removing the last possible trace of after-dinner mint.

'Abolish crime,' I warned her, 'and you abolish the very basis of our existence!'

'Oh, come now, Horace!' Featherstone was smiling at me tolerantly.

'He's right,' Hilda told him. 'Rumpole knows about bloodstains.'

'Abolish crime and we should all vanish.' I felt a rush of words to the head. 'All the barristers and solicitors and dock officers and the dear old matron down the Old Bailey who gives aspirins away with sentences of life imprisonment. There'd be no judges, no Lord Chancellor. The Commissioner of the Metropolitan Police would have to go out selling encyclopaedias.' I leant back, grabbed the wine from the bucket, and started to refill all our glasses. 'Why are we here? Why've we got prawn cocktail and *duck à l'orange* and selections from dear old *Oklahoma?* All because a few villains down the East End are kind enough to keep us in a regular supply of crime.'

A slightly hurt waiter took the bottle from me and continued my work.

'Don't you *help* them?' Marigold looked at me, doubtfully.

'Don't I *what?*'

'Help them. Doing all these crimes. After all. You get them off.'

'Today,' I said, not without a certain pride. 'Today, let me tell you, Marigold, I was no help to them at all. I showed them ... no gratitude!'

'You got him off!'

'What?'

'You got Peter Delgardo off.'

'Just for one reason.'

'What was that?'

'He happened to be innocent.'

'Come on, Horace. How can you be sure of that?' Featherstone was smiling tolerantly but I leant forward and gave him the truth of the matter.

'You know, it's a terrifying thing, my learned friend. We go through all that mumbo jumbo. We put on our wigs and gowns and mutter the ritual prayers. "My Lord, I humbly submit." "Ladies and gentlemen of the jury, you have listened with admirable patience..." Abracadabra. Fee Fo Fi Bloody Fum. And just when everyone thinks you're going to produce the most ludicrously faked bit of cheese-cloth ectoplasm, or a phoney rap on the table, it comes. Clear as a bell. Quite unexpected. The voice of truth!'

I was vaguely aware of a worried figure in a dinner jacket coming towards us across the floor.

'Have you ever found that, Featherstone? Bloody scaring sometimes. All the trouble we take to cloud the issues and divert the attention. Suddenly we've done it. There it is! Naked and embarrassing. The truth!'

I looked up as the figure joined us. It was my late instructing solicitor.

'Nooks. "Shady" Nooks!' I greeted him, but he seemed in no mood to notice me. He pulled up a chair and sat down beside Featherstone.

'Apparently it was on the nine o'clock news. They've just arrested Leslie Delgardo. Charged him with the murder of Tosher MacBride. I'll want a con with you in the morning.'

I was left out of this conversation, but I didn't mind. Music started again, playing a tune which I found vaguely familiar. Nooks was muttering on; it seemed that the police now knew Tosher worked for Leslie, and that some member of the rival Watson family may have spotted him at the scene of the crime. An extraordinary sensation overcame me, something I hadn't felt for a long time, which could only be described as happiness.

'I don't know whether you'll want to brief me for Leslie, Nooks,' I raised a glass to old 'Shady'. 'Or would that be rather over-egging the pudding?'

And then an even more extraordinary sensation, a totally irrational impulse for which I can find no logical explanation, overcame me. I put out a hand and touched She Who Must Be Obeyed on the powdered shoulder.

'Hilda.'

'Oh, yes, Rumpole?' It seemed I was interrupting some confidential chat with Marigold. 'What do you want now?'

'I honestly think.' I could find no coherent explanation. 'I think I want to dance with you.'

I suppose it was a waltz. As I steered Hilda out onto the great open spaces it seemed quite easy to go round and round, vaguely in time to the music. I heard a strange sound, as if from a long way off.

> *I'll have the last waltz with you,*
> *Two sleepy people together...*

Or words to that effect. I was in fact singing. Singing and dancing to celebrate a great victory in a case I was never meant to win.

Samuel Butler
SOME EREWHONIAN TRIALS*

IN EREWHON as in other countries there are some courts of justice that deal with special subjects. Misfortune generally is considered more or less criminal, but it admits of classification, and a court is assigned to each of the main heads under which it can be supposed to fall. Not very long after I had reached the capital I strolled into the Personal Bereavement Court, and was much both interested and pained by listening to the trial of a man who was accused of having just lost a wife to whom he had been tenderly attached, and who had left him with three little children, of whom the eldest was only three years old.

The defence which the prisoner's counsel endeavoured to establish was, that the prisoner had never really loved his wife; but it broke down completely, for the public prosecutor called witness after witness who deposed to the fact that the couple had been devoted to one another, and the prisoner repeatedly wept as incidents were put in evidence that reminded him of the irreparable nature of the loss he had sustained. The jury returned a verdict of guilty after very little deliberation, but recommended the prisoner to mercy on the ground that he had but recently insured his wife's life for a considerable sum, and might be deemed lucky inasmuch as he had received the money without demur from the insurance company, though he had only paid two premiums.

I have just said that the jury found the prisoner guilty. When the judge passed sentence, I was struck with the way in which the

---

* Excerpted from Ch. 11 of Butler's famous satire *Erewhon: or Over the Range*, 1863.

prisoner's counsel was rebuked for having referred to a work in which the guilt of such misfortunes as the prisoner's was extenuated to a degree that roused the indignation of the court.

"We shall have," said the judge, "these crude and subversionary books from time to time until it is recognised as an axiom of morality that luck is the only fit object of human veneration. How far a man has any right to be more lucky and hence more venerable than his neighbours, is a point that always has been, and always will be, settled proximately by a kind of higgling and haggling of the market, and ultimately by brute force; but however this may be, it stands to reason that no man should be allowed to be unlucky to more than a very moderate extent."

Then, turning to the prisoner, the judge continued: "You have suffered a great loss. Nature attaches a severe penalty to such offences, and human law must emphasise the decrees of nature. But for the recommendation of the jury I should have given you six months' hard labour. I will, however, commute your sentence to one of three months, with the option of a fine of twenty-five per cent of the money you have received from the insurance company."

The prisoner thanked the judge, and said that as he had no one to look after his children if he was sent to prison, he would embrace the option mercifully permitted him by his lordship, and pay the sum he had named. He was then removed from the dock.

The next case was that of a youth barely arrived at man's estate, who was charged with having been swindled out of large property during his minority by his guardian, who was also one of his nearest relations. His father had been long dead, and it was for this reason that his offence came on for trial in the Personal Bereavement Court. The lad, who was undefended, pleaded that he was young, inexperienced, greatly in awe of his guardian, and without independent professional advice. "Young man," said the judge sternly, "do not talk nonsense. People have no right to be young, inexperienced, greatly in awe of their guardians, and without independent professional advice. If by such indiscretions they outrage the moral sense of their friends, they must expect to suffer accordingly." He then ordered the prisoner to apologise to his guardian, and to receive twelve strokes with a cat-of-nine-tails.

Groucho Marx
LETTERS TO WARNER BROTHERS*

> When the Marx Brothers were about to make a movie called *A Night in Casablanca,* there were threats of legal action from the Warner Brothers, who, five years before, had made a picture called, simply, *Casablanca.* Whereupon Groucho, speaking for his brothers and himself, immediately dispatched the following letters:**

Dear Warner Brothers:

Apparently there is more than one way of conquering a city and holding it as your own. For example, up to the time that we contemplated making this picture, I had no idea that the city of Casablanca belonged exclusively to Warner Brothers. However, it was only a few days after our announcement appeared that we received your long, ominous legal document warning us not to use the name Casablanca.

It seems that in 1471, Ferdinand Balboa Warner, your great-great-grandfather, while looking for a shortcut to the city of Burbank, had stumbled on the shores of Africa and, raising his alpenstock (which he later turned in for a hundred shares of the common), named it Casablanca.

I just don't understand your attitude. Even if you plan on re-releasing your picture, I am sure that the average movie fan could learn in time to distinguish between Ingrid Bergman and Harpo. I

---

* Reprinted from *The Groucho Letters.* Copyright © 1967 by Groucho Marx. Reprinted by permission of Simon & Schuster, Inc.
**This note and the following notes were supplied by the editor of the original collection of letters.

don't know whether I could, but I certainly would like to try.

You claim you own Casablanca and that no one else can use that name without your permission. What about "Warner Brothers"? Do you own that, too? You probably have the right to use the name Warner, but what about Brothers? Professionally, we were brothers long before you were. We were touring the sticks as The Marx Brothers when Vitaphone was still a gleam in the inventor's eye, and even before us there had been other brothers—the Smith Brothers; the Brothers Karamazov; Dan Brothers, an outfielder with Detroit; and "Brother, Can You Spare a Dime?" (This was originally "Brothers, Can You Spare a Dime?" but this was spreading a dime pretty thin, so they threw out one brother, gave all the money to the other one and whittled it down to, "Brother, Can You Spare a Dime?")

Now Jack, how about you? Do you maintain that yours is an original name? Well, it's not. It was used long before you were born. Offhand, I can think of two Jacks—there was Jack of "Jack and the Beanstalk," and Jack the Ripper, who cut quite a figure in his day.

As for you, Harry, you probably sign your checks, sure in the belief that you are the first Harry of all time and that all other Harrys are imposters. I can think of two Harrys that preceded you. There was Lighthouse Harry of Revolutionary fame and a Harry Appelbaum who lived on the corner of 93rd Street and Lexington Avenue. Unfortunately, Appelbaum wasn't too well known. The last I heard of him, he was selling neckties at Weber and Heilbroner.

Now about the Burbank studio. I

believe this is what you brothers call
your place. Old man Burbank is gone. Perhaps you remember him. He was a great man
in a garden. His wife often said Luther
had ten green thumbs. What a witty woman
she must have been! Burbank was the
wizard who crossed all those fruits and
vegetables until he had the poor plants
in such a confused and jittery condition
that they could never decide whether to
enter the dining room on the meat platter
or the dessert dish.

This is pure conjecture, of course,
but who knows——perhaps Burbank's sur-
vivors aren't too happy with the fact
that a plant that grinds out pictures on
a quota settled in their town, appropri-
ated Burbank's name and uses it as a
front for their films. It is even possible that the Burbank family is prouder
of the potato produced by the old man
than they are of the fact that from your
studio emerged "Casablanca" or even "Gold
Diggers of 1931."

This all seems to add up to a pretty bitter tirade, but I assure you it's
not meant to. I love Warners. Some of my
best friends are Warner Brothers. It is
even possible that I am doing you an injustice and that you, yourselves, know
nothing at all about this dog-in-the-
Wanger attitude. It wouldn't surprise me
at all to discover that the heads of your
legal department are unaware of this absurd dispute, for I am acquainted with
many of them and they are fine fellows
with curly black hair, double-breasted
suits and a love of their fellow man that
out-Saroyans Saroyan.

I have a hunch that this attempt to
prevent us from using the title is the
brainchild of some ferret-faced shyster,

serving a brief apprenticeship in your
legal department. I know the type well—
hot out of law school, hungry for success
and too ambitious to follow the natural
laws of promotion. This bar sinister
probably needled your attorneys, most of
whom are fine fellows with curly black
hair, double-breasted suits, etc., into
attempting to enjoin us. Well, he won't
get away with it! We'll fight him to the
highest court! No pasty-faced legal adven-
turer is going to cause bad blood between
the Warners and the Marxes. We are all
brothers under the skin and we'll remain
friends till the last reel of "A Night in
Casablanca" goes tumbling over the spool.

                              Sincerely,

                              Groucho Marx

For some curious reason, this letter seemed to puzzle the
Warner Brothers legal department. They wrote—in all serious-
ness—and asked if the Marxes could give them some idea of
what their story was about. They felt that something might be
worked out. So Groucho replied:

Dear Warners:
        There isn't much I can tell you
about the story. In it I play a Doctor of
Divinity who ministers to the natives
and, as a sideline, hawks can openers and
pea jackets to the savages along the Gold
Coast of Africa.
        When I first meet Chico, he is work-
ing in a saloon, selling sponges to
barflies who are unable to carry their
liquor. Harpo is an Arabian caddie who
lives in a small Grecian urn on the outskirts of the city.
        As the picture opens, Porridge, a
mealy-mouthed native girl, is sharpening
some arrows for the hunt. Paul Hangover,
our hero, is constantly lighting two
cigarettes simultaneously. He apparently

"King James's? Revised Version? New English?
With or without Apocrypha?"

Reprinted by permission of *Punch.*

is unaware of the cigarette shortage.
      There are many scenes of splendor
and fierce antagonisms, and Color, an
Abyssinian messenger boy, runs Riot.
Riot, in case you have never been there,
is a small night club on the edge of town.
      There's a lot more I could tell
you, but I don't want to spoil it for
you. All this has been okayed by the Hays
Office, Good Housekeeping and the sur-
vivors of the Haymarket Riots; and if the
times are ripe, this picture can be the
opening gun in a new worldwide disaster.

                  Cordially,

                  Groucho Marx

Instead of mollifying them, this note seemed to puzzle the attorneys even more; they wrote back and said they still didn't understand the story line and they would appreciate it if Mr. Marx would explain the plot in more detail. So Groucho obliged with the following:

Dear Brothers:

Since I last wrote you, I regret to say there have been some changes in the plot of our new picture, "A Night in Casablanca." In the new version I play Bordello, the sweetheart of Humphrey Bogart. Harpo and Chico are itinerant rug peddlers who are weary of laying rugs and enter a monastery just for a lark. This is a good joke on them, as there hasn't been a lark in the place for fifteen years.

Across from this monastery, hard by a jetty, is a waterfront hotel, chockfull of apple-cheeked damsels, most of whom have been barred by the Hays Office for soliciting. In the fifth reel, Gladstone makes a speech that sets the House of Commons in a uproar and the King promptly asks for his resignation. Harpo marries a hotel detective; Chico operates an ostrich farm. Humphrey Bogart's girl, Bordello, spends her last years in a Bacall house.

This, as you can see, is a very skimpy outline. The only thing that can save us from extinction is a continuation of the film shortage.

Fondly,

Groucho Marx

After that, the Marxes heard no more from the Warner Brothers legal department.

Robert T. Sloan
DAISY WHIFFLE v.
TWITTER BIRD SEED COMPANY

I AM VERY MUCH COMPLIMENTED by the remarks of your toastmaster. I am also highly complimented that in recognition of my vast knowledge of the law your association should invite me here to speak on a subject peculiarly suited to my personality and attainments: abnormal jurisprudence. Your recognition makes me feel that at last I am becoming a lawyer's lawyer. Blessed be he who serves the poor! I shall not hesitate to speak freely.

Your program committee has specifically requested me to review a written case I tried here several years ago, my famous case of *Daisy Whiffle* v. *The Twitter Bird Seed Company*. Of course, the members of the bar are completely familiar with the details of that case. It created quite a sensation here at the time in justice court circles. As I recall I tried it in 1935. Let me see—yes, it was in the spring of 1935. For the benefit of our out-of-town guests and visitors, let me explain that it is not my most recent case, but I wanted to bring up one where I had been successful. So I am very grateful for the happy coincidence or rare tact, whichever it was, that inspired your program committee to select that old case, *Whiffle* v. *The Twitter Bird Seed Company*.

Although I realize that to many lawyers it is the most important consideration of all, I am not going to tell you at this time how I got the case. Suffice it to say that it came to me under rather extraordinary circumstances—practically an act of God. Indeed, if it hadn't been for the pluck and the remarkable perseverance of my client, Daisy Whiffle, a perseverance that sent her around from one law office to another even after twenty or thirty lawyers had turned her down, I might not even have represented her at all. Such are the ways of chance.

The facts of the case are comparatively simple. Daisy Whiffle was a professional woman, a snake charmer in a circus. She owned in her own right a baby rattlesnake, for which she felt the deepest affection, and which she generally carried coiled around her neck. Now, on the day of the misfortune I am about to relate, Daisy was out riding in an open touring car with her beloved pet encircling her neck as usual. The day was rather wintry and as a result the little snake became cold and stiff. Daisy happened to glance down and thought the poor creature was dead. Well, horrified and woman-like, she released both hands from the steering wheel and clutched the snake to her bosom. Meanwhile, the driver of another car, approaching from the opposite direction, in an effort to avoid a collision, drove up on the sidewalk and tried to scale an adjoining building, but gravity forced him down again in the path of the oncoming car, with the resulting collision. Neither driver was hurt, but Daisy's rattlesnake, frozen and stiff as it was, and therefore unable to relax, was fatally cracked in three places. So that by a strange twist of fate the illusion of death which caused the accident now became a hideous reality.

Now, I saw in these facts some of the elements of a perfect case. There was Daisy Whiffle, a woman. I looked at her and for the first time I saw she was beautiful—all clients look beautiful to me. There was a strong emotional appeal, a woman's love for her deceased pet. Plenty of damages—after all, you can't buy a live rattlesnake every day. But what it obviously lacked was a corporation defendant. In order to remedy this defect I took the deposition of the driver of the other car. I found that he owned his own car, that he was unemployed at the time of the accident, and that never in his entire life had he worked for a corporation. I also discovered, however, that eleven years prior to the accident in question, he had purchased a package of bird seed from The Twitter Bird Seed Company. It was a simple little transaction, and yet I thought I saw in it a sort of embryonic master and servant relationship, and I thought of that great maxim of law, *"olim proquerator semper procurator,"* or once an agent always an agent, and that other even more useful maxim, *"quid jurores non facient,"* or what won't a jury do; and I knew I had my corporation hooked.

I immediately filed suit against The Twitter Bird Seed Company. This company was represented by a very able corporation lawyer, a member of what in certain respects was the largest firm in our city. I say in certain respects, because of the seventeen partners in his firm only two were actually living, so that the size of the firm depends upon your point of view, heaven or earth. But any way you look at it, my distinguished adversary, through his contacts with the departed, was in an excellent position to secure divine guidance in handling cases....

I awaited the day for the trial with calm confidence. Only one thing happened to disturb my equilibrium, and that only temporarily. The defendant offered to settle for $10.00. Immediately I was precipitated into a great emotional conflict. Did I want a trial reputation or did I want $10.00 cold cash? That was my dilemma. For several days I was in the throes of agonizing indecision, and even now I don't know how I would have decided if again fate had not intervened, as it so frequently does in the lives of men of destiny. The choice was taken from my hands. The defendant withdrew his offer! The case had to be tried.

I made no preparations for the trial. It is not my policy to look up law in advance of the trial of a lawsuit. I have learned from experience that no matter how strange and fantastic is my own notion of the law, it is safe to assume that somewhere in the reports there will be a decision that will support it. And maybe I won't have to look it up at all. I really have, I must confess, a singular aversion to looking up law. At one time I seriously considered specializing exclusively in a certain class of cases dealing with what is commonly referred to as "the unwritten law," but I didn't seem able to work up that type of practice.

For a long time I was very discouraged about my laziness—or shall I call it my love of profound inactivity? I was so discouraged that I went to a psychiatrist for treatment, Dr. Elmer Good. Maybe you have heard of him. He is the author of several well-known books, *Good on Emotions, Good on Hallucinations,* and *Good on Everything.*

At first this great doctor had difficulty diagnosing my case. He couldn't locate my unconscious mind. He said he didn't know where to draw the line. But, after he talked with me a while, he said he didn't think it made any difference. Then he located my complex, the cause of my trouble. He said I was suffering from a suppressed desire to be President of the United States. Well, of course my presidential ambitions are no secret. My mother raised me to be President. I selected my studies in high school and at college with this goal in mind. And now, here I am of presidential age, fully trained and equipped, but there isn't any opening! And, God knows, Roosevelt may live to ninety!

Then the doctor, this psychiatrist, told me: "In a case of an ordinary individual with such an emotional thwarting as yours I recommend a substitute activity. For instance," he said, "if a man is jilted by a girl, he marries another girl and what is the difference. Or if he fails at a profession like the law, he goes to the Lake City

Munitions Plant and finds solace in the increased remuneration the government pays for that sort of work. But," he said, "when a man has a magnificent ambition like yours, there isn't any adequate substitute. And rather than desecrate such a fine, noble impulse with an unworthy substitute, I think you are justified in doing nothing."

Well, I tell you, that opened up a new world for me. To think that, like the story in the Bluebird, I should find my supreme happiness in what I was already doing—nothing! If the doctor had recommended any alteration in my character, it would have implied dissatisfaction with myself as I was, and consequently would have been a blow to my ego. But here he was able to restore my self-esteem without prescribing the slightest change in my character.

Now, to get back to my subject—there comes a time when every speaker must get back to his subject. We are trying the case of *Daisy Whiffle* v. *The Twitter Bird Seed Company.*

I didn't coach Daisy for the trial. I didn't have to. When she stalked into that courtroom with her superb animal magnetism, she was a sensation. She was dressed in canary-yellow and sheer nerve. Immediately she started broadcasting certain feminine psychical waves that made contact with the jury and the judge with devastating effect.

As I recall she was rather quick at repartee, too. I remember one instance in cross-examination. Opposing counsel, trying to ascertain the market value of her dead rattlesnake, very properly asked her whether it was a male or a female, and she turned to him and said, "Sir, that is a question which should be of interest only to another rattlesnake."

But I know this learned audience is interested not so much in the wit and humor displayed at the trial, as in the judicial significance of the case itself, and its place in the history of jurisprudence. I don't think there is any case that has gone so far as this one to clarify the law of negligence relating to personal injuries.

The judge issued only one instruction, but it was unusually lucid and comprehensive. He charged the jury in effect that "If you find from the evidence the plaintiff was a woman and the defendant was a corporation, your verdict will naturally be for the lady." And it was. But isn't that a masterful instruction? Doesn't it completely express the realities of modern law? The law is ever striving for certainty and simplicity, and there we have it in that simple little instruction.

I believe we have here tonight several educators, several great law teachers. I wish they would read the opinion of the justice in this case, *Whiffle* v. *The Twitter Bird Seed Company*. Let them read and reread it, and go back and tell it to their students, because, if they will pardon my saying so, it seems to me that our young law graduates commence the practice of law with a most grotesque conception of what constitutes the law of negligence. In their misguided zeal, they will read a great mass of authorities, trying to ascertain what a certain mythical figure they call the reasonable man would do under these or those circumstances. What an unnecessarily tedious way to practice law! They are also mastered by a fear, amounting almost to a phobia, that there won't be sufficient evidence to take the case to the jury. Let them cross that bridge when they come to it. There are lawyers who have traveled for years without sighting the bridge.

Now, in closing I want to point out that, if there are present here tonight any unusually erudite individuals, students of higher jurisprudence, who want to consult with me in private after the program is over, I shall be happy to place my learning at their disposal. It is my considered opinion, based on a certain amount of actual experience, that I am not likely to be invited back again, and I want to do as much for them as I can while I am here.

Tom Q. Ellis
A Dying Confession*

A young man fired with pep and zeal approached his
      doting Paw,
And said "Above all other things, I wish I knew the Law."
So Law it was, he entered school and wafted like a breeze
To topmost heights where he was crowned with all the
      Law Degrees.
And then he hung his shingle out and folks from far and
      near

* Reprinted by permission of *Mississippi Law Journal*.

Came rushing in to learn the Law from one who had no
    peer.
And soon he mounted to the Bench, the highest in the land,
And there as Judge and Counsellor dispensed blind Justice
    grand.
For years and years his word was Law, his reputation grew,
And none would dare to challenge him about the law he
    knew.
But Father Time must take his toll, when years have
    quickly sped,
And so this Judge and Counsellor came down to his last bed.
His breathing gasps came quick and short, his life was
    ebbing fast,
And many gathered 'round to hear some wise words as
    his last.
They huddled close and bended low—and listened, jaw to
    jaw,
But shocked they were when he confessed, "I wish I knew
    the Law."

There was a young lawyer who showed up at a
revival meeting and was asked to deliver a
prayer. Unprepared, he gave a prayer straight
from his lawyer's heart: "Stir up much strife
amongst the people, Lord," he prayed, "lest thy
servant perish." — *U.S. Sen. Sam Ervin*

As one gets older, litigation replaces sex.
                    —*Gore Vidal*

If you can eat sawdust without butter, you can be
a success in the law. —*Oliver Wendell Holmes*

"What do you do?"

"I'm a lawyer."
"The law."
"I do law."
"I practice law."
"I'm an attorney."
"Something legal."

LAWYERS

George Ade
THE FABLE OF THE BOOKWORM AND THE
BUTTERFLY WHO WENT INTO THE LAW*

TWO BROTHERS started away to College at the same Time. Just before they boarded the Train, Pa led them aside and handed them some splendid Advice. He told them that they were now ready to mold their Futures. He said he wanted them to stay in of Evenings and Bone hard, and he hoped they would mind the Faculty and keep away from the Cigarette Fiends who play the Banjo and talk about Actresses. He wanted them to stand high in their Classes and devote their Spare Moments to Reading rather than to the Whimsies and Mimical Fooleries of a University Town.

William listened solemnly and promised to Behave. Cholley fidgeted in his Chair and said it was nearly Train-Time.

So they rode away on the Varnished Cars, William reading about the Goths and Vandals and Cholley playing Seven Up with a Shoe Drummer from Lowell.

At the University William remembered what Pa had said, so he cooped himself up in his Room and became a Dig and soon enough was greatly despised as a Pet of the Professors. Cholley wore a striped Jersey and joined the Track Team and worked into the Glee Club. He went to his Room when all the other Places had closed up. Every Time a Show struck Town he was in the Front Row to guy the Performers and pick up some new Gags. He went calling on all the Town Girls who would stand for his Fresh Ways, and he was known as the best Dancer in the Ki Ki Chapter of the Gamma Oopsilon Greek Letter Fraternity. The Reports sent Home indicated that William was corralling the Honors in Scholarship and Cholley was getting through each Exam by the Skin of his Teeth, but he had

---

* The author of this piece, American humorist and playwright George Ade, is remembered especially for his fables. This one was originally published in his *Forty Modern Fables*, 1901.

been elected a Yell Captain and could do his 100 Yards in Ten Seconds Flat. Pa would write to Cholley now and then and tell him to Brace Up and give him a Hunch that Life was full of Sober Responsibilities and therefore he had better store his Mind with Useful Knowledge and Chop on all the Frivols and Fopperies, whereupon Cholley would write back that he needed Fifty by Return Mail to pay for Chemicals used in the Laboratory.

By the Time that both were Seniors, William had grown a fuzzy Climber in front of each Ear and was troubled with Weak Eyes. He always had a Volume of Kant under his Arm and seemed to be in a Brown Study as he walked across the Campus. Cholley kept himself Neat and Nobby and seemed always Cheerful, even though he had two or three Conditions to his discredit and had only an Outside Chance of taking his Degree. He was Manager of the Football Team, and he had earned the affectionate Nickname of "Rocks." He was a great Hand to get acquainted with any Girl who dared to show herself near the Halls of Learning and by constant Practice he had developed into a Star Chinner, so that he could Talk Low to almost any one of them and make her believe that of all the Flowers that ever bloomed she was the one and only $30,000 Carnation.

William kept away from Hops and Promenades because he remembered what Pa had said about the Distracting Influence of Fripperies and the Tittle-Tattle of Artificial Society. The only Girl he knew was a Professor's Sister, aged 51, with whom he was wont to discuss the Theory of Unconscious Cerebration. Then he would drink a Cup of Young Hyson Tea and go Home at 8:45 p.m. Cholley at about that Time would be starting out in his Primrose and Dockstader Suit to write his Name on Dance Cards and get acquainted with the Real Folks.

On Commencement Day William received the Cyrus J. Blinker Prize of a Set of Books for getting the Highest General Average of any one in the Class. Cholley just managed to Squeeze Through. The Faculty gave him a Degree for fear that if it didn't he might come back and stay another Year.

After they had graduated, Pa gave them another Talk. He said he was proud of William, but Cholley had been a Trial to him. Still he hoped it was not too late to set the Boy on the Right Track. He was going to put both of them into a Law Office and he wanted them to Read Law for all they were worth and not be lured away from their Work by the Glittering Temptations of Life in a Big City.

William said he was prepared to Read Law until he was Black in the Face. Cholley said he wouldn't mind pacing a few Heats with Blackstone and Cooley now and then, if he found that he could spare the Time. The Father groaned inwardly and did not see much Hope for Cholley.

When the two Sons became Fixtures in the Office of an established Law Firm, William kept his Nose between the Leaves of a Supreme Court Report and Cholley was out in the other Room warming up to the Influential Clients and making Dates for Luncheons and Golf Foursomes.

Within three Months after they started at the Office, William had read all the Books in the Place and Cholley was out spending three weeks at the Summer Home of the President of a Construction Company, who was stuck on Cholley's Dialect Stories and liked to have him around because he was such a good Dresser and made it lively for the Women.

Out at this Country Place it happened that Cholley met a Girl who didn't know how much she was worth, so Cholley thought it would be an Act of Kindness to help her find out. When he sat out with her in the Cool of the Evening and gave her the Burning Gaze

THE WILLING PERFORMER

and the low entrancing Love Purr that he had practised for Four Years at the University, she stopped him before he was half finished, and told him that he need not work Overtime, because he was the Boy for Nellie. She said she had had him Picked Out from the Moment that she noticed how well his Coat set in the Back.

In one of the large Office Buildings of the City there is a Suite finished in Dark Wood. At a massive roll-top Desk sits Cholley, the handsome Lawyer, who is acquainted with all the Club Fellows, Society Bucks and Golf Demons. When a Client comes in with a Knotty Question, Cholley calls in a

Blonde Stenographer to jot down all the Points in the Case. Then the Client departs. Cholley rings a Bell and Brother William comes out of a Side Room with his Coat bunched in the Back and his Trousers bagged at the Knees. His Cravat is tied on one Side only and he needs a Shave, but he is full of the Law. Cholley turns all the papers over to him and tells him to wrestle with the Authorities for a few Days and Nights. Then William slips back into his Hole and Humps himself over the calf-bound Volumes while Cholley puts on his slate-colored Gloves and Top Coat and goes out to where Simpson is holding a Carriage Door open for him. He and Nellie take the air in the $2,200 Victoria that he bought with her Money and later in the Day they dine with the Stockson-Bonds and finish at the Theater.

Cholley often reflects that it was a great Piece of Foresight on Pa's part to counsel Studious Habits and Rigid Mental Discipline, for if William had not been a Grind at College probably he would not have proved to be such a Help around the Office, and although William gets the Loser's End of the Fees and is never Called on to make a Witty Speech at a Banquet given by the Bar Association, he has the Satisfaction of knowing that he is the Silent Partner of the best-dressed Attorney in Town and one who is welcome wherever he goes.

MORAL: *There are at least two Kinds of Education.*

Charles Dickens
A VERY RESPECTABLE MAN*

MR. VHOLES is a very respectable man. He has not a large business, but he is a very respectable man. He is allowed by the greater attorneys who have made good fortunes, or are making them, to be a most respectable man. He never misses a chance in his practice; which is a mark of respectability. He never takes any pleasure; which is another mark of respectability. He is reserved and serious; which is another mark of respectability. His digestion is impaired, which is highly respectable. And he is making hay of

---

* Excerpted from *Bleak House,* 1852.

the grass which is flesh, for his three daughters. And his father is dependent on him in the Vale of Taunton.

The one great principle of the English law is, to make business for itself. There is no other principle distinctly, certainly, and consistently maintained through all its narrow turnings. Viewed by this light it becomes a coherent scheme, and not the monstrous maze the laity are apt to think it. Let them but once clearly perceive that its grand principle is to make business for itself at their expense, and surely they will cease to grumble.

But, not perceiving this quite plainly—only seeing it by halves in a confused way—the laity sometimes suffer in peace and pocket, with a bad grace, and *do* grumble very much. Then this respectability of Mr. Vholes is brought into powerful play against them. "Repeal this statute, my good sir?" says Mr. Kenge, to a smarting client, "repeal it, my dear sir? Never, with my consent. Alter this law, sir, and what will be the effect of your rash proceeding on a class of practitioners very worthily represented, allow me to say to you, by the opposite attorney in the case, Mr. Vholes? Sir, that class of practitioners would be swept from the face of the earth. Now you cannot afford—I will say, the social system cannot afford—to lose an order of men like Mr. Vholes. Diligent, persevering, steady, acute in business. My dear sir, I understand your present feelings against the existing state of things, which I grant to be a little hard in your case; but I can never raise my voice for the demolition of a class of men like Mr. Vholes." The respectability of Mr. Vholes has even been cited with crushing effect before Parliamentary committees, as in the following blue minutes of a distinguished attorney's evidence. "Question (number five hundred and seventeen thousand eight hundred and sixty-nine). If I understand you, these forms of practice indisputably occasion delay? Answer. Yes, some delay. Question. And great expense? Answer. Most assuredly they cannot be gone through for nothing. Question. And unspeakable vexation? Answer. I am not prepared to say that. They have never given *me* any vexation; quite the contrary. Question. But you think that their abolition would damage a class of practitioners? Answer. I have no doubt of it. Question. Can you instance any type of that class? Answer. Yes. I would unhesitatingly mention Mr. Vholes. He would be ruined. Question. Mr. Vholes is considered, in the profession, a respectable man? Answer"—which proved fatal to the inquiry for ten years—"Mr. Vholes is considered, in the profession, a *most* respectable man."

So in familiar conversation, private authorities no less disinterested will remark that they don't know what this age is come to; that we are plunging down precipices; that now here is something else gone; that these changes are death to people like Vholes: a man of undoubted respectability, with a father in the Vale of Taunton, and three daughters at home. Take a few steps more in this direction, say they, and what is to become of Vhole's father? Is he to perish? And of Vhole's daughters? Are they to be shirt-makers, or governesses? As though, Mr. Vholes and his relations being minor cannibal chiefs, and it being proposed to abolish cannibalism, indignant champions were to put the case thus: Make man-eating unlawful, and you starve the Vholeses!

In a word, Mr. Vholes, with his three daughters and his father in the Vale of Taunton, is continually doing duty, like a piece of timber, to shore up some decayed foundation that has become a pitfall and a nuisance. And with a great many people in a great many instances, the question is never one of a change from Wrong to Right (which is quite an extraneous consideration), but is always one of injury or advantage to that eminently respectable legion, Vholes.

Edward A. Hogan, Jr.
HOW A LAW PROFESSOR TELLS HIS CHILDREN
THE STORY OF THE THREE BEARS*

ONCE UPON A TIME (the exact date is not known, but it is not likely to be put in issue, since the memory of man runneth not to the contrary), a little girl (about whose parentage there is no issue and who will be presumed therefore to be legitimate) named Goldilocks wanted to visit her grandmother (whether paternal or maternal is immaterial) who lived on the other side of the forest (the exact location of which may be determined in metes and bounds by consulting the records of the Registry of Deeds in the county in which the said premises are located). Little Goldilocks was given permission by her parents. Throughout this narrative the parents

---

* At the time this story was published in the *Harvard Law School Record* (March 23, 1949), Prof. Hogan was dean of the University of San Francisco School of Law.

will be presumed to be reasonable and prudent parents because they warned little Goldilocks of all known and foreseeable dangers and instructed her to be guided accordingly.

No Attractive Nuisance

When little Goldilocks was perambulating the perimeter of the forest, she was attracted by a single dwelling of unusual construction set back from the highway in a manner which conformed exactly to the zoning regulations lawfully enacted and promulgated. This was not, as you will note, an attractive nuisance since the object was one with which all children are familiar and the dangers of which, if any, are obvious.

"Once upon a time, allegedly..."

Blackstone's Imaginary Fence

Disregarding the instructions of her prudent parents, she entered the land by crossing over the imaginary white fence which Blackstone says surrounds each parcel of realty. For this she became guilty of trespass *quare clausum fregit pedibus ambulando.* Knocking at the door and receiving no reply, she turned the knob, gave a good push and entered. This, as you know, was trespass *quare clausum fregit vi et armis.*

Trespass de Bonis Asportatis

She saw on the table three bowls of porridge. The first was too hot and the second was too cold. The third was just right so she ate it all up. This was trespass *de bonis asportatis.*

Inside the house she spied three chairs. She sat in the big chair, which belonged quite obviously to the Daddy bear, but it was too hard. (Since she did no harm this could be no trespass.) The medium-sized chair was too soft, so she sat in the little chair, which, she assumed, belonged to the baby bear. Since her weight exceeded the capacity of the chair, she broke it all down. Harm being done, she committed an ordinary trespass to personal property.

Two Schools of Thought

By that time little Goldilocks was tired. She found a bedroom with three beds. She tried the first and found it too hard, the second was too soft but the third was just right. So she lay down in the third, or baby bear's bed, and soon was fast asleep. It is not so easy to tell what kind of wrong this happens to be, and it may well be that on this point there are two schools of thought. It is not however tresspass *quare clausum fregit vi et armis ab initio* since this misfeasance did not follow an entry under license of law.

The Proprietors Returned

While she was fast asleep, the proprietors of the premises returned. Angered and aroused at the torts and trespasses they sought out the tortfeasor. Baby Bear found her in his own little bed and raised a hue and cry. Just then little Goldilocks woke up, realized her predicament and ran home as fast as she could with the three bears in fresh and hot pursuit. She got home just in time to slam the door in the faces of three angry bears. It is a good thing she did too because now we do not have to decide if a bear can be guilty of assault and battery.

And now I think it would be a good idea for you to go to sleep before you make the discovery, made by judges in the courts before which I practiced, once upon a time, that most of what I have to say is incompetent, irrelevant and immaterial.

Daniel R. White
A POET'S DREAM OF LITIGATION*

Had I but world enough, and time, to seek my true vocation,
I'd act without a nanosecond's thought or hesitation.
This chore of rhyme I'd chuck, this dull semantic mastication,
And trade it for a world of life-enhancing litigation.

Poesy's fine for those who hold no higher aspiration
Than tinkering with syllables and verbal colligation,
Who ask no more of life on earth than palest imitation
Of true fulfillment: decades spent in costly litigation.

Whatever made me join this muse-dependent occupation?
I've taken on my share, and more, of worldly obligation,
And law can never yield but bare subsistence compensation.
Ergo I rhyme, with precious little time for litigation.

True, my poems always find their way to publication,
Products of my Perry Mason-urge in sublimation,
But prosody for me is just a way around starvation,
A second-rate alternative to joyous litigation.

How is one to tolerate a life of such frustration?
Fantasy is key—escape through one's imagination,
Wherefore all my evenings spent in soothing contemplation
Of a case—one perfect case—to get me back to litigation.

*

I'd need, of course, a client filled with righteous indignation,
Hungry for revenge, and thus immune to perturbation
By costs that to results obtained might bear but chance
     relation,
Yet costs without whose payment there could be no litigation.

A client little prone to second thoughts and vacillation,
Or concern about his bank account's complete
     exsanguination,
A sturdy sort in whom my bills might trigger palpitation,
But nothing worse, nothing that could stop the litigation.

With wealth enough to buy a full-size yacht or mid-size
     nation,
Anything except a way to shed his reputation
For thoroughgoing rottenness—and hence his jubilation
That I would represent him in the current litigation.

A man considered lower than some mud-besmeared
     crustacean,
Whose very mother recommends his life incarceration,
Whose priest-confessor prays for his eternal condemnation—
And victory for whom would make me King of Litigation.

*

I'd also need associates, the kind whose dedication
To law is pathological—a Freudian fixation,
Who live to work and ask no other form of recreation
Than weekends at the office helping out with litigation.

They wouldn't be the products of northeastern education,
Trained at Yale in things like Roman transubstantiation,
Filling every brief with highfalutin' lucubration,
Irritating judges who could kill the litigation.

No, they'd be a rougher kind, whose fundamental motivation
Is hunger for a paycheck, not their mothers' approbation.
Disciplined, incapable of insubordination,
They'd march—young Spartans, unafraid of death—to
     litigation.

*

Secretaries not averse to taking lap dictation
(Regardless of their gender or their nuptial situation),
Massaging backs and egos, and providing titillation—
Anything for anyone involved in litigation.

Who think my cursive quite as nice as monks' illumination
Of medieval Bibles, and in need of no translation,
Who answer ringing phones before the tintinnabulation
Unhinges me and renders me unfit for litigation.

Who ask but paltry pay, and even less appreciation,
Enduring all my vices, never yielding to temptation
To quit or to attempt my much deserved defenestration,
Selflessly devoted to the cause of litigation.

Working 'round the clock for months, but taking no vacation,
And never showing pain from the resulting ulceration,
Disinclined to music, books, or carnal excitation,
Unless convinced that somehow it will help the litigation.

*

Hordes of paralegals who know proper case citation,
Every jurisdiction's rules on footnote numeration,
And all the other things that give the law its reputation
For pettiness, but constitute the core of litigation.

How to find the history of a piece of legislation,
From Congress, to the White House, to the courts for
        explication,
Always coming up with the "preferred" interpretation,
The one I've got to have if I'm to win the litigation.

Handling tasks indecorous, like record mutilation,
Memo alteration, even alibi creation,
All without my knowledge, lest some nasty allegation
Arise—to my surprise!—and undermine the litigation.

*

Last, I'd need the ultimate in office automation,
From dictaphones that stay awake through any peroration,
To copiers designed as much for paper duplication
As tearing up originals required for litigation.

Machines that work as people do, but need no exhortation
To do what they're expected to, no threat of termination;
That never fall asleep, or ask for more remuneration,
But live for just one purpose, to assist in litigation.

*

My client would be charged with crimes involving violation
Of laws both old and new (some still awaiting promulgation),
From negligence, to recklessness, to rank premeditation—
Each one good for several years, at least, of litigation.

Arson, incest, auto theft, police impersonation,
Murder, mayhem, forging bank notes, parrot strangulation,
Adultery, polygamy, attempted molestation
Of pets of certain jurors in this very litigation.

Word-based crimes—sedition, slander, riot incitation,
And the William Buckley, Jr., crime: undue syllabication
(Or using mammoth words to prove your higher education)—
A surefire way, in jury trials, to lose the litigation.

Crimes against good taste, for instance, public eructation,
Polyester suits (without some real good explanation),
Spitting down a manhole, or discussing constipation
At a State Department dinner—ample cause for litigation.

In sum, this wretch would stand accused of every
          permutation
Of behavior unacceptable within this constellation,
Resulting in a trial with no real hope of termination—
A lovely thought for someone who, like me, loves litigation.

*

Like all great lawsuits, this would be a paper altercation,
Every brief a multi-volume Ph.Dissertation,
More dazzling for its weight than for its ratiocination—
Ah, those noble forests, turned to pulp for litigation.

The judge in charge would end up on his knees in
          supplication,
Beset by scores of every form of legal complication,
Revealing law's capacity for trivialization,
Of things already trivial, but hey, that's litigation.

My basic goal would be, of course, my client's exculpation,
But also, for myself, the other lawyer's subjugation,
So word would spread that nothing but complete humiliation
Awaits the fool who tries to take me on in litigation.

Allowed at last to prove my skills at legal confrontation,
I'd stretch the bounds of sophistry and verbal obfuscation,
Attaining in the end the other side's capitulation,
And fear of ever facing me again in litigation.

Yes, I'd win, and win by knockout; I would wreak my
    devastation
In a manner Clarence Darrow would have viewed with
    approbation,
Ensuring my enshrinement and eternal consecration
In the (soon-to-be-established) Hall of Fame of Litigation.

My curse, that I must heed the siren call of disputation,
That courtrooms always offer me supreme exhilaration;
But there alone must I continue seeking my salvation,
For my idea of Heaven is eternal litigation.

Arnold B. Kanter
PRACTICING MICE AND OTHER AMAZING TALES*

FED UP WITH THE LEGAL MUMBO-JUMBO that chokes law reviews from coast to coast, a marauding band of lawyer-sociologists decided to take matters into their own hands. Striking swiftly, they wrenched the foundation research arms of bar associations into hammerlocks that would have done Vern Gagne (in my humble opinion, the greatest wrestler, save only Killer Kawalski, in the days when wrestlers were wrestlers, with stepover toe-holds and everything) proud.

---

* The author of this piece, Arnold B. Kanter, is perhaps best known for his
memoranda of the mythical firm Fairweather, Winters & Sommers, which have
appeared in *Chicago Lawyer* and often in *ABA Journal*. Reprinted from 8 *Barrister*
18-20, 37 (Autumn 1981) by permission of the author.

The research foundations quickly cried uncle, agreeing to sire bar research journals which serve to keep thousands of lawyer-sociologists off the streets. This, clearly, is good. These important bar research journals, some with circulations of well over 30 at last count, have succeeded in virtually stamping out legal gibble gabble, replacing it, instead, with sociological twaddle.

I have long felt that much of what appears in today's research journals would be of great interest to the Bar in general, were it only comprehensible. To test this hypothesis, I contacted Dr. Heinz Knibble regarding a popularized, made-for-BARRISTER version of his latest research article, "The Composition of the Legal Profession: A Socio-Psychological, Historico-Economic, Cross-Cultural and Neo-Political Peek."

Dr. Knibble kindly allowed access to his manuscript which, unfortunately, proved totally unintelligible. Rather than abandon the project, space already having been set aside for it, I coaxed him into the following exclusive interview.

BARRISTER: *Dr. Knibble, you are not a lawyer, is that correct?*

DR. KNIBBLE: I am not a lawyer, that is correct.

However, that is also not unusual.

One of the early studies I did unmasked the fact that a substantial majority of the people in this country are not lawyers. This is true even in Washington, D.C.

My finding came as a shock to most lawyers, who generally think that only they exist. They have responded by questioning my methodology and blithely continuing to speak alternately in Latin and arcane English.

Doctor, would you please tell us how you selected the subjects for your recent study of the legal profession?

Why not? I first considered selecting a random group of practicing attorneys for the study, but I was afraid there would be great difficulty in imposing the necessary controls on this group, thereby affecting the validity and reliability of the data collected. So, instead, I decided to create my own experimental group by purchasing 10,000 mice and putting them through law school.

That must have been very expensive. Where did you get the funds?

Initially I was funded by a $2 million research grant awarded to me, prehumously, by the American Bar Foundation. Naturally, that amount barely got me out of the blocks. Of the initial 10,000 mice, some 834 dropped or flunked out of law school. Many of them became insurance salesmice and, grateful to me for having given them their start, contributed generously to my project when the first two mil ran out.

What happened to the 9,166 who graduated?

Well, despite heroic efforts by the placement directors of many law schools, 3,842 were simply unable to find productive work. Of these, 3,787 took up residence in the homes of some of the most prominent citizens around the country. The other 55 are teaching in law schools.

You call the remaining 5,379 mice that form the basis of your study "practicing mice." What information did you gather about them?

Information as to all of the following independent variables was gathered for each practicing mouse: socioeconomic status, color, religion, sex, parents' occupation, cheese preference, length of tail, age and sexual preference. We then examined the covariation of this data with each of the following: LSAT score; law school; class rank; law journal, moot court and clinical experience; type of practice (e.g. corporate, small firm, government); average annual earnings and area of practice.

What did you discover from all of this?

From the cross-tabulation of data, certain moderately shocking correlations emerged, the most important of which are: LSAT score correlated most closely with cheese preference, those scoring over 700 almost invariably choosing camembert or brie, and those in the 400-500 range favoring Kraft American, preferably in individual cellophane-wrapped slices. The statistical significance of this correlation was .89, or 8.7 on the Richter scale. Sexual preference correlated most closely with law school; those attending the so-called elite law schools most often expressing no sexual preference. Average annual income correlated strongly with both length of tail and law school class rank, varying directly with the former and inversely with the latter.

How did you gather information about your subjects?

We circulated questionnaires to all practicing mice, soliciting information regarding their experiences. The results, however, proved inconclusive since of the 5,379 questionnaires sent out, only eight were returned.

We tried personal interviews, but ditched that technique when 69 of the first 71 interviews were terminated abruptly when the lawyers realized that the interviewers were not potential clients. We were forced then to observe the behavior and characteristics of our subjects through the installation of covert electronic audio and visual devices in the homes and workplaces of the mice.

Wasn't this a terrible intrusion on the privacy rights of the subjects?

Of course it was, but you're talking about important scientific research here.

What other findings did you turn up?

Practicing mice who went into ERISA work had no sense of humor.

How were you able to gauge sense of humor?

We attached electrodes to the temples of practicing mice and I rattled off some of my favorite one-liners. For example, "You are so dumb that you think Brandeis briefs are made by Fruit of the Loom." We then measured the electrical responses. Our results gave us some momentary concern, as it appeared that 18 of the ERISA mice had died. Though we have as yet been unable to determine whether or not these mice are alive, our concern has dissipated, since in either case they appear to be performing adequately in their specialty.

Can you give us examples of characteristics that you observed in mice in various types of practices?

Natch. We found that legal aid mice quickly experienced burnout and began to hate their clients. Economically, they were veritable churchmice. Those who opted for large law firms frequently developed drinking problems and despised their partners, as well as their clients. Mice who formed small law firms, e.g., Hickory, Dickory & Dock, P.C., often made big bucks, but suffered from both burnout and drinking problems.

The eight government mice were the only eight who returned our questionnaire.

Politically, what happened to your control group? Did they unite on areas of common interest?

You are prescient, they did indeed.

They quickly formed a bar association, the Mouso-American Federation of Important Attorneys (MAFIA), and lobbied successfully for a seat in the ABA House of Delegates. There, they pushed for reforms that would help future generations of Mouso-Americans, including a guideline aimed at denying ABA accreditation to any law school which discriminates against mice.

Two cunning tactical maneuvers rendered success inevitable. First, sensing that the mood of the ABA House was not quite right for a resolution directed solely at protecting rodents, the resolution was drafted to prohibit discrimination against anybody based on height, thus eliciting the support of many shorter non-vermin House members. Secondly, they avoided having either Young Lawyer or Individual Rights and Responsibilities delegates speak on behalf of their resolution.

Unfortunately, Oral Roberts University later sued the ABA and the principle was changed to prohibit discrimination based on height unless it is directly related to a religious tradition of the law school.

The MAFIA now functions largely like any other ethnic bar association. President Mary-Beth "Squeaky" Danish-Blue noted, at a recent press conference, that in its almost 200-year history the Supreme Court has never had a rodent justice.

Have mice experienced much discrimination?

Yes. At first, insensitive interviewers would frequently greet them with "Eeek!" And there were the inevitable mouse-and-elephant jokes. Because of their reputed timidity, mice were often pushed into probate work. Gradually, though, as inter-marriage has spread the barriers have dropped and Mouso-Americans have begun to achieve a new level of dignity.

Are your findings as to practicing mice generalizable to the entire lawyer population?

We thought we were well on our way to establishing generalizability when we discovered that one of our researchers was a CPA who, instead of using a least squares regression analysis, had applied the sum of the years digits method. This lowered our taxes, but invalidated our results. Now we're back at square one. You know, the best-laid schemes....

W. S. Gilbert
DAMON v. PYTHIAS*

Two better friends you wouldn't pass
Throughout a summer's day,
Than DAMON and his PYTHIAS,—
Two merchant princes they.

At school together they contrived
All sorts of boyish larks;
And, later on, together thrived
As merry mechants' clerks.

And then, when many years had flown,
They rose together till
They bought a business of their own—
And they conduct it still.

They loved each other all their lives,
Dissent they never knew,
And, stranger still, their very wives
Were rather friendly too.

Perhaps you think, to serve my ends,
These statements I refute,
When I admit that these dear friends
Were parties to a suit?

But 'twas a friendly action, for
Good PYTHIAS, as you see,
Fought merely as executor,
And DAMON as trustee.

* Reprinted from W. S. Gilbert, *The Bab Ballads,* 1871.

They laughed to think, as through the throng
Of suitors sad they passed,
That they, who'd lived and loved so long,
Should go to law at last.

The junior briefs they kindly let
Two sucking counsel hold;
These learned persons never yet
Had fingered suitors' gold.

But though the happy suitors two
Were friendly as could be,
Not so the junior counsel
Who were earning maiden fee.

They too, till then, were friends. At school
They'd done each other's sums,
And under Oxford's gentle rule
Had been the closest chums.

But now they met with scowl and grin
In every public place,
And often snapped their fingers in
Each other's learned face.

It almost ended in a fight
When they on path or stair
Met face to face. They made it quite
A personal affair.

(Enthusiastically high
Your sense of legal strife,
When it affects the sanctity
Of your domestic life.)

And when at length the case was called
(It came on rather late),
Spectators really were appalled
To see their deadly hate.

One junior rose—with eyeballs tense,
And swollen frontal veins:
To all his powers of eloquence
He gave the fullest reins.
His argument was novel—for
A verdict he relied
On blackening the junior
Upon the other side.

"Oh," said the Judge, in robe and fur,
"The matter in dispute
To arbitration pray refer—
This is a friendly suit."

And Pythias, in merry mood,
Digged Damon in the side;
And Damon, tickled with the feud,
With other digs replied.

But oh! those deadly counsel twain,
Who were such friends before,
Were never reconciled again—
They quarrelled more and more.

At length it happened that they met
On Alpine heights one day,
And thus they paid each one his debt,
Their fury had its way—

They seized each other in a trice,
With scorn and hatred filled,
And, falling from a precipice,
They, both of them, were killed.

Will Rogers
TWO LETTERS AND A DEDICATION*

MOST BOOKS have to have an Excuse by some one for the Author, but this is the only Book ever written that has to have an Alibi for the Title, too. About 4 years ago, out in California, I was writing sayings for the Screen and I called it *The Illiterate Digest*. Well one day up bobs the following letter from this N.Y. Lawyer. It and the answer are absolutely just as they were exchanged at that time.

WILLIAM BEVERLY WINSLOW
LAWYER
55 Liberty Street
New York, N.Y.

Nov. 5th, 1920.

Will Rogers, Esq.
c/o Goldwyn Studios,
Culver City, Calif.

Dear Sir:—
My client, the Funk & Wagnalls Company, publishers of the "Literary Digest" have requested me to write to you in regard to your use of the phrase, "The Illiterate Digest," as a title to a moving picture subject gotten up by you,

---

* This was the dedication to one of Will Rogers' best-known books, *The Illiterate Digest*, Boni, 1924. Reprinted by permission of the Will Rogers Memorial Commission, Claremore, Oklahoma.

the consequence of which may have escaped
your consideration.

For more than two years past it (my
client) has placed upon the moving picture screen a short reel subject carrying
the title "Topics of the Day," selected
from the Press of the World by "The
Literary Digest." This subject has
achieved a wide popularity both because
of the character and renown of "The
Literary Digest" and through the expendi-
ture of much time, effort and money by
its owners in presenting the subject to
the public. "The Literary Digest" is a
publication nearly thirty years old, and
from a small beginning has become probably the most influential weekly publication in the world. Its name and the
phrase "Topics of the Day" are fully
covered by usage as trademarks as well as
by registration as such in the United
States Patent Office.

During several months past your
"title," "The Illiterate Digest," has
been repeatedly called to our attention
and we are told that the prestige of "The
Literary Digest" is being lowered by the
subject matter of your film as well as by
the title of your film because the public
naturally confuse the two subjects. We
are also told that exhibitors are being
misled by the similarity of titles and
that some of them install your subject in
the expectation that they are securing
"The Literary Digest Topics of the Day."

It seems to me self-evident that
your title would scarcely have been
thought of or adopted had it not been for
our magazine and for our film. If this
were not the case the title which you use
would be without significance to the
general public.

I have advised the publishers that they may proceed against you through the Federal Trade Commission in Washington calling upon you to there defend yourself against the charge of "unfair competition," because of your simulation of their title, or that they can proceed against you, the producers of your film, its distributors and exhibitors in court for an injunction restraining you from use of the title, "The Illiterate Digest."

Before, however, instituting any proceedings in either direction they have suggested that I write directly to you to see if your sense of fairness will not cause you to voluntarily withdraw the use of the objectionable title.

Unless I hear favorably from you on or before the first of December, I shall conclude that you are not willing to accede to this suggestion and will take such steps as I may deem advisable.

Yours truly,

William Beverly Winslow

WBW/als

Los Angeles, Cal.
Nov. 15, 1920

MR WM BEVERLY WINSLOW

Dear Sir,
        Your letter in regard to my competi-
tion with the Literary Digest received
and I never felt as swelled up in my
life, And am glad you wrote directly to
me instead of communicating with my
Lawyers, As I have not yet reached that
stage of prominence where I was commiting
unlawful acts and requireing a Lawyer,
Now if the Literary Digest feels that the
competition is to keen for them——to show
you my good sportsmanship I will
withdraw, In fact I had already quit as
the gentlemen who put it out were behind
in their payments and my humor kinder
waned, in fact after a few weeks of no
payments I couldent think of a single
joke. And now I want to inform you truly
that this is the first that I knew my
Title of the Illiterate Digest was an
infringement on yours as they mean the
direct opposite, If a magazine was published called Yes and another Bird put
one out called No I suppose he would be
infringeing. But you are a Lawyer and its
your business to change the meaning of
words, so I lose before I start,
        Now I have not written for these
people in months and they havent put any
gags out unless it is some of the old
ones still playing. If they are using
gags that I wrote on topical things 6
months ago then I must admit that they
would be in competition with the ones the
Literary Digest Screen uses now. I will
gladly furnish you with their address, in
case you want to enter suit, And as I

have no Lawyer you can take my case too
and whatever we get out of them we will
split at the usual Lawyer rates of 80-20,
the client of course getting the 20,

Now you inform your Editors at once
that their most dangerous rival has
withdrawn, and that they can go ahead and
resume publication, But you inform Your
clients that if they ever take up Rope
Throwing or chewing gum that I will consider it a direct infringement of my
rights and will protect it with one of
the best Kosher Lawyers in Oklahoma,

Your letter to me telling me I was
in competition with the Digest would be
just like Harding writing to Cox and telling him he took some of his votes,

So long Beverly if you ever come to
California, come out to Beverly where I
live and see me

Illiterately yours

WILL ROGERS

When I sent him my answer I read it to some of the Movie Company
I was working with at the time and they kept asking me afterwards
if I had received an answer. I did not, and I just thought, oh well,
there I go and waste a letter on some High Brow Lawyer with no
sense of humor. I was sore at myself for writing it. About 6 months
later I came back to join the Follies and who should come to call on
me but the nicest old Gentleman I had ever met, especially in the
law profession. He was the one I had written the letter to, and he
had had Photographic Copies made of my letter and had given them
around to all his Lawyer friends.

So it is to him and his sense of humor, that I dedicate this
Volume of deep thought.

Talk of the Town
THE LEGAL MIND*

PINNING ANOTHER STORY on the innocent college professor may be taking advantage of a helpless class, but in this case there is no help for it; for the Professor tells it on himself.

He went into an antique shop in Italy and was rash enough to enthuse over a painting by an old master. "But of course," he said to the dealer, "I'm not one who can afford such things." And buying a small article he returned to his *pension*.

The next day the picture arrived. "Oh, yes," said the dealer, coldly when he went to protest, "You definitely bought this picture yesterday, and I'm afraid you'll have to pay for it. I intend to bring suit."

Wounded, confused, and despairing, the Professor went to an Italian friend of his—a lawyer. "Certainly I'll take the case," the lawyer said, after carefully examining the picture, "and you don't need to worry about the fee. By the way, was there anyone else in the shop when you were there?"

"No," said the Professor. "That's the trouble."

He had very little hope. And when at the trial the dealer produced two witnesses who swore they had heard the Professor order the picture sent to his *pension*, the last ray flickered and went out. Then his own lawyer got up.

"Did you leave the shop before my client, here?" he asked the witnesses.

"Yes."

"Well," he said, producing three respectable-looking citizens, "I have three witnesses who were in the shop later and who saw my client pay for the picture."

In this way the professor became the owner of an exceedingly valuable work of art. Then the lawyer called. "I won't bother you with a fee," he said affably. "I'll just take the picture." And putting it in his cab, he departed.

The Professor is still confused.

* Reprinted by permission; © 1926, 1954 The New Yorker Magazine, Inc.

Lawyer
He sits with spongy dignity
And waits for great thoughts to arrive
And censures the malignity
That gave him jowls at thirty-five.
—*Maxwell Bodenheim*

BLONDIE ®

by Dean Young and Stan Drake

LAWYERS IN WAITING

R. Emmett Kane, M.D.
THE BENCH AND BAR*

If you've got a son or daughter
Who ain't livin' like they orter,
If they'd suck an egg and peddle you the shell;
If the neighbors and the preacher,
The policemen and the teacher,
Are convinced that they are headed straight for hell;
If their instincts are possessive
And their ego is excessive,
If they're short on brains but very long on jaw,
Don't sit up nights and worry,
Make your mind up in a hurry,
Chuck 'em off to school and make 'em study law.
Have 'em learn the art of stalling,
How to howl like Virtue bawling,
And to make their betters think that they are tops;
How to wheedle fortunes stealthy
From a clientele that's wealthy,
And to be elected judge in case they're flops.
To become a politician
Must, of course, be their ambition,
Help 'em buy up all the ghosts they can afford.
It's a lawyer's bounden duty,
Be he moron, shyster, cootie,
When the gravy train is moving, be aboard.
He, of course, must hold his licker,
Be a Latin-spouting slicker,
Fill the human race with wholesome fear and awe,
For the life of Riley waits him
Till the Devil ups and dates him
When he's finished with the practice of the Law.

---

* Reprinted by permission of The Missouri Bar. Excerpted from a speech given to the
Missouri Bar Assoc. on Oct. 4, 1947.

J. S. Marcus
CENTAURS*

THE SMARTEST MAN in our law-school class told me he wanted to be an actor. He is short and awkward, and he has a comical problem with his "R"s. Once, he grabbed my hand and said, "Sheila, I made a terrible mistake leaving the stage." I like the idea of private failure. There must be chief executive officers who harbor secret dreams of teaching high-school English.

Inertia seems to be getting me through law school. I don't move much. I wait for a professor to intimidate me into the subject at hand: arson, divorce, whatever. I am particularly fascinated with the predicament of battered husbands. Not fascinated enough to do anything about it, but I don't mind reading the cases. My tax professor told me that I am not so different from my classmates. I suppose he meant the remark to be comforting.

If some man—say, X—runs a mink farm, and another, Y, is exploding dynamite next door, Y does not have to pay X in the event the mink eat their kittens from the shock of the explosion. It's the law.

I have a private life but not a personal one. Mostly, I smoke Dunhill cigarettes, put unwhipped cream on things, and reread early Evelyn Waugh novels. In private, I'm English.

A man from Yale who wants to go into entertainment law offered to buy me dinner. We chatted about the various apartments he'd had in New York, his stint in television, his Midwestern roots. When we got back to his apartment and undressed, he said, "Do it to me, sweetie." Now when we see each other, which is about twelve times a day, he acts as if we were once partners in some sort of class project.

If a railroad employee, X, thinks he is tripping over a bundle of newspapers, but is in fact tripping over a can of dynamite, and the explosion causes Y to drop a valuable family heirloom, could Y sue the railroad company for the cost of her grandmother's Hum-

---

* Reprinted by permission; © 1985 J. S. Marcus. Originally in *The New Yorker*.

mel figurine? I don't know, because I wasn't paying attention that day.

At a mandatory law-school party, a lady law professor from another university asked me to show her which were the law students and which were the dates. She just assumed I wasn't a date. After most of the guests had left, she broached the subject of alternative families. She said that Lesbian motherhood was fascinating but doomed as an institution. I told her that I liked her Laura Ashley dress.

I have one friend. He's a homosexual and also likes Evelyn Waugh. Sometimes he even does imitations of the characters. He calls most people philistines, and often walks into Evidence and says, "I got positively no sleep last night." I usually believe him.

*

At a mandatory tea at the Dean's house, I met the Dean's wife. She's an illustrator of children's books and a gourmet cook. After a few preliminary remarks, she asked if I wanted her recipe for *crème brûlée*. I suppose she thought I was different from the other law students.

The editor of the law review lives across the street. She used to be a nun, but now she wears hiking boots and smokes mentholated cigarettes. After she left the convent and before she entered law school, she worked at the men's cologne counter of a large department store. Sometimes she has dinner parties and drinks a lot of Scotch. I guess another "terrible beauty is born." But how and when? Did she just wake up one morning and head for the nearest men's cologne counter? Perhaps it happened gradually (she's about forty-five)—a rosary in one hand, a Budweiser in the other; half saint, half goat.

People in law school, like people in general, try to be pleasant, and like people in general they often fail. Law students, I have noticed, tend to eat three-quarters of a sandwich and then wrap the remainder in foil, right there out in the open. One law student who is handicapped asks people to buy him hot chocolate around lunchtime; his wheelchair can't get near the vending machines. The other law students, busy wrapping, usually don't hear him.

My Jurisprudence professor decided to hold class in his apartment so it could turn into a party. He had a copy of *Soviet Life* in the bathroom and talked about how much money he'd be making if he weren't a law professor. He lives with one of his former students.

She's a judge and wears the same clothes as he does: boots, bluejeans, blazers. They are both, as fate would have it, from the same Chicago suburb. She came up to me with a plate full of cucumbers and smiled. I wanted to tell her that while insanity may be a defense for homicide, it is not a defense for a plate full of cucumbers; she always has a ravaged, insane look on her face.

As a child, I wanted to be an actress. More recently I've toyed with the idea of becoming a chief executive officer.

Each year, we eagerly await the Malpractice party and the White-Collar Crime party. The Malpractice party comes in October and is made up of law students and medical students. The White-Collar Crime party comes in February and is made up of law students and business students. One wonders: Left to their own devices, do the medical students and business students meet on their own? Is there such an animal as the Hospital Administrators' party?

Soon we will be reading about a woman who signed up for thirty thousand dollars' worth of dance lessons. I'm not sure if she was hit by a car on the way to her first lesson and wanted all her money back, or if she never learned to dance and blew up the studio with dynamite. Perhaps she was black, or a man, or handicapped, and they gave her inferior lessons. I just don't know.

In law school, you can feel boredom go from the benign to the malignant. You can see people run around with a quarter of a tuna-salad sandwich in their briefcase and argue about mink farms. You can, with a little patience and finesse, get yourself invited to a party where the food and liquor are free.

*

Law students, unlike other students, tend to have umbrellas. I feel even more English when it rains, and often say things like "Excuse me, I have to go to the loo."

Some of the more interesting stereotyped characteristics of law students: unshaven, impotent, dirty, overweight, devout, narrow-minded, humorless. Or if they're women: frigid, tall, overweight, giddy. If you've ever seen a law school catalogue, you know there are very few pictures.

I could be wrong, of course. Perhaps the man from Yale said, "Do it to me, Mama," not "sweetie." This would make more sense, since I am taller than he is. But if I had to go through it all over again and he did say "sweetie," I would tell him never under any circumstances to use both an imperative and a diminutive in the same sentence—especially in bed.

The other day, I was on my way to class when the man from Yale came out of nowhere and said to me, "Where are you galloping off to?"

At law-school parties, men and women talk to each other as if there were no difference between men and women. The law students and the dates act as if there were no difference between the law students and the dates. Of course, the dates don't understand all this talk about law, unless they happen to be judges. Sometimes the women talk about feminism, and sometimes the men talk about sports. But we eventually leave those topics to the extremists and drift off onto less sacred subjects. I have never heard Evelyn Waugh's name brought up at a law-school party—not even at the ex-nun's house. My homosexual friend has better things to do, and I usually don't open my mouth, even though I am a baseball fan.

Transformations, sublimations, things becoming other things. Yesterday, I had a Reuben potato—certainly the centaur of modern delicatessen food. Prodding the melted cheese for some trace of Russian dressing, I tried to recall if any of the law-school parties so far had been catered. I am becoming a lawyer.

Incompetent. Tenured. —*Robert J. Morris*

Robert D. Abrahams
THE LAW OF LIBEL*

Law Offices
Barr, Disbarr & Krohbar

November 15, 1938

Editor
Shoddy Stories
City

Dear Editor:

Your letter, marked "urgent," asking for an opinion on the Law of Libel, with respect to a certain article you are thinking of publishing, arrived today, and this being Saturday, I hasten to tell you that all the partners and assistants have gone fishing, leaving me in charge. My instructions were to do nothing but to answer the telephone, but if you had called by telephone, I would have answered, so I see no reason why I should not answer the mail, as well. After all, I am a second-year law student, and did pretty well in my classes last year, flunking in only two subjects, neither of which was the Law of Libel, so I can assure you that my ideas on the subject will be of help to you.

I can well understand how you need advice on Libel. I don't read your magazine, because my tastes are superior to that, but I realize that almost everything you publish would be a libel on somebody.

* Reprinted from the long-defunct humor magazine *Judge*, 12-38.

The article you sent for our opinion is undoubtedly libelous. You ought to know by this time that you can't say that the Senator is a polygamist, or that he killed his last wife at breakfast, in a fit of rage when his name was left out of the morning paper by mistake, or that he keeps a stable of horses on money he steals from the WPA. Really, Mr. Editor, you ought not to need a lawyer to tell you that—especially at the rates charged by Barr, Disbarr & Krohbar. Confidentially, when I have graduated I will probably be opening an office of my own, and will be very pleased to serve you for much less than they do.

Even to your suggestion that you change the article to say it is *alleged* that the Senator is a polygamist, and it is *said* that the Senator killed his wife at breakfast, in a fit of rage when his name was left out of the morning paper by mistake, and it is *whispered* that the Senator keeps a stable of horses on money he steals from the WPA will not let you out. Changing "polygamist" to "bigamist" won't do, either.

After much thought, and having spent at least fifteen minutes in our law library, I have come to the conclusion that there is one way in which you can save the situation. *Run a quiz.* You know what a quiz is, don't you, Mr. Editor? They begin: "How Intelligent Are You? One out of four of the following is correct. If you're smart, you'll know which one it is. If you're dumb, you won't." Then they go on with something like this:

> *The George Washington Bridge is:*
> (1) A game played at Mt. Vernon.
> (2) A dental invention, much used among the Japanese.
> (3) A figment of the imagination.
> (4) A span across the Hudson.

Well, Mr. Editor, you can get around this libel in the same way. Just say:

> *Three of the following four statements are wrong:*
> Senator So-and-Such is:
> (1) A polygamist.
> (2) A man who killed his wife at breakfast in a fit of rage when his name was left out of the morning paper by mistake.
> (3) A man who keeps a stable of horses on money he steals from the WPA.
> (4) A United States Senator.

Then, way back among the advertisements, you put a little bit of a thing reading, in very small type:

> *Nos. 1, 2, 3.*

You see, in that way, Mr. Editor, you aren't *saying* that the Senator is any one of the other things, and I think it will be O.K. if you're even a little careless, and put the answers where nobody would read them anyhow, like among the editorials.

I'm not allowed to take money for legal services, because I'm not yet admitted. Instead of that, if it's O.K. with you. I'll take it out in trade. All I want is to draw up your quizzes on certain people in the news.

Yours very truly,

Robert D. Abrahams

Fred Rodell
NON-NEGOTIABLE YOU

(Music by Harold Rome)

I study law
With the proper awe,
I'm an earnest sort of lad;
But I've got a flair
For a lady fair
Who's no way to be had;
She won't be hugged and she won't be kissed
Though I've tried to be empiric;
So I sing to the girl who *can* resist
This legalistic lyric:

You're the note
That's got my goat,
Non-negotiable you.
You've got class
That I can't pass,
Non-negotiable you.
You've the only form that I endorse,
I've not used fraud and I've not used force,
And I want to be your holder in due course,
'Cause you're due!

You're the Jill
That fills the bill,
Non-negotiable you.
You've set the date
And payment's late,
Non-negotiable you.
Another slip wants me for a taker,
Her sum is certain, but I'd still forsake her
To be your own accommodation maker,
Non-negotiable you!

D. W. P.
THE LAW STUDENT'S WIFE*

He's got books,
He's got classes,
He's got notes
And horn-rimmed glasses.

He's got abstracts,
Trial cases,
And he trots
The legal paces.

He's got bills,
He's got notes,
He's got Profs
On whom he dotes.

He's got loves,
He's got hates,
Based upon
The mark he rates.

He's got friends,
They're law students.
They dispute
Jurisprudence.

He's got Langdell
And the Libe,
Lots of places
To imbibe.

Knowledge, whisky,
Beer or gin,
At his law club
Or The Inn.

He can argue,
He can chatter,
Night or day
It doesn't matter.

But with so much
Joy and strife,
Why'd he ever
Take a wife?

He seldom sees her,
When he does
The air's with
Legal terms a-buzz.

Her neat house
Is a mess of papers,
While he rants
'Bout wills and rapers.

She hears cases
Cause and why,
Till she'd love
To pop that guy.

They play bridge,
Well, bridge of sorts,
Till he recalls
That case in Torts.

When he's late
For every meal,
He goes and blames
Professor Beale.

* Reprinted from *Docket*, 4-33, by permission of West Publishing Company.

And should she try
To have a guest,
If nonlegal
She's a pest.

And so, your Honor,
May I say:
To hell with Law
And its *in re.*

For he must explain
The law he knows;
Then it's too late
For movie shows.

My next marriage,
Though less prudent,
Sure won't be to
A law student.

William L. Prosser
NEEDLEMANN ON MORTGAGES*

IN THE LAW OF CALIFORNIA, the distinction between a mortgage and a deed of trust is, I am told, a matter of great intricacy, and its consequences are sometimes peculiarly perplexing to lawyers, and even more to students of the law. As their ramifications are explored at the Law School of the University of California at Berkeley, in the course on Security Transactions given by Professor Stefan A. Riesenfeld, they are reported to lead to mental anguish in an extreme degree. At the end of the course stands an examination, which, I am informed, is looked upon by the class with much the same unfavorable eye with which the prophet Mahomet looked upon marriage. It will be recalled that he likened it to an ordeal, wherein a man putteth his hand into a sack containing a thousand asps and one eel, and it is by the favor of Allah alone that he may draw forth the eel. The fact that law school generations have taken the course, and the examination, and have lived to tell the tale is, of course, considered quite immaterial.

Especially harrowing to the soul of the California student is the fact that there is no textbook to which he may resort for solace and aid. The student view of the profound and learned *Hornbook on Mortgages,* written by Professor George E. Osborne, of Stanford, is that it is an excellent book, and doubtless sufficient and satisfactory

---

* The author of this piece, William L. Prosser, was recognized not only as an authority on tort law, but also as a leading legal humorists and editor of *The Judicial Humorist: A Collection of Judicial Opinions and Other Frivolities,* Little, Brown, 1952. Reprinted from 9 *Journal of Legal Education* 489-494 (1957) by permission of the *Journal of Legal Education.*

for Stanford, but that is signally fails to come to grips with many of
the highly complex problems discovered by Professor Riesenfeld in
the California law. There is no other short text. This is an aching
void and the cause of infinite student woe.

On a dull Sunday afternoon, when the usual dismal January
rain was drizzling down on Berkeley, two of the student assistants
behind the library desk, with nothing else to do, decided that it was
time that this void should be filled. The thought was father to the
deed. They proceeded to prepare and to insert in the card catalogue
of the Law School library a card reading as follows:

294r	Needlemann, Sol H. 1910-
N76	
1956	California Law of Mortgages
	West Publishing Co., St. Paul, Minn., 1956
	—126 pages
	1. Current Law
	2. Mortgages and Deeds of Trust—
	Distinguished and Explained

In addition to this the name of *Needlemann on Mortgages* was
inserted in the "flip card" index, designed for quick location of
books expected to be used frequently. A second card was prepared
for the library desk, indicating that on this particular rainy Sunday,
the book had been called for and taken out by some person uniden-
tified, whose name was signed on the back. All that remained was
to mention to two or three members of Professor Riesenfeld's class,
selected as those most likely to disseminate news, that the library
had acquired *Needlemann on Mortgages* and that it was the complete
answer to all prayers.

Wildfire spread. In a day or two, word was around the school
that manna had descended from heaven. The library desk was
stormed. The book was, unhappily, out. The desk card was
produced. The signature on the back of it was utterly illegible. It
began with something like an A or an O, which might equally be a
B, a D, a Q, an R, or an N. In the middle of it there was a tall letter,
possibly a b, an f, an l, a d, or an uncrossed t. It ended, in all
probability, with an n or an m, which might, perhaps, be a double
s. The name might have been Anderson, Androsian, Oberlin or
Ostermann. It might, with almost equal probability, have been
Doublecross or Qrxfvmcn. It is, perhaps, not surprising that
presently dark forebodings were voiced that the Russians might be

at work. It was even suggested that the book might have been taken out by Needlemann.

For several days, the siege of the library desk continued; but the book was not returned. A diligent search of all of the offices of the faculty, beginning, of course, with that of the dean, failed to discover it. Suspicion grew that some hound in human form, seeking an unfair advantage in the competition for grades, had purloined the book, deliberately leaving behind him a specimen of his examination book handwriting which even Osborn—meaning, of course, *Osborn on Questioned Documents*—could not decipher. Appeals to the desk men to do something at once drew forth only grim mutterings that for this, someone's head would roll in the basket; and demands that another copy of the book be ordered forthwith received the answer that this had, of course, been done. There was, however, some unaccountable delay in St. Paul, and no book came.

At the meeting of the second-year class, the class president made an earnest and impassioned appeal to the unknown individual who had the book to play fair with his classmates and return it at once. This proved to be entirely futile. Professor Riesenfeld was approached by some of the class and asked where to obtain a copy of *Needlemann on Mortgages*. He made confusion worse confounded by asserting categorically that there was no such book—a statement obviously incredible in the face of the card in the catalogue. He would, he said, know. "The only book on the California law of mortgages," he declared, "is the one I am writing." Rumor, which is rife, has it that he then retired to his office and spent $16.75 on long distance telephone calls in an effort to track down this sudden and mysterious competitor. This, however, has not been verified. However it may be, student perplexity was in no way diminished when Professor Riesenfeld, in a subsequent class hour, referred in an offhand manner to *Needlemann on Mortgages* as containing an excellent discussion of a minor point into which he had no time to go.

With all of the magnificent resources of the Law School broken down and lying prostrate at their feet, the indefatigable student body, with a persistence worthy of the fine traditions of the school, sought elsewhere. The San Francisco County Law Library turned out not to have the book, nor did the Alameda County Law Library in Oakland. Calls were made to the law schools of Hastings and Stanford, but these excellent and worthy institutions proved, once again, to be broken reeds. A careful and exhaustive search of Martindale-Hubbell, ranging through all the cities and towns of California, found no lawyer named Needlemann. The identity of the learned author remained shrouded in mystery and silence.

Again, rumor, emanating from the library desk, supplied a clue. It was suggested that this Needlemann must be none other than the well-known Father Needlemann, until recently a professor of the Law School of Loyola University in Los Angeles, who two or three years ago had left his position and the state. Los Angeles is a large city more than four hundred miles to the southward, concerning which any report, of whatever character, tends to be received in Berkeley with implicit belief. The telephone to Los Angeles produced, however, no enlightenment. Neither at Loyola, nor at the University of Southern California, nor at our sister school of the University of California at Los Angeles, had any one ever heard of Father Needlemann or of *Needlemann on Mortgages*.

One member of the class discovered that the West Publishing Company had an office in San Francisco. He journeyed to that city, expending fifty cents on bridge tolls and as much more for parking, only to be told that the Company had published no such book and was confident that it had been published by no one else. This stu-

G. B. Trudeau, DOONESBURY

dent, I am informed, feels himself aggrieved. He considers that he has a cause of action against the University of California, under the doctrine of *respondeat superior,* for his dollar and the value, if any, of his wasted time. This cause of action is believed to sound in deceit. As to whether he has also a cause of action for the intentional infliction of severe mental distress by extreme and outrageous conduct, see Prosser, *Insult and Outrage,* 44 Calif.L.Rev.40 (1956).

Meanwhile, vaulting ambition soared in the hearts of the conspirators behind the desk. They discussed plans of a student forum, at which some one with a thick Teutonic accent should appear to impersonate Needlemann, and deliver an utterly incomprehensible lecture on the law of mortgages. These were the best laid plans of mice. They came crashing to the earth when suddenly, one rainy morning, unfounded rumor stalked the corridors that Assistant Dean William N. Keeler had become interested in the matter and was about to make a personal investigation to discover what had become of *Needlemann on Mortgages.* Dean Keeler is a mild and gentle man, but he is reliably reported to have defeated his weight in mountain lions in single combat. Faced with this dire inquisition, the morale of the culprits disintegrated like a haystack in a hurricane. They came forward and confessed. Consternation and righ-

teous indignation reigned in the class on Security Transactions.No one, however, was lynched. I am told that this was only because it was felt that the dean would not like it. The dean is familiarly known to the student body as Wild Bill, and there is a legend that when aroused to fury, he spits chemically pure sulphuric acid. It is also understood that somewhere in the law school of the University of Minnesota, there is the skin of a rattlesnake which he strangled with his bare hands.

Thus, there is lost to California, to legal scholarship, and to posterity, a masterpiece, unique of its kind and of ineffable value to the world. Before the curtain descends on the little drama, I should like to add, for the benefit of future historians, a few words about the distinguished legal scholar whose great work has perished in this distressing manner in the halls of our Law School.

Sol Humperdinck Needlemann* was born on April 1, 1910, in the city of Pilsen. As his name indicates, he was the descendant of a long line of English tailors. The founder of the continental branch of the family was kidnapped while traveling in Prussia and was impressed into the regiment of giant grenadiers maintained by Friedrich Wilhelm I. During the Seven Years War, while in the invading army of Friedrich II, he was wounded while retreating after the battle of Prague and remained behind to settle in Pilsen, where he became a brewer. His beer, which is named after the town, is still manufactured by the family. It is, of course, a household word both in Germany and in the United States.

The future author was educated originally to be a rabbi. Even during his childish years, he displayed remarkable talents—among them, an unusual skill at the game of chess. At the age of four, he defeated his father, no mean player; and at fourteen, he had become a grandmaster of the game. His greatest single feat was at the tournament at Bad Order in 1928, when he finished first over a field of the twenty-four best players in the world, including Capablanca, Lasker, Alekhine, Nimzovitch, Bogoljubov, Moussorgsky, Prokofieff, Shostakovich, Borodin, Rimski, and Korsakov. His 32 4-move draw with Lasker, lasting more than sixteen hours, is still renowned

---

* Not under any circumstances to be confused with Professor Kurt H. Nadelmann of New York University, to whom humble apologies are due for the coincidence of the similarity in names. I am informed by the students in question that "needlemann" had no other connotation than that of "needling" their fellows.

as the only master tournament game which was finished in solitude and total darkness—after the spectators and the referee had gone home and the janitor had turned out the lights. This one game completely demolished Schinken's move in the Eier line in the Bratwurst variation of the Queen's Gambit Declined, which never has been played in any master tournament since.

In 1930, an event occurred which profoundly affected the future career of this young genius. While he was swimming in the River Main, he was saved from drowning by the Archbishop of Worms, who, at the time, was descending the river in a flatboat on his way from Kulmbach to Würzburg. The pious prelate jumped overboard, pulled the youth ashore, expertly administered artificial resuscitation, and conferred his benediction.

This rescue had three natural and inevitable consequences in young Needlemann's life. One was his immediate conversion to the Catholic faith. The second was a determination to study law. The third was a burning desire to come to California.

There followed years of study, during which this double master of chess and law amassed a record of university degrees believed to be unequaled in the entire history of legal education. No known compilation of all of them exists, but included in the list were doctorates from Heidelberg, Göttingen, Tübingen, Jena, Magdeburg, Breslau, Berlin, Vienna, Aarhus, Padua, Bologna, Milan, Paris, Louvain, Salamanca, Barcelona, Oxford, Cambridge, Edinburgh, Mexico, Lima, Chicago, the University of Kansas City, the St. Paul College of Law, Stanford, and, of course, Yale. Included also was a degree of Doctor of Legal Hermeneutics from the University of Omsk, earned during a brief interval while Needlemann was a prisoner in Siberia. The suggestion of Russian influence is, thus, not entirely without foundation, although so far as I have been able to discover, it never led to a congressional investigation.

From the beginning, and as a product of his career as a chess master, Needlemann was fascinated by the law of mortgages. The marked similarity between the positional problems arising, for example, after the twelfth move in the Tchigorin defense to the Ruy Lopez and the problems arising in the law of subrogation will be readily apparent to any student of both subjects. Needleman's first contribution to legal scholarship was his noted article on circuity of lien, which appeared in the *Ausgewählte Beitrage zum Vergleichenden Pfandrecht*, published in 1933 under the auspices of the University of Bologna, in company with articles by such other distinguished legal scholars as Reulbach, Overall, Pfiester, Brown, Kling, Schulte, Hofmann, Scheckard, Steinfeldt, Tinker, Evers, and Chance.

Having attained an enviable international reputation Needlemann achieved in 1947 the ambition of his life and came to California. He became a professor of law at Loyola, giving courses in Comparative Law and Security Transactions. His first accomplishment within the state was the completion of an exhaustive sociological and economic survey, conducted with a grant in aid from the Uplift Foundation, of the mortgage situation in Los Angeles. This survey finally and conclusively demonstrated that a mortgagor is invariably a person who needs to borrow money; and on this basis, it has become the foundation stone for many economics textbooks since.

Although Needlemann never had taken holy orders, his plump, beaming personality soon won for him the affectionate student nickname of Father Needlemann. Anyone who has had the singular good fortune to attend a symposium * held by the genial Father Donovan at the meetings of the Association of American Law Schools will undoubtedly remember Needlemann as a jolly, rotund, broad, expansive, fair-haired individual with a slight, but attractive, Swedish accent, bubbling over with new discoveries in the law of his beloved mortgages, gesturing dramatically with a cluster of hors d'oeuvres in one hand and a glass in the other, and enthusiastically sharing the refreshments with all comers.

His departure from Loyola in 1953 was not, as has been so unkindly suggested in San Francisco, due to a violent dislike for Los Angeles and the feeling that human endurance could stand no more. He loved the place, and especially he loved Loyola. He left only to write his book, which was to be, and was, the *magnum opus* of his life. He retired to a little cattle ranch in northwestern Mexico, on the outskirts of Aguardiente, where he labored for three years to untangle the California law of mortgages and deeds of trusts. He needed no library and no cases, because he had memorized them

---

* "*Symposium.* In ancient Greece, a drinking together, usually following the banquet proper, with music, singing, and conversation; hence, a banquet or social gathering at which there is free interchange of ideas." *Webster's Collegiate Dictionary* 1011 (5th ed. 1945).

all. He finally completed the book, which was at once accepted for publication by West.

Before it was published, he was called to his ultimate reward. Without warning, Sol Humperdinck Needlemann suddenly died, of a surfeit. At this distance, there is no available information as to a surfeit of what. Professor Riesenfeld thinks that it may have been a surfeit of rolling options. Be that as it may, it was a happy death. His great work was done.

Thus perished, in the flower of his achievement, this remarkable genius, this distinguished legal scholar, this author of a lost masterpiece. The tradition, I might even say the legend, remains behind him as a enduring monument to the things that are done in the state of California.

As to what became of the book, no one knows.

Edward J. Bander
ON THE CASE SYSTEM*

(with apologies to Mr. Dooley and "th' backers iv th' system.")

"I SEE BE TH' PA-APERS," observed Mr. Dooley, "that all th' gr-reat instatooshuns iv laygal l'arnin' in th' country have taken to th' case system."

"Niver heard iv a system that did me much good," muttered Mr. Hennessy.

"'Tis that kind iv system, Hinnissy, but 'tis not likely it'll bother ye. 'Tis not backed be gamblers but be collidge perfessers and its victims aren't hodcarriers but those like Hogan, who must lose a few years becomin' lawyers before runnin' fer Congress. There are those Hinnissy, whose l'arnin' has gone to their tongues, who prefers callin' it th' cha-os method, but that's a bit too much fer ye.

"'Twas someone with th' rich name iv Christopher Columbus

---

* A legal librarian, Edward J. Bander edited a collection of Finley Peter Dunne's writings under the name *Mr. Dooley on the Choice of Law*, The Michie Co., 1963. This imitation comes from that volume. For another takeoff on Dunne, see James M. Marsh's "Mr. Dooley Discovers a Unanimous Dissent" (p. 174), and for the real thing, see "Cross-Examinations" (p. 146). © The Michie Company, reprinted by permission of the publisher.

Langsyne who started th' business. This here feller got lost in th' shelvin' in th' Harvid Lib'ry, an be th' time they discovered him, he'd gone an' read all th' cases from Doomsday to th' lates' Supreem Coort dispatches. He was niver th' same afther th' experience an' neither was th' law. 'Tis said he read more cases than John L. drank, and there are those who'll wager John L. could walk th' sthraighter line.

"First thing ye know they made old Langsyne Dean, an' he began advertisin' in th' Boston pa-apers that a feller cud l'arn a bit iv law without studyin' wan wor-rd iv lessons an' definitions th' same as in school. This pa-aper said there was some gr-reat lawyer-men there at Harvid, an' they knew so much law all a feller had to do was to dally around ferninst thim fer a year 'r two an' let it sink in—ivry mornin' readin' what Holmes, J. or Cardozo, J. or Marshall, J.—all Harvid men be th' way—have to say about gas stokin', automobiles or fay-ries, about which ye'd think they'd know nawthin'.

"It made hayroes iv these judges Hinnissy an' twudden't surprise me some day if I heer some little kiddies swappin' five Frankfurters fer four Blacks or two Potted Stuarts fer wan law clark—'twud at laste be good fer th' bubble gum industhry. Anny-how, to make th' system work, th' men who wud profit most from it, printed a rosy raypoort iv this most scandalous scheme an' it caught on like chain letters. 'Twas like Congress votin' itself a raise.

"In th' ol' days Hinnissy mention case to a lawyer an' he'd say Ol' Crow—at laste be th' beeographies—an' there are those who say th' law didn't suffer be it although it was th' death iv manny a good liver. Rough-house Choate didn't need *Buster on Pleadin'* to l'arn a jury how to be his. Dinny Webster—ah, I cud use th' man to pay me rent—an' Fallon an' Darrow were all case method men iv a kind Langsyne wud hold his nose up to, but 'tis not to say they weren't book-l'arn'd.

"There was manny story books on th' law thin, an' Kent did some writin' ontil he saw th' jig was up an' wint into th' cigarette business in th' nick iv time, an' there was an' old English wan called Cook on Littleton which I forbid Hogan to bring into me estab-lishment. 'Twas a simple matter thin. In thim days all ye had to do was to sit at th' feet of an imminent lawyer—no mean feat, Hinnis-sy—read a little law as they say, and, if ye had th' looks, th' voice an' ye'er father in th' business ye was set fer lifers.

"Today, Hinnissy, ye go to law school fer three y'ars an' then ye have to ask th' sthreet car conductor where th' Coorthouse is. Ye'eve read all th' cases fr'm here to Chinee an' whin ye get into coort ye make ye'er first mistake be cross-examinin' th' bailiff an' ye'er secon' be commentin' on what a shtupid lookin' jury ye have to contind with as ye look at th' men in th' nice chairs behind ye. Ye think th' clerk iv coort sells dhry goods—if he did, he'd be sartin' to make th' briefs too long—an' ye think a charge to th' jury means which side can get to thim first. Hinnissy fer what most lawyers wind up doin' 'tis like tachin' a boy to run a cash raygister be sindin' him to that other timple of l'arnin' on th' wrong side iv th' Charles.

"Ye shud see th' kind iv problems they give th' boys before they let 'em loose on a suspectin' public. Hogan showed me his exam pa-aper wancet, an' niver again. 'Twas as sad an' sorry a story as I've ever read, like a woman's magazine, excipt it had no endin'. Th' poor hayroe was left bleedin', lost an' shellshock. 'Hogan,' I said, 'what's th' rest iv th' story. Me heart is sore fr'm cryin'.' Ye wudden't believe what Hogan told me. In th' story there was a little feller. Hogan, mercy be, called him an attractive nuisance. They had a saintly girl testifyin' to foul deeds. Hogan, impudent as iver, says not to believe a word she says because of a Hershey bar. An' ivry time I thought I was comin' to th' punch line Hogan wud puff his chest an' smile wisely an' say 'see Leach *v* Nutshell' or 'see Simpson *v* Stupidity' or some such nonsense. I'll see 'em, Hinnissy, but not in these familiar surroundin's.

"But to get back to l'arnin' be th' cha-os method—if ye please. 'Tis a game iv cards Hinnissy, an' th' house always wins. Each lawyer-to-be has to buy a stacked deck an' th' house always comes up with th' Jack-Ace to make a donkey out iv ye. An' whin ye think ye'eve got th' cards marked an' can give th' taycher a run fer ye'er money, don't ye think he knows it an' turns aroun' an' makes ye buy another deck. In th' ol' days a book iv law was good fer years on end but did ye iver here iv a case book outlivin' th' author. Not if his successor can help it. 'Tis a game an' like all games it has its followers includin' those that spend three years tryin' to bate it, a few who lave off in a week or so lackin' th' spoortin' blood as they do, an' wan or two brainy wans that laves off afther a year or two an' go into th' writin' business.

"An' thim that plays th' game—oh, 'tis a pitiful thing, Hinnissy,—'tis awful. They git th' mos' turr'ble gamblin' fayver. Whin thim boys ain't aytin' or slaypin'—which they seldom ar-re—they do nawthin' but play solitaries with thim packs iv cases. They take wan case an' rade it over an' over, an' thin wancet again, an' they sip'rate ivry line fr'm th' wan nix' above an' below be gr-reat black borders, so's not to git wan mixed up with t'other, an' they puzzle over ivry wor-rd, an' they bile it all down—or bile it away accordin' to th' run iv th' luck—an' thin they put th' bilin's into a schrap-book an' call thim 'abshtracts,' an' thin they bile thim abshtracts down, an' whin, afther they're all thru mixin' an' bilin', they go to tak' a fin'l invinth'ry iv what's in th' kittle, they foind it's full iv hot air.

"Be that as it may Hinnissy, 'tis a valuable experience an' I have often thought that manny a horse-player belonged in law school for 'tis on th' track that abshtractin' an' underlinin' is no lost art—an' there are those who'll say vicey-versey.

"But ye have to see a case book to believe it. Ivry wan sued in these cases has a middle name beginnin' with a 'v'. Wan iv these days it'll be St. Vincent battlin' Morgan Memorial. An' the names. Armry v Delamire, Buick v McPherson, Eugene v Debs. Thin comes his honor—a feller always havin' a 'J' fer a first name. I suppose 'tis as good a way iv pickin' thim as electin' thim or havin' th' guv'ner pick 'em, that way it's called judicial selection, but me frind Dochney, in th' eighth ward calls it courtship. Thin th' case begins.

"Hinnissy wan day I'll read ye th' case about th' constituchin followin' th' flag. Each case has a p'int—if ye can find it—an' wan p'int builds on another p'int an' sometimes a case takes away a p'int an' be th' time Hogan came in fr'm class to do his studying'—wan p'int leadin' to another—he'd soon be edycatin' me patroons on th' finer p'ints iv th' law—excipt in th' matter iv holdin' 'em.

"Now all that don' sound exactly enlightenin', Hinnissy, but afther raydin' it over a couple iv hundther' times with th' help iv a few dicsch'neries an' grammers, an' givin' yer imaginash'n a bit iv play, ye'd be surproised th' way th' pictoor gradooley onfolds befure yer eager eyes. Whin on th' next day th' taycher sez, 'Mr. Hinnissy, shtat th' nix' case,' here's what ye say: 'Whin A said, "Deed, I do," he sold Blackacre to B, and whin B promised to act like a father to th' young immigrant girl on a promise to will th' land to her, 'twas a misdeed.'

"'Indeed,' says th' perfesser who gets a handsome sum fer writin' introductions to books, and he then adds p'ints to th' case an' takes 'em away ontil th' lawyers-to-be agree that Blackacre is a stained glass window an' that's what th' case meant. Some students who read th' case ar-re given a boost, an' those who haven't read it are made to feel they have ontil it is suggested with as much cruelty as th' law will allow, that there is a shortage of French Legionnaires in Algeria. Th' treatment is such as th' case may require.

"'Tis th' Suecratic method, Hinnissy. Suecrats was a Greek who cured ivrybody's problem but his own. Th' lawyers like him because he proved wancet fer all that if ye thry to be ye'er own lawyer ye have a ninny fer a client. He talked himsilf into th' lockstep an' th' hemlock, which is a drink, me frind, that me neighbor across th' sthreet makes ye pay to take."

"I don't undherstand," said Hennessy, who was not easily confused.

"I'll give ye an example iv th' Suecratic method. Whin th' case is discussed to th' satisfaction iv th' taycher he says, 'Shtat th' nix' case.'

"'Excuse me,' sez a student who has read all about Suecrats, 'but what does this case decide?'

"'What shud ye say?' sez th' taycher.

"'Oive not th' raymotes' idea,' sez th' student.

"'Thin' sez th' taycher, 'Ye shtat th' nix' case.'"

Accuracy and diligence are much more necessary to a lawyer than great comprehension of mind, or brilliancy of talent. His business is to refine, define, split hairs, look into authorities, and compare cases. A man can never gallop over the fields of law on Pegasus, nor fly across them on the wings of oratory. If he would stand on terra firma, he must descend. If he would be a great lawyer, he must first consent to become a great drudge. —Daniel Webster

Daniel R. White
YES AND MAYBE LETTERS*

THE "YES" LETTER   What the firm *said:*

QUEEN & SPRAWLING
1 Peachtree Street
Atlanta, Georgia 30319

November 23, 1983

Mr. James T. Pinch
906 Johnson Hall
Columbia Law School
New York, New York 10027

Dear Mr. Pinch:
       I enjoyed talking with you when I
was at Columbia. You have an excellent
record, and on behalf of the firm I would
like to extend you an offer of employment.
       We would be pleased to have you
visit our offices to meet more of our
attorneys. If you would be interested in
pursuing this invitation, please call me
or our recruitment coordinator Ellen
Shady to arrange a mutually convenient
time for your visit.
       I look forward to hearing from you
soon.

                    Sincerely,

                    Barbara J. Bookman

---

* These letters, purporting to be responses from big-time lawyers to law students
  whom they have recently interviewed for jobs, are reprinted from D. Robert White,
  The Official Lawyer's Handbook, Simon & Schuster, 1983.

What the firm *meant:*

QUEEN & SPRAWLING
1 Peachtree Street
Atlanta, Georgia 30319

November 23, 1983

Mr. James T. Pinch
906 Johnson Hall
Columbia Law School
New York, New York 10027

Dear Mr. Pinch:

For a guy from a trade school in Harlem, you make quite an impression. Your pale complexion and emaciated physique, combined with your incredibly high grade point average, suggest that you are precisely the sort of compulsive, library-loving grind we're looking for.

No doubt you will have a lot of offers, because hard-core zealots like you aren't a dime-a-dozen. Someone so patently willing to sacrifice his health and social life is a real find.

I wouldn't want to introduce you to a client or have to eat a meal with you, but I'll bet you could rack up enough billable hours in a year to reduce your salary to the equivalent of $1.95 per hour.

I hope we can sign you up.

Sincerely,

Barbara J. Bookman

THE "MAYBE" LETTER   What the firm *said:*

CRAVEN, SWINE & LESS
43 Park Avenue
New York, New York 10000

November 23, 1983

Mr. Russell A. Williams
413 Johnson Hall
Columbia Law School
New York, New York 10027

Dear Mr. Williams:

I enjoyed talking with you when I was at Columbia. You have an excellent record, and although I am not able to make you an offer of employment based on our meeting, I would like very much to have you visit our offices for further interviews.

If you would be interested in pursuing this invitation, please call our recruitment coordinator Laurie Munch to arrange a mutually convenient time for your visit.

I look forward to seeing you again.

Sincerely,

G. Carter Covington

What the firm *meant:*

CRAVEN, SWINE & LESS
43 Park Avenue
New York, New York 10000

November 23, 1983

Mr. Russell A. Williams
413 Johnson Hall
Columbia Law School
New York, New York 10027

Dear Mr. Williams:

I must say I was surprised that a person like you would bother to interview with Craven, Swine & Less. Your record gives new meaning to the word mediocre.

On the other hand, a bald willingness to ask for something you have no right to is worth something in this line of work, as you'd understand if you could have heard some of the arguments we used recently in a big antitrust suit. You've definitely got guts.

You couldn't possibly have a real future with us. We always need more bodies, however, and you might be okay for two or three years. Besides, we can bill your time as highly as that of our good associates.

I'm not willing to take sole responsibility for hiring you, so you'd better come down and meet some others. Since you're in the same city it won't cost us much to have you in.

Sincerely,

G. Carter Covington

Signs of Life

1. *Light burning brightly. (Tape the light switch in the "on" position, so the clean-up crew won't flip it off in your absence.)*
2. *Coat on back of chair.*
3. *Uncapped pen.*
4. *Full cup of coffee. (Make sure it's full. Half-cups are common.)*
5. *Smoking cigarette. (Check your local novelty store for those Perma-lite cigarettes that give off smoke for hours.)*
6. *Half-eaten sandwich. (How long could you last on a half-empty stomach?)*
7. *Phone with blinking "Hold" button. (Dial your home phone, which will ring until you get in from your night on the town, and punch the "Hold" button and leave.)*
8. *Open Federal Reporter.*
9. *Shoes. (How far could you get without your shoes?)*
10. *Open briefcase. (Keep a second one around for this purpose. You should be carrying your first one with you when you leave.)*
11. *Open drawer. (Partners are too fastidious to believe you'd leave it that way all night.)*
12. *Legal pad with writing cut off in mid-sentence . . . even mid-word.*

LEGAL PRACTICE

Arnold B. Kanter
THE ALL-PURPOSE, MODEL
PARTNERSHIP AGREEMENT FORM*

ONE OF THE PERENNIAL PROBLEMS of the law firm is its partnership agreement. Firms are always curious about what another firm is doing, and they look for "model" forms of agreement. The following agreement was found in an abandoned Xerox copier and sent to us. It may be helpful to others.

Partnership Agreement

WHEREAS, just about everybody wants something in writing; NOW THEREFORE, the parties will settle for the following:

Article I. Partners

1.1 Certain of the partners are Corner Partners. Life is unfair.

1.2 Certain of the partners are known as the "Others" (and occasionally as "Partners," when the Corner Partners are feeling expansive).

1.3 The rest of the lawyers are known as "Associates" (which shall mean any person who, with the fullness of time and the ripeness of old age, may have the ability or dumb luck to become an "Other").

Article II. Percentages

2.1 Any Partner who has more than 3 per cent is hereinafter sometimes known as a "Big Hitter," and shall be entitled to one Associate at his beck and call for each quarter of a percentage point in excess of 3.

---

* Reprinted from 68 *ABA Journal* 1166-67 (Sept. 1982) by permission of the author.

2.2 In case of disputes regarding partnership percentages, the principle "to each according to his needs" shall apply. All Partners agree that Big Hitters have big needs.

Article III. Billing

3.1 All Partners shall bill the required rate unless a member of the Billing Committee approves a lower bill. The "required rate" shall mean that rate per hour which, when multiplied by the number of hours worked, will permit Corner Partners to live at the RLAF ("Required Level of Affluence").

3.2 The Billing Committee shall be composed, from time to time, of the five meanest, toughest sons-of-bitches in The Firm.

Article IV. Associate Salaries

4.1 Associates shall be paid the going rate.

4.2 The going rate shall mean the minimum salary that Associates will accept before going.

Article V. Use of Associates

5.1 Those Partners without Associates at their beck and call must request Associates from the Headhunters Committee.

5.2 The Headhunters Committee is responsible for overseeing the development of Associates, which everybody admits is painfully slow.

5.3 Those Associates who have survived three or more years at The Firm or 1,150 cups of The Firm's coffee (whichever comes first) shall be deemed to be in the Free Fire Zone.

5.4 All Associates in the Free Fire Zone may be used by any Partner, provided such Associate is properly trapped by a Partner in any office or common area of The Firm. Bathrooms shall be deemed sanctuaries from the Free Fire Zone. The Geneva Convention shall not apply, since The Firm was not a party.

Article VI. Blame and Credit

6.1 Partners do not make mistakes. Blame for anything that goes wrong with respect to a particular file shall be allocated to the Associate who last worked on the file.

6.2 Credit shall continue to be distributed, in accordance with the accepted firm practice, on the principle of LRP ("Least Responsible Partner").

Article VII. Voting

7.1 All Corner Partners and Others shall have one vote on all matters which properly come before the partnership.

7.2 The Big Hitters All-Star Committee shall determine what matters properly come before the partnership.

Article VIII. All-Star Committee

8.1 The Big Hitters All-Star Committee shall be composed of those partners having the five largest partnership percentages. The Big Hitters All-Star Committee shall have the power to make such decisions as it may, from time to time, damn well want to.

8.2 The committee shall, every now and then, submit matters to the full partnership for the uh-huh.

Article IX. Committees

9.1 The Firm shall be governed by committees.

9.2 The initial appointment of members to committees shall occur mystically. Thereafter, committees shall be self-perpetuating.

Article X. Retirement

10.1 Retirement shall be mandatory at the age of 70.

10.2 Notwithstanding the foregoing, retirement shall not be mandatory at the age of 70.

Article XI. Resignation of Partners

11.1 Any partner may resign by tendering his or her written resignation to the Big Hitters All-Star Committee or by the Big Hitters All-Star Committee tendering the resignation to itself on such partner's behalf. Either type of resignation shall be deemed voluntary.

11.2 A resigning partner shall be entitled to bupkus.

11.3 Any partner who resigns from The Firm shall not provide any legal services to any client or potential client of The Firm for five years after his resignation. "Client" means any person or entity for whom legal services were being performed by The Firm at the time of the Partner's resignation. "Potential client" means any person or entity for whom legal services were not being provided by The Firm at the time of the Partner's resignation.

Article XII. Amendment

12.1 This agreement may not be amended.

12.2 Notwithstanding the foregoing, this agreement may be amended at any time on the whims of those Big Hitters who are members of the Chosen People. They know who they are.

Thurman Arnold
A MEMORANDUM*

MEMORANDUM: Partners, Associates, and Staff of Arnold, Fortas and Porter and their Heirs and Assigns forever.

FROM: Thurman Arnold

The Department of Health and Sanitation of the District of Columbia is about to indict the firm of Arnold, Fortas and Porter for conditions of chaos, disorder, and general litter in their offices which the Department alleges are a menace to health and safety and an affront to the aesthetic sensibilities of the entire population of the District, which the last census shows to be nearly a million people.

The Committee on Un-American Activities has informed me that the office looks like the kind of an office in which Communists congregate and multiply.

---

* The author of this piece, Thurman Arnold, was not only the founder of one of Washington, D.C.'s largest law firms, but also one of American law's funniest practitioners. This memorandum is reprinted from Thurman Arnold, *Selections from the Letters and Legal Papers*, Arnold, Fortas & Porter, 1961, by permission of Victor H. Kramer and Arnold & Porter.

For these reasons I have given Miss
Dorothy Bailey the responsibility of raising sufficient hell with everyone from
the partners up, to the end that the
papers, gadgets, files, books, briefcases and other flotsam and jetsam which
are now scattered around the place from
hell to breakfast shall be removed and
the semblance of order restored and con-
tinuously maintained during the balance
of this year of our Lord, 1951.

More specifically, Dorothy Bailey
is directed to remove the files which
Paul A. Porter has placed on the floor of
the library. She is directed to inform
Paul A. Porter that the reason we put
shelves in the library was to keep things
off the floor, an idea which might auto-
matically occur to a more reflective
mind. She is further directed to inform
Walton Hamilton that the disreputable
looking file which he keeps on the floor
of the large room must be removed to a
less conspicuous site, preferably in his
own office although he may keep it in the
men's room if he finds it more convenient.

The so-called Conference Room is to
be re-arranged according to more adequate
aesthetic principles. In this connection
I offer the strong suggestion that the
couch is a singularly inappropriate piece
of equipment for any purposes for which
the said conference room is intended to
be used.

No one seems to remember to close
cabinet doors. It will lighten Miss
Bailey's task greatly if anyone who opens
them will immediately thereafter close
them again. This technique may be difficult at first, but, like riding a
bicycle, once acquired it is never lost.
It is also a very beneficial exercise

which I hope may tend to reduce the
weight of some of the heavier members of
our little group. The same observation
holds for books left on the library
table. Replacing them after use creates
better circulation of the blood and im-
proves one's metabolism.

The partners, associates, and staff
may have access at all reasonable times
to my own office so that they can observe
how a well-kept office looks.

Yours for a better life in
the future,

Thurman Arnold

S. Sponte, Esq.
A VINCULO PARTNERMONIIS*

I HAVE THIS FRIEND, and I am partial to him. We have known each
other for a long time, and together we have endured the passions
of professional youth and the mellowness of middle age. As practitioners of the same art, we have prospered in parallel, apart, but
never too far. I had lunch with him recently, the first time I had seen
him for a while, and the metamorphosis he had undergone in the
interim was astonishing. His eyes did not have their customary
gleam, and his appetite, once legendary, was insulting to the short-
order cook. Although he was at first reluctant to discuss his *rigor
mentis,* under careful cross-examination he admitted that the source
of his consternation was the impending dissolution of his long-
standing partnership. It seemed that, after many years of professional bliss, he and his partner had come to a parting of the fees.
Not wishing to intrude further into his melancholy, I abandoned

---

* S. Sponte, Esq. is the pseudonym used by David J. Millstein, an attorney who
practices in Westmoreland County, Pennsylvania. This piece is reprinted from *The
Pennyslvania Lawyer,* 1978, by permission of the author.

the line of questioning in favor of the less perturbing subjects of marital infidelity and child abuse.

In my tenure at the bar, I have seen a lot of partnerships that pass in the night. Once I even had one, and it was better than most. Where I was weak, my partner was strong. Where I could laugh, he could cry. My colleagues on more than one occasion remarked that my partner was diligent, patient, tactful, clever and kind, and the reason we got on so well together was because we were so dissimilar. As our professional interests went their separate ways, so did our firm, but to this day we remain good friends.

Some partnerships, alas, do not sever so well. Most older lawyers no doubt recall a well-known partnership of some years ago that had earned a certain preeminence at the local bar, but, when it erupted, it put Cracatoa to shame. The partners at first attempted to distribute the assets with the same grace characteristic of their practice. However, when they could not amicably agree upon an equitable division of the caseload, one partner hurdled the impasse by grabbing some 400 active files and dropping them, time slips and all, from a private plane over Lake Erie. A Court of Admiralty assumed jurisdiction of the dispute, but, when the parties could not decide who should be the petitioner and who the respondent, the court awarded salvage to the itinerant bass fisherman whose boat had been sunk by the weight of the caseload, and who spent his declining years in retirement, living off the referral fees.

It has always seemed to me that those partnerships that survive the ravages of barristry are those in which the whole exceeds the sum of its partners. Like marriages of the flesh, the successful firm assumes a distinct personality all its own. Partnerships can have a certain style or lack of it, a special grace or a predisposition for ineptitude, all of which may be totally unrelated to the qualities of the individual partners. While this *sui lexis* is ethereal, it is *sui* nevertheless, and is borne of the delicate intercourse between the members of the firm, a process so subtle as to often escape discernment. There are, however, a few maxims I have been able to extrapolate from my observations of partnerships and their survival, and I pass them on to you herewith, regardless of their merit:

1. Do not treat your partners with respect. They aren't used to it and it may make them nervous;

2. Share your secretaries equally with your partners during office hours;

3. Always let your partners think they are earning their keep;

4. Be gracious when your partners are named defendants in a malpractice suit, or they may join you as an additional defendant;

5. Pay for the toilet paper yourself if to do otherwise means going without;

6. Neither sign your name to a partner's pleading nor your partner's name to a firm check;

7. Trust your partners implicitly. The truth is too high a price to pay to gratify one's suspicions.

It is, I suppose, a basic instinct of all lawyers to be combative, competitive and hostile. Accordingly, a law partnership is contrary to nature and, like "a friendship among women," is "only a suspension of hostilities." If in some way I have added one minute to that armistice or have contributed to the salvation of a single partnership, that will be fee enough for my effort, though a partner may prefer cash.

Art Buchwald
THE BOOMING LAW BUSINESS*

THIS HAS PROBABLY BEEN the greatest year in history for criminal lawyers. Thanks to the Watergate fallout, every law firm in this city is now on a twenty-four-hour, seven-day week schedule. Whereas most law offices were sedate, quiet places, they now resemble brokerage offices with everyone screaming into the phones.

I stopped in to see a friend of mine who works for one of the top criminal law firms in Washington. He had his coat off, his shirt open at the collar, his tie askew, and he was writing furiously on a yellow pad. He motioned for me to sit down. Then he yelled into the phone, "Right, I got you. Forty-three indictments in Jersey. We'll take them. Tell them to put the money in the bank." He hung up.

"Boy, what a day," he told me. "I just—" The phone rang.

"Yeah ... yeah ... we take perjury. How many cases you got? ... Fifteen ... grand jury or Senate? ... Both ... Okay ... Send them over.

* Reprinted from "I Am Not a Crook," Putnam, 1970, by permission of the author.

No, not today ... We can't see them for two weeks.... You can't wait that long? ... So get yourself another lawyer." He hung up.

"You really must be doing well to turn away business."

"Every time someone gets indicted he wants to see his lawyer *right* away. They'll call back. Most law firms have a one-month waiting list for perjurers."

My friend's secretary came in. "Mr. McIntosh, we have a mayor outside who is being indicted for income tax evasion."

"Tell him we don't take mayors anymore. You have to be either a president of a corporation or a high official of the administration."

A law partner rushed in. "We've been offered three hundred bribery cases in Baltimore County. Should we take them?"

"Take two hundred," my friend shouted. "We can't put all our eggs in bribery."

"What price should I quote?"

"One hundred thousand a case in advance, two hundred thousand before we go to trial. Vote fraud is fifty thousand extra."

"Wow," I said, "you people are really raking in the money."

"Watergate's been very good to us," my friend said. "You know, before Watergate all we got were a lot of priests and students being indicted by the government. Most of them didn't have a dime. But now you're getting a much higher class of defendant. They come from the best families, they went to the best schools, and they all have short hair. Most of the people being indicted these days are lawyers, so you don't have to explain things to them twice. I tell you it's a pleasure doing business with them."

The phone rang. He picked it up. "Oh, hi, Buzz. You offering us forty-three kickback cases in New York? Sure, we'll take them if your law firm doesn't want them.... I see you have sixty-three judges coming up for trial.... Look, while I have you on the phone, would you take thirty-three wiretapping trials in Los Angeles? We just don't have the troops to send to L.A.... Thanks a lot...."

The secretary came back in. "There's a delegation of ex-White House aides to see you. They say it's very important."

"Send them to the White House department down on the second floor."

Another law partner came in. "You interested in a former Attorney General and a former Secretary of Commerce?"

"Good God," my friend said in exasperation, "I've only got two hands."

The phone buzzed. He picked it up.

"Oh, yes, sir, Mr. Vice President. Uh-huh ... uh-huh.... Yes I've been reading about it in the newspapers.... I see.... Well we usually don't handle Vice Presidents, but we might make an exception in your case.... Now could you start at the beginning?..."

"I certainly made that judge look silly."

Drawing by Robt. Day; © 1933, 1961
The New Yorker Magazine, Inc.

John G. Saxe
THE BRIEFLESS BARRISTER*

An Attorney was taking a turn,
In shabby habiliments drest;
His coat it was shockingly worn,
And the rust had invested his vest.

His breeches had suffered a breach,
His linen and worsted were worse;
He had scarce a whole crown in his hat,
And not half a crown in his purse.

And thus as he wandered along,
A cheerless and comfortless elf,
He sought for relief in a song,
Or complainingly talked to himself:—

"Unfortunate man that I am!
I've never a client but grief:
The case is, I've no case at all,
And in brief, I've ne'er had a brief!

"I've waited and waited in vain,
Expecting an 'opening' to find,
Where an honest young lawyer might gain
Some reward for toil of his mind.

"'T is not that I'm wanting in law,
Or lack an intelligent face,
That others have cases to plead,
While I have to plead for a case.

* The author of this piece, John G. Saxe, was a prominent nineteenth-century
Vermont attorney, newspaper editor, and wit.

"O, how can a modest young man
E'er hope for the smallest progression,—
The profession's already so full
Of lawyers so full of profession!"

While thus he was strolling around,
His eye accidentally fell
On a very deep hole in the ground,
And he sighed to himself, "It is well!"

To curb his emotions, he sat
On the curbstone the space of a minute,
Then cried, "Here's an opening at last!"
And in less than a jiffy was in it!

Next morning twelve citizens came
('T was the coroner bade them attend),
To the end that it might be determined
How the man had determined his end!

"The man was a lawyer, I hear,"
Quoth the foreman who sat on the corse.
"A lawyer? Alas!" said another,
"Undoubtedly died of remorse!"

A third said, "He knew the deceased,
An attorney well versed in the laws,
And as to the cause of his death,
'T was no doubt for the want of a cause."

The jury decided at length,
After solemnly weighing the matter,
That the lawyer was drownded, because
He could not keep his head above water!

A. A. Milne
THE BARRISTER*

THE NEW BAILEY was crowded with a gay and fashionable throng. It was a remarkable case of shop-lifting. Aurora Delaine, 19, was charged with feloniously stealing and conveying certain articles the property of the Universal Stores, to wit, thirty-five yards of book muslin, ten pairs of gloves, a sponge, two gimlets, five jars of cold cream, a copy of the Clergy List, three hat-guards, a mariner's compass, a box of drawing-pins, an egg-breaker, six blouses, and a cabman's whistle. The theft had been proved by Albert Jobson, a shopwalker, who gave evidence to the effect that he followed her through the different departments and saw her take the things mentioned in the indictment.

"Just a moment," interrupted the Judge. "Who is defending the prisoner?"

There was an unexpected silence. Rupert Carleton, who had dropped idly into court, looked round in sudden excitement. The poor girl had no counsel! What if he—yes, he would seize the chance! He stood up boldly. "I am, my Lord," he said.

Rupert Carleton was still in the twenties, but he had been a briefless barrister for some years. Yet, though briefs would not come, he had been very far from idle. He had stood for Parliament in both the Conservative and Liberal interests (not to mention his own), he had written half-a-dozen unproduced plays, and he was engaged to be married. But success in his own profession had been delayed. Now at last was his opportunity.

He pulled his wig down firmly over his ears, took out a pair of *pince-nez* and rose to cross-examine. It was the cross-examination which was to make him famous, the cross-examination which is now given as a model in every legal textbook.

"Mr. Jobson," he began suavely, "you say that you saw the

* The author of this piece, A. A. Milne, was a British writer of diverse talents. His satirical and dramatic works have been overshadowed by his children's books, notably *Winnie-the-Pooh*. Reprinted from A. A. Milne, *Happy Days*, 1915, by permission of Curtis Brown & John Farquharson. Originally published in *Punch*.

accused steal these various articles, and that they were afterwards found upon her?"

"Yes."

"I put it to you," said Rupert, and waited intently for the answer, "that that is a pure invention on your part?"

"No."

With a superhuman effort Rupert hid his disappointment. Unexpected as the answer was, he preserved his impassivity.

"I suggest," he tried again, "that you followed her about and concealed this collection of things in her cloak with a view to advertising your winter sale?"

"No. I saw her steal them."

Rupert frowned; the man seemed impervious to the simplest suggestion. With masterly decision he tapped his *pince-nez* and fell back upon his third line of defence. "You saw her steal them? What you mean is that you saw her take them from the different counters and put them in her bag?"

"Yes."

"With the intention of paying for them in the ordinary way?"

"No."

"Please be very careful. You said in your evidence that prisoner when told she would be charged, cried, 'To think that I should have come to this! Will no one save me?' I suggest that she went up to you with her collection of purchases, pulled out her purse, and said, 'What does all this come to? I can't get any one to serve me.'"

"No."

The obstinacy of some people! Rupert put back his *pince-nez* in his pocket and brought out another pair. The historic cross-examination continued.

"We will let that pass for the moment," he said. He consulted a blank sheet of paper and then looked sternly at Mr. Jobson. "Mr. Jobson, how many times have you been married?"

"Once."

"Quite so." He hesitated and then decided to risk it. "I suggest that your wife left you?"

"Yes."

It was a long shot, but once again the bold course had paid. Rupert heaved a sigh of relief.

"Will you tell the gentlemen of the jury," he said with deadly politeness, "*why* she left you."

"She died."

A lesser man might have been embarrassed, but Rupert's iron nerve did not fail him.

"Exactly!" he said. "And was that or was that not on the night when you were turned out of the Hampstead Parliament for intoxication?"

"I never was."

"Indeed? Will you cast your mind back to the night of April 24th, 1897? What were you doing on that night?"

"I have no idea," said Jobson, after casting his mind back and waiting in vain for some result.

"In that case you cannot swear that you were not being turned out of the Hampstead Parliament—"

"But I never belonged to it."

Rupert leaped at the damaging admission.

"What? You told the Court you lived at Hampstead, and yet you say that you never belonged to the Hampstead Parliament? Is *that* your idea of patriotism?"

Karel Capek

"I said I lived at Hackney."

"To the Hackney Parliament, I should say. I am suggesting that you were turned out of the Hackney Parliament—"

"I don't belong to that either."

"Exactly!" said Rupert triumphantly. "Having been turned out for intoxication?"

"And never did belong."

"Indeed? May I take it then that you prefer to spend your evenings in the public-house?"

"If you want to know," said Jobson angrily, "I belong to the Hackney Chess Circle, and that takes up most of my evenings."

Rupert gave a sigh of satisfaction and turned to the jury.

"*At last,* gentlemen, we have got it. I thought we should arrive at the truth in the end, in spite of Mr. Jobson's prevarications." He turned to the witness. "Now, Sir," he said sternly, "you have already told the Court that you have no idea what you were doing on the night of April 24th, 1897. I put it to you once more that this blankness of memory is due to the fact that you were in a state of intoxication on the premises of the Hackney Chess Circle. Can you swear on your oath that this is not so?"

A murmur of admiration for the relentless way in which the truth had been tracked down ran through the Court. Rupert drew himself up and put on both pairs of *pince-nez* at once.

"Come, Sir!" he said; "the jury is waiting."

But it was not Albert Jobson who answered. It was the counsel for the prosecution. "My lord," he said, getting up slowly, "this has come as a complete surprise to me. In the circumstances I must advise my clients to withdraw from the case."

"A very proper decision," said his lordship. "The prisoner is discharged without a stain on her character."

*   *   *   *   *

Briefs poured in upon Rupert next day, and he was engaged for all the big Chancery cases. Within a week his six plays were accepted, and within a fortnight he had entered Parliament as the miners' Member for Coalville. His marriage took place at the end of a month. The wedding presents were even more numerous and costly than usual, and included thirty-five yards of book-muslin, ten pairs of gloves, a sponge, two gimlets, five jars of cold cream, a copy of the Clergy List, three hat guards, a mariner's compass, a box of drawing-pins, an egg-breaker, six blouses, and a cabman's whistle. They were marked quite simply, "From a grateful friend."

A. J. Shannon
THE FIRST CASE*

The little office.
The diploma on the wall.
The picture of the Supreme Court.
The months of waiting.
The swivel chair beneath the steam pipe.
The endless perusal of magazines.
The doze.
The unexpected knock at the door.
The search for a pen.
The rustling of papers.
The busy air.
The visions of a wealthy client.
The dream of a fat fee.
The palpitation of the heart.
The brisk "Come in."
The destitute washerwoman.
The quarrel over a hog.
The scrambled recital of facts.
The retainer of two dollars.
The search for the law.
The failure to find anything.
The remembrance of the Digest.
The vast collection of cases.
The hours of labor.
The bringing of suit.
The trials.
The fight with counsel.
The unfair judge.
The prejudiced jury.
The recalcitrant witness.
The laugh at your expense.
The speech to the jury.
The cold sweat.

* Reprinted from *Docket* by permission of West Publishing Company.

The words that will not come.
The sleeping juror.
The instructions you ask for.
The instructions you get.
The adverse verdict.
The lame explanation.
The anger of your client.
The loud criticism of your ability.
The fee you never receive.

Theobald O. Mathew
THE YOUNG SOLICITOR AND
THE SAGACIOUS OLD BUFFER*

THERE WAS ONCE a Young Solicitor who Began to Fear that he
would Never Get On. He Worked Hard, but, Try as he Might, he
Could not Learn any Law. Persons who Sought his Advice were
Clearly Disappointed when the Young Solicitor Told them he
would Look it Up and Let Them Know To-morrow. The Young
Solicitor therefore Determined to Consult a Sagacious Old Buffer
whose Name was a Household Word in the Profession. The Street
in which the Old Buffer's Palatial Offices were Situate was Blocked
from Morning to Night by the Rolls-Royces of the Bankers, Ladies
in Distress, Shipowners, Jockeys, and Dignitaries of the Church
who Desired his Assistance. The Old Buffer Made them Pay through
the Nose, but they all Went Away Satisfied that they had Received
Good Value for their Money. Nor was this Surprising. For the Old
Buffer Possessed both a Dignified Appearance and a Sympathetic
Manner, and was Never at a Loss when a Complicated Legal Problem had to be Solved. The Old Buffer Always Remembered that
Baron Parke, or Cairns, or Blackburn had discussed the Topic in an
Old Case. He would then Tell his Clerk to Bring him "2 Meeson &
Welsby," "6 Term Reports," or "4 Barnewall & Cresswell"; and, Lo
and Behold, the Volume was Sure to Contain Something Apposite

---

* The author of this piece, Theobald O. Mathew, was a British legal humorist who
  published under the pseudonym "O." In the 1920s he put out three volumes of
  "Forensic Fables," the second of which, *Further Forensic Fables*, Butterworth & Co.,
  1928, included this fable.

and Helpful. When the Client Expressed his Astonishment at the Old Buffer's Amazing Feat of Memory he would Smile Quietly and Say it was Nothing. The Old Buffer Received the Young Solicitor with the Utmost Courtesy and Listened Attentively to his Story. When he had Finished, the Old Buffer Locked the Door and Whispered to the Young Solicitor that, if he would Swear Never to Divulge it to a Soul, he would Impart to him the Secret of his Success. "Like you," said the Old Buffer, with Tears in his Eyes, "I Knew no Law and Could not Learn any of the Beastly Stuff. But One Day I Found on a Railway Book-Stall an Admirable Work Entitled 'Law for the Million.' It Cost Two Shillings and Six Pence. I Saw at once that it was a Mine of Useful Information. I Purchased Three Copies and had them Rebound. One is Called '2 Meeson & Welsby,' Another is '6 Term Reports,' and the Third is '4 Barnewell & Cresswell.' When I am Asked to Advise about a Charter Party, a Bill of Sale, a Gambling Debt, or a Faculty I Turn Up the Appropriate Heading with the Happiest Results. I Strongly Advise You to Do the Same. The Book is Arranged Alphabetically," the Old Buffer Concluded, "so that it is Quite Easy to Find what you Want."

The Young Solicitor Thanked the Old Buffer Warmly and Withdrew.

Within Five Years the Young Solicitor was a Knight, a Member of Parliament, the Owner of Three Cars, and a Resident in Carlton House Terrace. And if the Old Buffer had not Retired from Practice meanwhile (with a Cool Quarter of a Million) the Young Solicitor would Assuredly have Cut him Out.

MORAL.—*Bind Your Books Carefully.*

Daniel R. White
WEEKEND WORK*
Avoiding It, Simulating It

A LEGAL CAREER inevitably involves weekend work. It was a lawyer who said, "Thank God it's Friday—only two more work days until Monday."

A question confronting all associates is how to know when weekend work is really necessary. Legal work is like school work, in that you could always do more in given area. (Or like psychoanalysis, in that the more you get into it, the uglier things look.)

Your goal, of course, is to minimize weekend work. Free weekends are what it's all about.

Weekend work is of two types. First, there is serious, big-time work that has been brewing for a long time. It could be a major antitrust suit that you've been involved in, the papers are due on Monday, and you are, by any test, the logical person to spend the necessary weekend time buffing up the brief.

There is no escape from such work. You should resign yourself to it, exploiting the opportunities it will afford to enhance your image as a hard worker. If the partner in charge takes the extraordinary step of *asking* whether you will be able to help out over the weekend, and you have sized up the situation and see that you are clearly the logical choice for the job, *do it!*

Pretend you are *glad* about it. Tell him you were already *planning* to be there. Tell him you *like* weekends because they give you a chance to hunker down without a lot of interruptions from the secretaries. (Do not worry about your credibility in this regard: lots of partners really *do* like weekends for that very reason.)

The second type of weekend work is emergency work: short-term, last-minute, run-of-the-mill work that any associate could do. *This* type of work you can avoid.

This isn't *your* emergency; it isn't something they need *you* to

---

* Reprinted from D. Robert White, *The Official Lawyer's Handbook,* Simon & Schuster, 1983.

handle. It might be that a judge has just asked some partner to brief an issue by Monday, or the local prosecutor has just summoned a client of the firm to appear before a grand jury.

More likely, some partner hasn't bothered taking care of a matter that has been around for a long time, because he knew there was a full stable of associates he could get to handle it at the last minute.

Any associate can handle these types of emergencies, and you shouldn't be concerned about the propriety of trying to avoid them. What you should be concerned about is *how* to avoid them. It can be done. See "Friday Afternoons," below.

Won't people get angry if you consistently manage to avoid weekend work? Most likely, no one will know. Still, it's worth covering your ass here, as everywhere. There are three especially handy devices for doing this.

First, many firms have a receptionist come in for all or part of each Saturday. This affords you a great opportunity. Whether you are at home, at the beach, or at a friend's place on Saturday morning engaged in some horizontal recreation, set the alarm for about 11:00 A.M., sit up, call the office and, using a false voice, have yourself paged.

Everyone who is really at the office will assume you are there, too, somewhere. Don't worry that the receptionist will know you haven't answered your page; she doesn't care.

Another handy device for simulating weekend work is more effective but also more demanding. It involves actually going in.

This doesn't have to ruin your picnic plans. You don't have to *stay* there. Just go in, look a bit fatigued (not *too* fatigued; you're supposed to be able to take the pressure), walk briskly through the library, grab two or three reference volumes, return to your office, turn on the light, and then head for the links.

Turning on your light is important. The cleaning personnel will have turned off all office lights on Friday evening, so anyone who sees your light burning on Saturday thinks you've been in.

The joy of this trick is that it keeps working all weekend. In most office buildings the cleaning personnel won't be around again until Monday night, so you get the benefit through Saturday evening, all Sunday, and even Monday at dawn.

As long as you're in on any weekend, consider leaving some kind of note on the desk of a partner, just to let him know you were in. You have to be careful with this device, because it can be a bit transparent. Don't do it *every* weekend, and don't write in red ink at the top of the note "SATURDAY, 7:00 P.M." Let the partner figure out when the note must have been written, as by observing that it was written on the back of that weekend's church bulletin.

The third method of simulating weekend work requires you to ingratiate yourself with the guard stationed at your office building on weekends. With flattery and a bottle of scotch, you may be able to persuade him to sign your name on the check-in list that office buildings maintain on Saturdays and Sundays.

All those who actually come by will see your name as they sign their own names. Better yet, they *won't* see a mark beside your name in the check-*out* column—clear evidence that you've outlasted them all.

Friday Afternoons (The art of laying low)

Friday afternoon is a critical time. That's when partners start checking their calendars to see what's on tap for Monday; that's when your weekend stands its greatest chance of being destroyed.

Try to avoid answering your phone over these hours. Definitely do not check with your secretary or receptionist for messages.

Avoid walking past any partners' offices on the way to the restroom. If possible, don't even go to the restroom over these hours. If you absolutely have to, consider finding a nice stall and staying there the entire afternoon.

Ideally you should arrange to be out of the building altogether. If that isn't possible, the next best strategy is to set up camp in an obscure corner of the library. Just take your books and papers and whatever you're working on with you. Don't worry about how it looks; lots of people keep mountains of garbage there.

Be sure it's an obscure corner of the library. Not infrequently, a partner needing bodies will actually prowl through the library in search of hapless associates for weekend duty. Also, you want to be able to ignore your name when it goes out over the paging system; if you're in a crowded area some jerk will tap you on the shoulder to say he thinks he just heard your name.

Two Lawyers

Two lawyers, when a knotty case was o'er,
Shook hands, and were as friendly as before:
"Zounds!" said the client, "I would fain know how
You can be friends, who were such foes just now?"
"You fool!" said one, "we lawyers, though as keen
As shears, ne'er cut ourselves, but what's between!"
                    —*Anonymous*

Time in Eternity

A lawyer at the pearly gate
Protested, "Set the record straight.
St. Peter, I'm too young to die."
The old saint raised a kindly eye
And sighed and put his coffee down,
Reviewed his books with puzzled frown,
Then smiled. "There's no mistake," said he.
"My ledger shows you're 83."
"How can that be?" in outraged tone
The lawyer cried. "I'm 51!"
The good saint shrugged and sipped his cup,
"We added all your time sheets up."
                    —*Allan J. Parker*

THE LAWYER'S PUBLIC IMAGE

Anonymous
A LAWYER AND THE DEVIL*

THERE ONCE WAS A LAWYER, pitiless and grasping, who traveled from town to town taking all he could from anyone within his power. One day, as he was hastening to a certain town for the purpose of exacting his tribute, the Devil, in the likeness of a man, joined him on his journey. He knew this was the Devil from the horror he felt as well as from the way the fellow talked, and he was very fearful of traveling with him; but he was unable, either by praying or by making the sign of the cross, to get him to go away.

As they walked together, a poor man approached, leading a pig by a rope. The pig ran hither and thither, causing the man to cry out angrily, "Devil take you!" Hearing this, the lawyer, who hoped to free himself from his companion, said to the Devil, "Listen, friend, that pig is yours now. Go and seize it." The fiend responded, "He is not given to me from the heart, so I cannot accept."

As they continued to walk, they heard a baby crying, and its mother, standing in the door of her house, exclaimed in a petulant tone, "Devil take you! Why do you trouble me with your crying?" At this point the lawyer said, "Well, you're richer now—by one soul. Take the baby. It's yours." As before, the Devil declined, saying, "It was not given to me from the heart. That is just the way people talk when they're angry."

But as they drew near the town to which they were headed, some men spotted them from afar and, knowing the purpose of the lawyer's visit, they cried out, "Devil take you!" and "To the Devil with you!" Hearing this, the fiend, wagging his head and laughing, said to the lawyer, "Now, *you* are a present they give me from the bottom of their hearts. Therefore you are mine."

---

* This is a medieval story, somewhat updated.

William E. Daly
THE ARGUMENT*

A surgeon and an architect
Were making great to-do,
Each claiming his profession
Was the older of the two.

The surgeon said, "When Eve was made
It took a surgeon's knife
To form from Adam's sturdy rib
The mate he took to wife.
So you can see that surgery
Goes back to Eden's time.
No other trade was active when
My trade was in its prime!"

"Come, come!" the architect replied,
"Before there was a man,
The earth was formed from chaos
In accordance with a plan.
It took a mighty Architect,
With compass, rule and gauge,
To build the world before your man
Could step upon the stage!"

A clever lawyer joined the two
And smiled with look benign.
"My friends," said he, "Your trades, though old
Are young compared with mine.
If chaos is the stuff from which
The universe was made,
Since *we* created chaos,
Ours is far the oldest trade."

---

* Reprinted from the *Journal of the Bar Association of the District of Columbia*, April
  1951, by permission of the publisher.

The surgeon and the architect
Had nothing more to say,
They knew their friend the lawyer won
The argument that day.
What's more! They knew that, if the world
Is subject to his plan,
All will revert to chaos,
As it was, ere time began.

Jerome K. Jerome
STAGE LAW*

THE STAGE LAWYER never has any office of his own. He transacts all his business at his clients' houses. He will travel hundreds of miles to tell them the most trivial piece of legal information.

It never occurs to him how much simpler it would be to write a letter. The item for "travelling expenses," in his bill of costs, must be something enormous.

There are two moments in the course of his client's career, that the Stage lawyer particularly enjoys. The first is when the client comes unexpectedly into a fortune; the second, when he unexpectedly loses it.

In the former case, upon learning the good news, the Stage lawyer at once leaves his business, and hurries off to the other end of the kingdom to bear the glad tidings. He arrives at the humble domicile of the beneficiary in question, sends up his card, and is ushered into the front parlour. He enters mysteriously, and sits left, client sits right. An ordinary, common lawyer would come to the point at once, state the matter in a plain, business-like way, and trust that he might have the pleasure of representing, &c., &c.; but such simple methods are not those of the Stage lawyer. He looks at the client, and says:

"You had a father."

The client starts. How on earth did this calm, thin, keen-eyed old man in black know that he had a father? He shuffles and

* Reprinted from Jerome K. Jerome, *Stage-land: Curious Habits and Customs of Its Inhabitants*, 1890.

stammers, but the quiet, impenetrable lawyer fixes his cold, glassy eye on him, and he is helpless. Subterfuge, he feels, is useless, and amazed, bewildered, at the knowledge of his most private affairs, possessed by his strange visitant, he admits the fact: he had a father.

The lawyer smiles with a quiet smile of triumph, and scratches his chin.

"You had a mother, too, if I am informed correctly," he continues.

The Stage Lawyer.

It is idle attempting to escape this man's supernatural acuteness, and the client owns up to having had a mother also.

From this, the lawyer goes on to communicate to the client, as a great secret, the whole of his (the client's) history from his cradle upwards, and also the history of his nearer relatives, and in less than half-an-hour from the old man's entrance, or, say, forty minutes, at the outside, the client almost knows what the business is about.

On the other occasion, when the client has lost his fortune, the Stage lawyer is even still happier. He comes down himself to tell the misfortune (he would not miss the job for worlds), and he takes care to choose the most unpropitious moment possible for breaking the news. On the eldest daughter's birthday, when there is a big party on, is his favourite time. He comes in about midnight, and tells them just as they are going down to supper.

He has no idea of business hours, has the Stage lawyer—to make the thing as unpleasant as possible seems to be his only anxiety.

If he cannot work it for a birthday, then he waits till there's a wedding on, and gets up early in the morning on purpose to run down and spoil the show. To enter among a crowd of happy, joyous fellow-creatures, and leave them utterly crushed and miserable is the Stage lawyer's hobby.

The Stage lawyer is a very talkative gentleman. He regards the telling of his client's most private affairs to every stranger that he meets, as part of his professional duties. A good gossip, with a few chance acquaintances, about the family secrets of his employers, is food and drink for the Stage lawyer. * * *

The good Stage lawyer has generally nursed the heroine on his knee, when a baby (when *she* was a baby, we mean)—when she was only so high. It seems to have been a part of his professional duties. The good Stage lawyer also kisses all the pretty girls in the play, and is expected to chuck the housemaid under the chin. It is good to be a good Stage lawyer.

The good Stage lawyer also wipes away a tear when sad things happen; and he turns away to do this, and blows his nose, and says he thinks he has a fly in his eye. This touching trait in his character is always held in great esteem by the audience, and is much applauded.

The good Stage lawyer is never, by any chance, a married man. (Few good men are, so we gather from our married lady friends.) He loved, in early life, the heroine's mother. That "sainted woman" (tear and nose business) died, and is now among the angels—the gentleman who did marry her, by-the-bye, is not quite so sure about this latter point, but the lawyer is fixed on the idea.

In stage literature of a frivolous nature, the lawyer is a very different individual. In comedy, he is young, he possesses chambers, and he is married (there is no doubt about this latter fact); and his wife and his mother-in-law spend most of the day in his office, and make the dull old place quite lively for him.

He only has one client. She is a nice lady, and affable, but her antecedents are doubtful, and she seems to be no better than she ought to be—possibly worse. But anyhow, she is the sole business that the poor fellow has—is, in fact, his only source of income, and might, one would think, under such circumstances, be accorded a welcome by his family. But his wife and his mother-in-law, on the contrary, take a violent dislike to her; and the lawyer has to put her in the coal scuttle, or lock her up in the safe, whenever he hears either of these female relatives of his coming up the stairs.

We should not care to be the client of a farcical comedy Stage lawyer. Legal transactions are trying to the nerves under the most favourable circumstances; conducted by a farcical Stage lawyer, the business would be too exciting for us.

*   *   *

Stage "law" may not be quite the most fearful and wonderful mystery in the whole universe, but it's near it—very near it. We were under the impression, at one time, that we ourselves knew something—just a little—about statutory and common law, but, after paying attention to the legal points of one or two plays, we found that we were mere children at it.

The only points of Stage "law" on which we are at all clear, are as follows:

That if a man dies, without leaving a will, then all his property goes to the nearest villain.

But that if a man dies, and leaves a will, then all his property goes to whoever can get possession of the will.

That the accidental loss of the three and sixpenny copy of a marriage certificate annuls the marriage.

That the evidence of one prejudiced witness, of shady antecedents, is quite sufficient to convict the most stainless and irreproachable gentleman of crimes for the committal of which he could have had no possible motive.

But that this evidence may be rebutted, years afterwards, and the conviction quashed without further trial, by the unsupported statement of the comic man.

That if A forges B's name to a check, then the law of the land is that B shall be sentenced to ten years' penal servitude.

That ten minutes' notice is all that is required to foreclose a mortgage.

That all trials of criminal cases take place in the front parlor of the victim's house, the villain acting as counsel, judge and jury rolled into one, and a couple of policemen being told off to follow his instructions. * * *

As for the Stage hero, the state of the law naturally confuses him, and the villain, who is the only human being who does seem to understand Stage legal questions, is easily able to fleece and ruin him. The simple-minded hero signs mortgages and bills of sale, and deeds of gift and such like things, under the impression that he is playing some sort of round game; and then, when he cannot pay the interest, they take his wife and children away from him, and turn him adrift into the world.

Being thrown upon his own resources, he naturally starves.

Stanley Jones
HE ALSO SERVES—*

THERE ARE FEW AVOCATIONS yielding the rich returns of subpoena serving. Here's a sideline combining the best features of stagecraft, contract bridge, snipe-shooting, and Prisoner's Base. I shall never forget the thrill of my first assignment.

"We're counting on you, lad," said the old marshal huskily. He laid a gnarled hand on my shoulder. "Counting on you to carry the message to—what's that name again?"

"Slabchellowitz," I said, reading the summons.

"Slabchellowitz it is, lad. He owes people he's never even heard of. Plaster it on him!"

I trotted forth, head up.

Mr. Slabchellowitz had his being on the top floor of an eight-story walk-up. As I panted warily against his door, the marshal's advice rang in my ears. "This guy is smart, see? Fox him."

Ten minutes' knocking finally elicited a crusty grunt from overhead. A troglodyte face was dimly apparent in the open transom. "Who the hell are you?"

"Sa-ay," I chuckled, keeping my hatbrim foxily pulled down, "don't pull this nonshaylunt stuff on me! Open up, you old umbrella!"

"Is that old Bill Stedberg?" he grinned at last.

Drawing by Leo Cullum; © 1988
The New Yorker Magazine, Inc.

"You called it," I bantered.

"Try this," he said suddenly, "you cheap so-and-so!" A pail of dirty water cascaded out, drenching my new subpoena-serving suit to the last cotton thread. The transom clicked shut, muffling raucous guffaws.

A favorite dodge of veteran subpoena-servers is the resort to different disguises. These open up fascinating possibilities for one possessing even moderate dramatic gifts. You may, for instance, take off well-known screen stars, state senators, or old-fashioned ottomans. Personally, I have had most success with a Western Union messenger suit. "Telegram for Mr. Wilson," in a quavering voice, is certainly hard to resist, even for gun-shy old tuskers. The thrill which comes when you thrust the subpoena into the trembling hand of an anxious old man—ah, that is a moment! Not until you have been recalled from the land of make-believe by a stunning blow from a crutch do you learn to depart the instant service has been rendered.

Another wrinkle that I have worked up rather neatly is the "Auld Lang Syne" approach. This prepares the ground, tends to allay suspicion, and often renders a difficult entrance surprisingly easy. You have designs, let us say, on a Mr. Ben Weevil. You call him up.

"Hello. Ben Weevil? This is Ed—how are you, anyway?" (You could, of course, say "This is Sylvester," or "This is Jules," just as easily, but it would increase the hazard. Every man knows at least one man named "Ed," and generally seven or eight.)

Mr. Weevil, nine times out of ten, will fall into the trap and will invite you, however uncertainly, to step over for a little visit. There are few more amusing sights than that afforded by Weevil when he opens the door and finds himself shaking hands with a piece of paper while you back off, convulsed with laughter.

*   *   *

One of the most effective bits of "business" (as you come to term it) was originated by a quaint old German named Philippe Zach. Craftily turning one of the most common human weaknesses to account, Herr Zach would telephone his quarry, the conversation running something like this:

"Hello. Iss dis Herr Hemoglobin?"

"It might be," suspiciously. "Who wants to know?"

"Der gas company. On dot last bill—"

"I paid it."

"Chust a minute, Herr Hemoglobin. I haff checked up, und dot stupid inspector has charged you mit two dollars und a haff too much. I come around mit a refund some time when you iss in."

"Oh, that's different. Can't you step over now?"

Through this artifice, so simple on the face of it, Zach set up a record which is still the envy of his guild. He might still be alive had he not unwittingly tried it on an official of a gas company, who of course recognized the utter absurdity of any such business emanating from a gas company.

Sinclair Lewis
LEGAL CORRESPONDENCE

Dear Lewis:

Have read a few of your works and would like to ask a few favors. Please send me a list of your stories, your autograph, picture, and a letter describing your life. How many children have you and their names.

Thanking you, I am

Yours very truly,

J. J. JONES, Esq.

To Which Lewis Answered:

My Dear Jim:

There was only one thing about your nice letter that I didn't like. It was so sort of formal. True, we have never met, and somehow I feel we aren't likely to, but, isn't this a democratic country? So let me call you Jim, and you call me Fatty, or any other friendly name.

Now Jim, I haven't got a photograph of me here, but I'll go right down to the junction and have one taken. I'm preparing a letter about my life, but it's been a pretty long one and a bad one, and that will take me several weeks.

But in the meantime, Jim, I'm awfully interested in lawyers, Kindly send me your picture, picture of your home and office, a list of your assets and liabilities, average income per month, list of the books you have read since 1914, if any. Kindly inform me whether you have ever defended a bootlegger and

why. Should be glad to have any other interesting personal information for use in
a story. How do you get along with your
wife? Kindly explain this in detail.

    Thanking you in advance, I remain,

        Yours affectionately,

        SINCLAIR LEWIS.

Why Lawyers Are So Much Increased

You ask me why lawyers are so much increased
Though most of the country already is fleeced;
The reason I'm sure is most strikingly plain:
The sheep are oft sheared yet the wool grows again.
And though you may think e'er so odd of the matter,
The oft'ner they're fleeced, the wool grows back the
      better.
Thus downy-chinned boys as oft I have heard
By frequently shaving obtain a large beard.
        —Anonymous

Law. A machine which you go into as a pig and
come out of as a sausage. *—Ambrose Bierce*

THE ELOQUENT DEFENCE ATTORNEY AND THE IMPRESSIONABLE JUROR

Drawing by Carl Rose; © 1932, 1960
The New Yorker Magazine, Inc.

THE LAWYER IN COURT

Robert Benchley
"TAKE THE WITNESS!"*

NEWSPAPER ACCOUNTS of trial cross-examinations always bring out the cleverest in me. They induce day dreams in which I am the witness on the stand, and if you don't know some of my imaginary comebacks to an imaginary cross-examiner (*Doe* v. *Benchley*, 482 U.S. 367-398), you have missed some of the most stimulating reading in the history of American jurisprudence.

These little reveries usually take place shortly after I have read the transcript of a trial, while I am on a long taxi ride or seated at a desk with plenty of other work to do. I like them best when I have work to do, as they deplete me mentally so that I am forced to go and lie down after a particularly sharp verbal rally. The knowledge that I have completely floored my adversary, and the imaginary congratulations of my friends (also imaginary), seem more worth while than any amount of fiddling work done.

During these cross-questionings I am always very calm. Calm in a nice way, that is—never cocky. However frantic my inquisitor may wax (and you should see his face at times—it's purple!), I just sit there, burning him up with each answer, winning the admiration of the courtroom, and, at times, even a smile from the judge himself. At the end of my examination, the judge is crazy about me.

Just what the trial is about, I never get quite clear in my mind. Sometimes the subject changes in the middle of the questioning, to allow for the insertion of an especially good crack on my part. I don't think that I am ever actually the defendant, although I don't know why I should feel that I am immune from trial by a jury of my peers—if such exist.

I am usually testifying in behalf of a friend, or perhaps as just

* Excerpt from "Take the Witness!" from *My Ten Years in a Quandary and How They Grew* (1936) by Robert Benchley. Copyright © 1964 Gertrude Benchley. Reprinted with the permission of Harper & Row, Publishers, Inc.

an impersonal witness for someone whom I do not know, who, naturally, later becomes my friend for life. It is Justice that I am after—Justice and a few well-spotted laughs.

Let us whip right into the middle of my cross-examination, as I naturally wouldn't want to pull my stuff until I had been insulted by the lawyer, and you can't really get insulted simply by having your name and address asked. I am absolutely fair about these things. If the lawyer will treat me right, I'll treat him right. He has got to start it. For a decent cross-examiner, there is no more tractable witness in the world than I am.

Advancing toward me, with a sneer on his face, he points a finger at me. (I have sometimes thought of pointing my finger back at him, but have discarded that as being too fresh. I don't have to resort to clowning.)

*   *   *   *   *   *

Q—You think you're pretty funny, don't you? (*I have evidently just made some mildly humorous comeback, nothing smart-alecky, but good enough to make him look silly.*)
A—I have never given the matter much thought.
Q—Oh, you haven't given the matter much thought, eh? Well, you

I just sit there, burning him up with each answer.

Gluyas Williams

seem to be treating this examination as if it were a minstrel show.

A (*very quietly and nicely*)—I have merely been taking my cue from your questions. (*You will notice that all this presupposes quite a barrage of silly questions on his part, and pat answers on mine, omitted here because I haven't thought them up. At any rate, it is* evident that I have already got him on the run before this reverie begins.)

Q—Perhaps you would rather that I conducted this inquiry in baby talk?

A—If it will make it any easier for you. (*Pandemonium, which the Court feels that it has to quell, although enjoying it obviously as much as the spectators.*)

Q (*furious*)—I see. Well, here is a question that I think will be simple enough to elicit an honest answer: Just how did you happen to know that it was eleven-fifteen when you saw the defendant?

A—Because I looked at my watch.

Q—And just why did you look at your watch at this particular time?

A—To see what time it was.

Q—Are you accustomed to looking at your watch often?

A—That is one of the uses to which I often put my watch.

Q—I see. Now, it couldn't, by any chance, have been ten-fifteen instead of eleven-fifteen when you looked at your watch this time, could it?

A—Yes, sir. It could.

Q—Oh, it could have been ten-fifteen?

A—Yes, sir—if I had been in Chicago. (*Not very good, really. I'll work up something better. I move to have that answer stricken from the record.*)

* * * * * *

When I feel myself lowering my standards by answering like that, I usually give myself a rest, and, unless something else awfully good pops into my head, I adjourn the court until next day. I can always convene it again when I hit my stride.

If possible, however, I like to drag it out until I have really given my antagonist a big final wallop which practically curls him up on the floor (I may think of one before this goes to press), and, wiping his forehead, he mutters, "Take the witness!"

As I step down from the stand, fresh as a daisy, there is a round of applause which the Court makes no attempt to silence. In fact, I have known certain judges to wink pleasantly at me as I take my seat. Judges are only human, after all.

My only fear is that, if I ever really am called upon to testify in court, I won't be asked the right questions. That would be a pretty kettle of fish!

George Ade
THE ATTENUATED ATTORNEY WHO RANG IN THE ASSOCIATE COUNSEL*

ONCE THERE WAS a sawed-off Attorney who had studied until he was Bleary around the Eyes and as lean as a Razor-Back. He knew the Law from Soup to Nuts, but much learning had put him a little bit to the Willies. And his Size was against him. He lacked Bellows.

He was an inconspicuous little Runt. When he stood up to Plead, he came a trifle higher than the Chair. Of the 90 pounds he carried, about 45 were Gray Matter. He had Mental Merchandise to burn but no way of delivering it.

When there was a Rally or some other Gabfest on the Bills, the Committee never asked him to make an Address. The Committee wanted a Wind-Jammer who could move the Leaves on a Tree 200 feet distant. The dried-up Lawyer could write Great Stuff that would charm a Bird out of a Tree, but he did not have the Tubes to enable him to Spout. When he got up to Talk, it was all he could do to hear himself. The juries used to go to sleep on him. He needed a Megaphone. And he had about as much Personal Magnetism as an Undertaker's Assistant.

The Runt lost many a Case because he could not Bark at the Jury and pound Holes in a Table. His Briefs had been greatly admired by the Supreme Court. Also it was known that he could draw up a copper-riveted Contract that would hold Water, but as a Pleader he was a Pickerel.

At one time he had an Important Suit on hand, and he was Worried, for he was opposed by a couple of living Gas Engines who could rare up and down in front of a yap jury for further Orders.

---

* Reprinted from George Ade, *People You Know*, 1903.

"I have the Law on my Side," said the Runt. "Now if I were only Six-Feet-Two with a sole-leather Thorax, I could swing the Verdict."

While he was repining, in came a Friend of his Youth, named Jim.

This Jim was a Book-Agent. He was as big as the Side of a House. He had a Voice that sounded as if it came up an Elevator Shaft. When he folded his Arms and looked Solemn, he was a colossal Picture of Power in Repose. He wore a Plug Hat and a large Black Coat. Nature intended him for the U.S. Senate, but used up all the Material early in the Job and failed to stock the Brain Cavity.

Jim had always been at the Foot of the Class in School. At the age of 40 he spelled Sure with an Sh and sank in a Heap when he tried to add 8 and 7. But he was a tall Success as a Book Peddler, because he learned his Piece and the 218 Pounds of Dignified Superiority did the Rest.

Wherever he went, he commanded Respect. He could go into a strange Hotel, and sit down at the Breakfast Table and say: "Please pass the Syrup," in a Tone that had all the majestic Significance of an Official Utterance. He would sit there in silent Meditation. Those who sized up that elephantine Form and noted the Gravity of his Countenance and the Fluted Wrinkles on his high Brow, imagined that he was pondering on the Immortality of the Soul. As a matter of Fact, Jim was wondering whether he would take Ham or Bacon with his Eggs.

Jim had the Bulk and the awe-inspiring Front. As long as he held to a Napoleonic silence he could carry out the Bluff. Little Boys tip-toed when they came near him, and Maiden Ladies sighed for an introduction. Nothing but a Post-Mortem Examination would have shown Jim up in his True Light. The midget Lawyer looked up in Envy at his mastodonic Acquaintance and sighed.

"If I could combine my intellect with your Horse-Power, I would be the largest Dandelion in the Legal Pasture," he said.

Then a Happy Idea struck him amidships.

"Jim, I want you to be my Associate Counsel," he said. "I understand, of course, that you do not know the difference between a Caveat and a Caviar Sandwich, but as long as you keep your Hair combed the way it is now and wear that Thoughtful Expression, you're just as good as the whole Choate Family. I will introduce you as an Eminent Attorney from the East. I will guard the Law Points and you will sit there and Dismay the Opposition by looking Wise."

So when the Case came up for Trial, the Runt led the august Jim into the Court Room and introduced him as Associate Counsel. A Murmur of Admiration ran throughout the Assemblage when Jim showed his Commanding Figure, a Law Book under his Arm and a look of Heavy Responsibility on his Face. Old Atlas, who carries the Globe on his Shoulders, did not seem to be in it with this grand and gloomy Stranger.

For two hours Jim had been rehearsing his Speech. He arose.

"Your Honor," he began.

At the Sound of that Voice, a scared silence fell upon the Court Room. It was like the Lower Octave of a Pipe Organ.

"Your Honor," said Jim, "we are ready for Trial."

The musical Rumble filled the Spacious Room and went echoing through the Corridors. The Sound beat out through the Open Windows and checked Traffic in the Street. It sang through the Telegraph Wires and lifted every drooping Flag.

The Jurors turned Pale and began to quiver. Opposing Counsel were as white as a Sheet. Their mute and frightened Faces seemed to ask, "What are we up against?"

Jim sat down and the Trial got under way.

Whenever Jim got his Cue he arose and said, "Your Honor and Gentlemen of the Jury, I quite agree with my learned Colleague."

Then he would relapse and throw on a Socrates Frown and the Other Side would go all to Pieces. Every time Jim cleared his Throat, you could hear a Pin drop. There was no getting away from the dominating Influence of the Master Mind.

The Jury was out only 10 Minutes. When the Verdict was rendered, the Runt, who had provided everything except the Air Pressure, was nearly trampled under foot in the general Rush to Congratulate the distinguished Attorney from the East. The Little Man gathered up his Books and did the customary Slink, while the False Alarm stood in awful Silence and permitted the Judge and others to shake him by the Hand.

MORAL: *An Associate Counsel should weigh at least 200 pounds.*

Charles Dickens
BARDELL v. PICKWICK*

"I AM FOR THE PLAINTIFF, my Lord," said, Mr. Serjeant Buzfuz.
"Who is with you, brother Buzfuz?" said the judge. Mr. Skimpin bowed, to intimate that he was.

"I appear for the defendant, my Lord," said Mr. Serjeant
Snubbin.

"Anybody with you, brother Snubbin?" inquired the court.

"Mr. Phunky, my Lord," replied Serjeant Snubbin.

"Serjeant Buzfuz and Mr. Skimpin for the plaintiff," said the
judge, writing down the names in his note-book, and reading as he
wrote; "for the defendant, Serjeant Snubbin and Mr. Monkey."

"Beg your Lordship's pardon, Phunky."

"Oh, very good," said the judge; "I never had the pleasure of
hearing the gentleman's name before." Here Mr. Phunky bowed
and smiled, and the judge bowed and smiled too, and then Mr.
Phunky, blushing into the very whites of his eyes, tried to look as
if he didn't know that everybody was gazing at him: a thing which
no man ever succeeded in doing yet, or in all reasonable probability,
ever will.

"Go on," said the judge.

The ushers again called silence, and Mr. Skimpin proceeded to
"open the case;" and the case appeared to have very little inside it
when he had opened it, for he kept such particulars as he knew,
completely to himself, and sat down, after a lapse of three minutes,
leaving the jury in precisely the same advanced stage of wisdom as
they were in before.

Serjeant Buzfuz then rose with all the majesty and dignity
which the grave nature of the proceedings demanded, and having
whispered to Dodson, and conferred briefly with Fogg, pulled his
gown over his shoulders, settled his wig, and addressed the jury.

Serjeant Buzfuz began by saying, that never, in the whole
course of his professional experience—never, from the very first
moment of his applying himself to the study and practice of the

---

* Excerpted from *The Pickwick Papers*, 1837.

law—had he approached a case with feelings of such deep emotion, or with such a heavy sense of the responsibility imposed upon him—a responsibility, he would say, which he could never have supported, were he not buoyed up and sustained by a conviction so strong, that it amounted to positive certainty that the cause of truth and justice, or, in other words, the cause of his much-injured and most oppressed client, must prevail with the high-minded and intelligent dozen of men whom he now saw in that box before him.

Counsel usually begin in this way, because it puts the jury on the very best terms with themselves, and makes them think what sharp fellows they must be. A visible effect was produced immediately; several jurymen beginning to take voluminous notes with the utmost eagerness.

"You have heard from my learned friend, gentlemen," continued Serjeant Buzfuz, well knowing that, from the learned friend alluded to, the gentlemen of the jury had heard just nothing at all—"you have heard from my learned friend, gentlemen, that this is an action for a breach of promise of marriage, in which the damages are laid at £1,500. But you have not heard from my learned friend, inasmuch as it did not come within my learned friend's province to tell facts and circumstances, gentlemen, you shall hear detailed by me, and proved by the unimpeachable female whom I will place in that box before you."

Here Mr. Serjeant Buzfuz, with a tremendous emphasis on the word "box," smote his table with a mighty sound, and glanced at Dodson and Fogg, who nodded admiration of the serjeant, and indignant defiance of the defendant.

"The plaintiff, gentlemen," continued Serjeant Buzfuz, in a soft and melancholy voice, "the plaintiff is a widow; yes, gentlemen, a widow. The late Mr. Bardell, after enjoying, for many years, the esteem and confidence of his sovereign, as one of the guardians of his royal revenues, glided almost imperceptibly from the world, to seek elsewhere for that repose and peace which a custom-house can never afford."

At this pathetic description of the decease of Mr. Bardell, who had been knocked on the head with a quart-pot in a public-house cellar, the learned serjeant's voice faltered, and he proceeded with emotion:

"Some time before his death, he had stamped his likeness upon a little boy. With this little boy, the only pledge of her departed exciseman, Mrs. Bardell shrunk from the world, and courted the retirement and tranquillity of Goswell Street; and here she placed in her front parlour-window a written placard, bearing this inscription—'Apartments furnished for a single gentleman. Inquire within.'" Here Serjeant Buzfuz paused, while several gentlemen of the jury took a note of the document. * * *

"Before the bill had been in the parlour-window three days— three days, gentlemen—a Being, erect upon two legs, and bearing all the outward semblance of a man, and not of a monster, knocked at the door of Mrs. Bardell's house. He inquired within; he took the lodgings; and on the very next day he entered into possession of them. This man was Pickwick—Pickwick, the defendant."

Serjeant Buzfuz, who had proceeded with such volubility that his face was perfectly crimson, here paused for breath. The silence awoke Mr. Justice Starleigh, who immediately wrote down something with a pen without any ink in it, and looked unusually profound, to impress the jury with the belief that he always thought most deeply with his eyes shut. Serjeant Buzfuz proceeded. * * *

"I shall show you, gentlemen, that for two years Pickwick continued to reside constantly, and without interruption or intermission, at Mrs. Bardell's house. I shall show you that Mrs. Bardell, during the whole of that time waited on him, attended to his comforts, cooked his meals, looked out his linen for the washerwoman when it went abroad, darned, aired, and prepared it for wear, when it came home, and, in short, enjoyed his fullest trust and confidence. I shall show you that, on many occasions, he gave halfpence, and on some occasions even sixpences, to her little boy; and I shall prove to you, by a witness whose testimony it will be impossible for my learned friend to weaken or controvert, that on one occasion he patted the boy on the head, and, after inquiring whether he had won any *alley tors* or *commoneys* lately (both of which I understand to be a particular species of marbles much prized by the youth of this town), made use of this remarkable expression: 'How should you like to have another father?' I shall prove to you, gentlemen, that about a year ago, Pickwick suddenly began to absent himself from home, during long intervals, as if with the intention of gradually breaking off from my client; but I shall show you also, that his resolution was not at that time sufficiently strong, or that his better feelings conquered, if better feelings he has, or that the charms and accomplishments of my client prevailed against his unmanly intentions; by proving to you, that on one occasion, when he returned from the country, he distinctly and in

Attorney Robert Macaire: "Gentlemen, the contract in question is manifoldly null and void, fraudulent and without force in law." *The President, interrupting:* "But you are arguing against your own client." *Attorney Macaire, aside:* "The Devil! It's true, I'm in trouble. *(aloud)* This is no doubt what my colleagues will try to tell you... But in fact, this contract is certainly sound, legal, and completely binding, etc., etc." He pleaded five hours without stopping to spit, and lost his case. —Honoré Daumier, *Caricaturana,* 1837.

terms, offered her marriage: previously however, taking special care that there should be no witness to their solemn contract; and I am in a situation to prove to you, on the testimony of three of his own friends—most unwilling witnesses, gentlemen, most unwilling witnesses—that on that morning he was discovered by them holding the plaintiff in his arms, and soothing her agitation by his caresses and endearments."

A visible impression was produced upon the auditors by this part of the learned serjeant's address. Drawing forth two very small scraps of paper, he proceeded:

"And now, gentlemen, but one word more. Two letters have passed between these parties, letters which are admitted to be in the hand-writing of the defendant, and which speak volumes indeed. These letters, too, bespeak the character of the man. They are not open, fervent, eloquent epistles, breathing nothing but the language of affectionate attachment. They are covert, sly, underhanded communications, but, fortunately, far more conclusive than if couched in the most glowing language and the most poetic imagery—letters that must be viewed with a cautious and suspicious eye—letters that were evidently intended at the time, by Pickwick, to mislead and delude any third parties into whose hands they might fall. Let me read the first:—'Garraway's, twelve o'clock. Dear Mrs. B.—Chops and Tomata sauce. Yours, PICKWICK.' Gentlemen, what does this mean? Chops and Tomata sauce. Yours, Pickwick! Chops! Gracious heavens! and Tomata sauce! Gentlemen, is the happiness of a sensitive and confiding female to be trifled away, by such shallow artifices as these? The next has no date whatever, which is in itself suspicious. 'Dear Mrs. B., I shall not be at home till to-morrow. Slow coach.' And then follows this very remarkable expression. 'Don't trouble yourself about the warming-pan.' The warming pan! Why, gentlemen, who does trouble himself about a warming-pan? When was the peace of mind of man or woman broken or disturbed by a warming-pan, which is in itself a harmless, a useful, and I will add, gentlemen, a comforting article of domestic furniture? Why is Mrs. Bardell so earnestly entreated not to agitate herself about this warming-pan, unless (as is no doubt the case) it is a mere cover for hidden fire—a mere substitute for some endearing word or promise, agreeably to a preconcerted system of correspondence, artfully contrived by Pickwick with a view to his contemplated desertion, and which I am not in a condition to explain? And what does this allusion to the slow coach mean? For aught I know, it may be a reference to Pickwick himself, who has most unquestionably been a criminally slow coach during the whole of this transaction, but whose speed will now be very unexpectedly accelerated, and whose wheels, gentlemen, as he will find to his cost, will very soon be greased by you!"

Mr. Serjeant Buzfuz paused in this place, to see whether the jury smiled at his joke; but as nobody took it but the green-grocer, whose sensitiveness on the subject was very probably occasioned by his having subjected a chaise-cart to the process in question on that identical morning, the learned serjeant considered it advisable to undergo a slight relapse into the dismals before he concluded.

"But enough of this, gentlemen," said Mr. Serjeant Buzfuz, "it is difficult to smile with an aching heart; it is ill jesting when our deepest sympathies are awakened. My client's hopes and prospects are ruined, and it is no figure of speech to say that her occupation is gone indeed. The bill is down—but there is no tenant. Eligible single gentlemen pass and repass—but there is no invitation for them to inquire within or without. All is gloom and silence in the house; even the voice of the child is hushed; his infant sports are disregarded when his mother weeps; his 'alley tors' and his 'commoneys' are alike neglected; he forgets the long familiar cry of 'knuckle down,' and at tip-cheese, or odd and even, his hand is out. But Pickwick, gentlemen, Pickwick, the ruthless destroyer of this domestic oasis in the desert of Goswell Street—Pickwick, who has choked up the well, and thrown ashes on the sward—Pickwick, who comes before you to-day with his heartless Tomata sauce and warming-pans—Pickwick still rears his head with unblushing effrontery, and gazes without a sigh on the ruin he has made. Damages, gentlemen—heavy damages—is the only punishment with which you can visit him; the only recompence you can award to my client. And for those damages she now appeals to an enlightened, a high-minded, a right-feeling, a conscientious, a dispassionate, a sympathising, a contemplative jury of her civilised countrymen." With this beautiful peroration, Mr. Serjeant Buzfuz sat down, and Mr. Justice Stareleigh woke up.

Daniel R. White
CIVIL PROCEDURE*

IF YOU WANT TO BE A TRIAL LAWYER, you need to know about civil procedure. Civil procedure covers the rules of court you must follow when suing someone or being sued. The word "civil" has nothing to do with politeness; it differentiates the rules that apply to a "civil" action from those that apply to a "criminal" action. The latter is what you'll face in most places if you stab someone, or if you jaywalk in Washington, D.C.

There are three basic concepts you need to understand about civil procedure.

---

* Reprinted from D. Robert White, *The Official Lawyer's Handbook,* Simon & Schuster, 1983.

Standing

"Standing" refers to a concrete, personal interest in a particular lawsuit. It's something you're required to have in order to stay in court. Such an interest is easy to prove when you've been run over by a truck. Your injuries constitute your interest. Your broken legs give you standing.

But what if you want to sue Congress for passing a law restricting fat people from walking on public sidewalks during the lunch hour? If you're skinny, say, 6'3" and 109 pounds, you don't have "standing," because the law in question doesn't affect you personally. Even dating a fat person isn't enough.

This explains why you often see six-year-old kids as the nominal plaintiffs in school desegregation cases, or senile derelicts as the nominal plaintiffs in welfare litigation. They've been recruited by lawyers. They don't know what the hell these people in suits are fighting about, but they have standing.

Jurisdiction

The concept of jurisdiction relates to which courts can hear which cases. You can't always get your case into a federal court, for example, even though that Oklahoma state judge won't read your papers and hates you because you have a beard, or don't have a beard, or anything else he feels like holding against you.

To understand jurisdiction, just recall how things worked when you were a kid: "cases" involving who got to use the family car probably fell within Dad's jurisdiction; those involving whose turn it was to do the dishes fell within Mom's. If it wasn't clear who had jurisdiction, you engaged in "forum shopping"—you went to the one most likely to give the answer you wanted.

The basic jurisdictional rule is that everything goes into the state courts unless there's a special reason it should go into a federal court. Lawyers would *rather* have their cases in federal court, partly because the judges are better and the rules of the game a lot clearer, but mainly because of prestige. A lawyer who says "I'm trying a case in *federal* court" is boasting. One who says "I'm trying a case in *state* court" is telling you where he's trying his case.

The reason for the prestige of federal cases is that they involve more money. The reason for the extra money goes back to the nature of jurisdiction.

There are two ways a federal court can get jurisdiction over a case. The first involves somebody going up against a federal law, *i.e.*, a law passed by the U.S. Congress (as opposed to one passed by a state, a city, or the Moral Majority).

A case involving a federal law usually involves a lot of money because Congress only passes laws on important subjects, like requiring those "Do Not Remove" labels on your pillows and mattresses that always make you tear the fabric to get them off. Congress leaves minor things like murder and rape to the states.

The second way a federal court can get jurisdiction over a case involves the state citizenship of the parties to the lawsuit. If the plaintiff (the fellow with the tire tracks on his face) is from Alabama, and the defendant (the fellow who was driving the cement truck) is from New York, the two parties have "diversity of citizenship." The case can get into federal court as a so-called "diversity suit."*

The theory behind this is that an Alabama jury might not take kindly to a New Yorker. The fact that *no one* takes kindly to a New Yorker is irrelevant. Supposedly the federal judge, appointed by the President, hates New Yorkers less than most people do, and he'll keep the Alabama jury from doing a bankroll-ectomy on the New Yorker.

Like cases involving federal laws, diversity suits tend to involve a lot of money—it costs more to run over somebody twelve states away than to run over your next-door neighbor. Hence the extra prestige of a federal case.

Service of Process

Long before you can begin to explain to a jury how you were sexually harassed by your lecherous boss, you have to give your boss notice of the lawsuit. She's entitled to defend herself.

You give her notice by delivering to her, or "serving" upon her, a copy of your complaint. This is called "service of process."

Service of process raises many practical questions. If you go to your boss's address and she won't open the door, how do you serve her? By placing it on her doorstep? Throwing it through her window? Beating her dog until she opens the door?

One option is to hire an independent agent to perform the

---

* Not to be confused with the plaid suit, striped shirt, and paisley tie that your Uncle Pollard from Kansas City wears to church.

service. A private process server, usually a former bar bouncer or mud wrestler, will lurk in the shadows of her home until he catches her, invariably scaring her into a coronary.

The problem with private process servers is that they are not known for their reliability. The job doesn't pay well, and not that many people enjoy lurking in the shadows of strangers' homes.

Private process servers are famous for tossing complaints into the nearest sewer—"sewer service." Then they report back to you for payment. Because private process servers outweigh you by 80 pounds, you pay without question.

Theobald O. Mathew
THE INEXPERIENCED ADVOCATE AND
THE HOLDER IN DUE COURSE*

A N INEXPERIENCED ADVOCATE was once Requested by a Learned Friend to "Devil" a Short Cause. As he had Never Raised his Voice in Court (except to Apply for a Case to Stand Out of the List till next Sittings, Keeping its Place) the Inexperienced Advocate was Rather Alarmed at the Prospect. But, being Ambitious, he Agreed to Do his Best. He Gathered that he was to Appear for the Defendant, and that the Plaintiff was the Holder in Due Course of a Bill of Exchange. Also that he was to Knock the Plaintiff About a Bit in Cross-Examination. Pulling himself Together he Went into Court and the Case was Soon Called on. The Plaintiff had a Slightly Red Nose and his Linen was not Unimpeachable, but he gave his Evidence Clearly and in a Firm Voice. When he Rose to Cross-Examine the Plaintiff, the Inexperienced Advocate Shook Very Much, Particularly at the Knees, and the Court seemed to be Spinning Round and Round. The Judge and the Plaintiff Completely Disappeared from his Vision and were Replaced by Strangely-Coloured Sparks and Chaos. His Jaw Dropped and his Eye was Glazed. He Became Unconscious of his Surroundings. The Plaintiff was so Horrified by the Inexperienced Advocate's Appearance that he Completely Lost his Nerve. Asking in Faltering Tones what he was Looking at him like That for, the Plaintiff Added

* Reprinted from Theobald O. Mathew, *Forensic Fables*, Butterworth & Co., 1926.

that he had been a Respectable Man Ever Since———. Here he
Paused. But the Judge Took up the Running, and Before the Inexperienced Advocate had Recovered his Senses, the Plaintiff had
Admitted that he had been Convicted of Fraud on Divers Occasions,
and the Judge had Given Judgment (with Costs) for the Defendant.
The Defendant's Solicitor was so Delighted with what he Regarded
as a Splendid Histrionic Display that he thereafter Showered Briefs
upon the Inexperienced Advocate.

MORAL.—*Silence is Golden.*

THE INEXPERIENCED ADVOCATE AND THE
HOLDER IN DUE COURSE

Anonymous
SILENCE IS GOLDEN*

A STOLID, BLANK-LOOKING INDIAN sat in the federal court-room to be arraigned for bootlegging. His case was called. The marshal told him to stand up; but he only stared, apparently not comprehending. The marshal motioned him to rise. He stood.

"What is your name?" the Judge asked.

No reply.

"Have you an attorney?"

Only a helpless stare from the Indian.

"Can you understand English?" queried the Judge.

Blank silence on the part of the prisoner.

"Mr. Attorney, what is this man charged with?" asked the Judge.

The District Attorney stated the case.

"It seems to me," said the Judge, "that this is a very trivial case. The poor thing doesn't seem to understand a word of English. He probably has no understanding that he has done wrong. Mr. Attorney, just enter a *nolle prosequi* in this case."

The Indian was told he could go; but stood staring and motionless. The marshal, with a gesture, ordered him to sit down. He obeyed, and stayed throughout the long afternoon session of court. In one case, the charge was similar to his own. Scott Miller, a noted local lawyer, was defending. Miller entered a plea of guilty for his client, and then made an impassioned plea for mercy. His pathos would have moved a marble statue to tears. He represented long and earnestly the wonderful virtues and manifold kindnesses of his client. When he sat down, the Judge said, "Five years in the penitentiary."

Court adjourned, and as the crowd passed out the Indian followed. He walked down the steps behind Miller. Suddenly he leaned over and whispered in the attorney's ear.

"White man talk too damn much."

---

* Reprinted from the *The Green Bag*, 1914, which was a popular American legal publication in the early part of this century.

Finley Peter Dunne
CROSS-EXAMINATIONS*

MR. DOOLEY put down his newspaper with the remark; "They cudden't get me into coort as a witness; no, sir, not if 't was to hang me best frind.

" 'T is hard enough," he said, "with newspapers an' cinsus officers an' th' mim'ry iv cab dhrivers to live down ye'er past without bein' foorced to dhrill it in a r-red coat an' with a brass band ahead befure th' eyes iv th' multitood. I did it wanst; I'll do it no more. Wanst I was summonsed to appear in th' high temple iv justice where Timothy Duffy is th' presidin' janius, as Hogan says, to give me priceless tistymony as to whether th' plumbin' in Harrigan's house was fitted to hold wather. 'T was me opinyon, havin' had a handful iv thrumps I held in Harrigan's parlor spiled be Lake Michigan dhroppin' through th' ceilin', that said plumbin' was conthrary to th' laws an' ordinances iv th' county iv Cook, State iv Illinois, S.S. made an' provided an' th' same. I put on a high hat an' a long-tailed coat an' left a man in charge iv me business an' wint down to Halsted Street an' swore to, as solemnly as I cud, knowin' that Harrigan wudden't pay th' rent annyhow. An' what come iv it? I was two minyits givin' me tistymony, an' two hours thryin' to convince th' hon'rable coort—a loafer be th' name iv Duffy—an' th' able jury that I hadn't stolen th' shirt on me back fr'm a laundhry wagon. Th' coort was goin' to confine me in jail f'r life f'r contimpt, th' lawyer f'r th' definse sthrongly intimated that I was in th' neighborhood whin Charlie Ross was kidnapped an' th' jury ast to be allowed to bring in a verdict iv manslaughter again me without exthra pay. As I wint out iv th' coort two or three women in large hats hissed me an' a man at th' dure threatened me with an umbrelly ontill I made a counther dimonsthration with me foot. Justice, says ye? I tell ye Hogan's r-right whin he says: 'Justice is

---

* This is the only one of three "Mr. Dooley" pieces in this book (for the imitations, see p. 83 and p. 174) that was actually written by Mr. Dooley's creator. Finley Peter Dunne was an Irish-American political humorist who may be best remembered for the following Dooley statement: "Whether th' Constitution follows th' flag or not, th' Supreme Court follows th' illiction returns."

blind.' Blind she is, an' deff an' dumb an' has a wooden leg! Niver again will they dhraw me to a coort. I'll take th' rude justice iv a piece iv lead pipe without costs or th' r-right iv appeal.

Mark Twain
SCIENCE *v.* LUCK*

A T THAT TIME, IN KENTUCKY (said the Hon. Mr. K—), the law was very strict against what is termed "games of chance." About a dozen of the boys were detected playing "seven-up" or "old sledge" for money, and the grand jury found a true bill against them. Jim Sturgis was retained to defend them when the case came up, of course. The more he studied over the matter, and looked into the evidence, the plainer it was that he must lose a case at last—there was no getting around that painful fact. Those boys had certainly been betting money on a game of chance. Even public sympathy was roused in behalf of Sturgis. People said it was a pity to see him mar his successful career with a big prominent case like this, which must go against him.

But after several restless nights an inspired idea flashed upon Sturgis, and he sprang out of bed delighted. He thought he saw his way through. The next day he whispered around a little among his clients and a few friends, and then when the case came up in court he acknowledged the seven-up and the betting, and, as his sole defense, had the astounding effrontery to put in the plea that old sledge was not a game of chance! There was the broadest sort of a smile all over the faces of that sophisticated audience. The judge smiled with the rest. But Sturgis maintained a countenance whose earnestness was even severe. The opposite counsel tried to ridicule him out of his position, and did not succeed. The judge jested in a ponderous judicial way about the thing, but did not move him. The matter was becoming grave. The judge lost a little of his patience, and said the joke had gone far enough. Jim Sturgis said he knew of no joke in the matter—his clients could not be punished for indulging in what some people chose to consider a game of chance until it was *proven* that it was a game of chance. Judge and counsel said

---

* This story was originally published in 1870.

that would be an easy matter, and forthwith called Deacons Job, Peters, Burke, and Johnson, and Dominies Wirt and Miggles, to testify; and they unanimously and with strong feeling put down the legal quibble of Sturgis by pronouncing that old sledge *was* a game of chance.

"What do you call it *now*?" said the judge.

"I call it a game of science!" retorted Sturgis; "and I'll prove it, too!"

They saw his little game.

He brought in a cloud of witnesses, and produced an overwhelming mass of testimony, to show that old sledge was not a game of chance but a game of science.

Instead of being the simplest case in the world, it had somehow turned out to be an excessively knotty one. The judge scratched his head over it awhile, and said there was no way of coming to a determination, because just as many men could be brought into court who would testify on one side as could be found to testify on the other. But he said he was willing to do the fair thing by all parties, and would act upon any suggestion Mr. Sturgis would make for the solution of the difficulty.

Mr. Sturgis was on his feet in a second.

"Impanel a jury of six of each, Luck *versus* Science. Give them candles and a couple of decks of cards. Send them into the jury-room, and just abide by the result!"

There was no disputing the fairness of the proposition. The four deacons and the two dominies were sworn in as the "chance" jurymen, and six inveterate old seven-up professors were chosen to represent the "science" side of the issue. They retired to the jury-room.

In about two hours Deacon Peters sent into court to borrow three dollars from a friend. (*Sensation.*) In about two hours more Dominie Miggles sent into court to borrow a "stake" from a friend. (*Sensation.*) During the next three or four hours the other dominie and the other deacons sent into court for small loans. And still the packed audience waited, for it was a prodigious occasion in Bull's Corners, and one in which every father of a family was necessarily interested.

The rest of the story can be told briefly. About daylight the jury came in, and Deacon Job, the foreman, read the following

Verdict

We, the jury in the case of the Commonwealth of Kentucky *v.* John Wheeler *et al.*, have carefully considered the points of the case, and tested the merits of the several theories advanced, and do hereby unanimously decide that the game commonly known as old sledge or seven-up is eminently a game of science and not of chance. In demonstration whereof it is hereby and herein stated, iterated, reiterated, set forth, and made manifest that, during the entire night, the "chance" men never won a game or turned a jack, although both feats were common and frequent to the opposition; and furthermore, in support of this our verdict, we call attention to the significant fact that the "chance" men are all busted, and the "science" men have got the money. It is the deliberate opinion of this jury, that the "chance" theory concerning seven-up is a pernicious doctrine, and calculated to inflict untold suffering and pecuniary loss upon any community that takes stock in it.

"That is the way that seven-up came to be set apart and particularized in the statue-books of Kentucky as being a game not of chance but of science, and therefore not punishable under the law," said Mr. K—. "That verdict is of record, and holds good to this day."

Arthur C. Train
THE DOG ANDREW*

"WHO IS ANDREW?" asked Mr. Tutt.

"Andrew is a dog," said Tutt, leaning against his senior partner's door jamb. "He bit one Tunnygate, and now the Grand Jury have indicted not the dog, as it is clear they should have done, but the dog's owner: Mr. Enoch Appleboy."

"What for?"

"Assault in the second degree with a dangerous weapon."

"What was the weapon?" inquired Mr. Tutt simply.

---

* Excerpted from the novel *Tutt and Mr. Tutt*, one of a series of humorous novels by Arthur C. Train, all centering on the lawyer Mr. Tutt.

"The dog."

"What are you talking about?" cried Mr. Tutt. "What nonsense!"

"Yes, it is nonsense!" agreed Tutt. "But they've done it all the same. Read it for yourself!" And he handed Mr. Tutt the indictment, which the latter proceeded to read. * * *

"It's no good," said Mr. Tutt. "There isn't any allegation of *scienter*, or malicious intent, in it."

"What of it? It says he assaulted Tunnygate with a dangerous weapon. You don't have to set forth that he knew it was a dangerous weapon if you assert that he did it willfully. You don't have to allege in an indictment charging an assault with a pistol that the defendant knew it was loaded."

"But a dog is different!" reasoned Mr. Tutt. "A dog is not *per se* a dangerous weapon. Saying so doesn't make it so, and that part of the indictment is bad on its face—unless, to be sure, it means that he hit him with a dead dog, which it is clear from the context that he didn't. The other part—that he set the dog on him—lacks the allegation that the dog was vicious and that Appleboy knew it; in other words an allegation of *scienter*. It ought to read that said Enoch Appleboy, well knowing that said dog Andrew was a dangerous and ferocious animal and would, if incited, provoked and encouraged, bite the legs and body of him the said Herman— did then and there feloniously, willfully and wrongfully incite, provoke and encourage the said Andrew, and so forth.'" * * *

"Well, the Appleboys are waiting to see you," said Tutt. "They are in my office. Bonnie Doon got the case for us off his local district leader, who's a member of the same lodge of the Abyssinian Mysteries—Bonnie's been Supreme Exalted Ruler of the Purple Mountain for over a year—and he's pulled in quite a lot of good stuff, not all dog cases either! Appleboy's an Abyssinian too."

"I'll see them," consented Mr. Tutt, "but I'm going to have you try the case. Dog trials aren't in my line. There are some things which are *infra dig**—even for Ephraim Tutt."

*   *   *

---

* *Ed.* Beneath dignity.

Mr. Appleboy sat stolidly at the bar of justice, pale but resolute. Beside him sat Mrs. Appleboy, also pale but even more resolute. A jury had been selected without much manifest attention by Tutt, who had nevertheless managed to slip in an Abyssinian brother on the back row, and an ex-dog fancier for Number Six. Also among those present were a delicatessen man from East Houston Street, a dealer in rubber novelties, a plumber and the editor of *Baby's World*. The foreman was almost as fat as Mr. Appleboy, but Tutt regarded this as an even break on account of the size of Tunnygate. As Tutt confidently whispered to Mrs. Appleboy, it was a rotten a jury as he could get. * * *

Upon the bench Judge Witherspoon, assigned from somewhere upstate, finished the letter he was writing to his wife in Genesee County, scaled it and settled back in his chair. An old war horse of the country bar, he had in his time been mixed up in almost every kind of litigation, but as he looked over the indictment he with difficulty repressed a smile. Thirty years ago he'd had a dog case himself; also of the form, style and breed known as bull.

"You may proceed, Mister District Attorney!" he announced, and little Pepperill, the youngest of the D.A.'s staff, just out of the law school, begoggled and with his hair plastered evenly down on either side of his small round head, rose with serious mien, and with a high piping voice opened the prosecution.

It was, he told them, a most unusual and hence most important case. The defendant Appleboy had maliciously procured a savage dog of the most vicious sort and loosed it upon the innocent complainant as he was on his way to work, with the result that the latter had nearly been torn to shreds. It was a horrible, dastardly, incredible, fiendish crime, he would expect them to do their full duty in the premises, and they should hear Mr. Tunnygate's story from his own lips.

Mr. Tunnygate limped with difficulty to the stand, and having been sworn gingerly sat down—partially. Then turning his broadside to the gaping jury he recounted his woes with indignant gasps.

"Have you the trousers which you wore upon that occasion?" inquired Pepperill.

Mr. Tunnygate bowed solemnly and lifted from the floor a paper parcel which he untied and from which he drew what remained of that now historic garment.

"These are they," he announced dramatically.

"I offer them in evidence," exclaimed Pepperill, "and I ask the jury to examine them with great care."

They did so.

Tutt waited until the trousers had been passed from hand to hand and returned to their owner; then, rotund, chipper and birdlike as ever, began his cross-examination much like a woodpecker attacking a stout stump. The witness had been an old friend of Mr. Appleboy's, had he not? Tunnygate admitted it, and Tutt pecked him again. Never had done him any wrong, had he? Nothing in particular. Well, any wrong? Tunnygate hesitated. Why, yes, Appleboy had tried to fence in the public beach that belonged to everybody. Well, did that do the witness any harm? The witness declared that it did; compelled him to go round when he had a right to go across. Oh! Tutt put his head on one side and glanced at the jury. How many feet? About twenty feet. Then Tutt pecked a little harder.

"Perhaps *this* will refresh your memory."

"Didn't you tear a hole in the hedge and stamp down the grass when by taking a few extra steps you could have reached the beach without difficulty?"

"I—I simply tried to remove an illegal obstruction!" declared Tunnygate indignantly.

"Didn't Mr. Appleboy ask you to keep off?"

"Sure—yes!"

"Didn't you obstinately refuse to do so?"

Mr. Pepperill objected to "obstinately" and it was stricken out.

"I wasn't going to stay off where I had a right to go," asserted the witness.

"And didn't you have warning that the dog was there?"

"Look here!" suddenly burst out Tunnygate. "You can't hector me into anything. Appleboy never had a dog before. He got a dog just to sic him on me! He put up a sign 'Beware of the dog,' but he knew that I'd think it was just a bluff. It was a plant, that's what it was! And just as soon as I got inside the hedge that dog went for me and nearly tore me to bits. It was a rotten thing to do and you know it!"

He subsided, panting. * * *

Tutt waved the witness from the stand contemptuously.

"Well, I'd like a chance to testify!" shrilled Mrs. Tunnygate, rising in full panoply.

"This way, madam," said the clerk, motioning her round the back of the jury box. And she swept ponderously into the offing like a full-rigged bark and came to anchor in the witness chair, her chin rising and falling upon her heaving bosom like the figurehead of a vessel upon a heavy harbor swell.

Now it has never been satisfactorily explained just why the character of an individual should be in any way deducible from such irrelevant attributes as facial anatomy, bodily structure or the shape of the cranium. Perhaps it is not, and in reality we discern disposition from something far more subtle—the tone of the voice, the expression of the eyes, the lines of the face or even from an aura unperceived by the senses. However that may be, the wisdom of the Constitutional safeguard guaranteeing that every person charged with crime shall be confronted by the witnesses against him was instantly made apparent when Mrs. Tunnygate took the stand, for without hearing a word from her firmly compressed lips the jury simultaneously swept her with one comprehensive glance and turned away. Students of women, experienced adventurers in matrimony, these plumbers, bird merchants, "delicatessens" and the rest looked, perceived and comprehended that here was the very devil of a woman—a virago, a shrew, a termagant, a natural-born trouble-maker; and they shivered and thanked God that she was Tunnygate's and not theirs. * * *

It was as naught to them that she testified to the outrageous illegality of the Appleboys' territorial ambitions, the irascibility of the wife, the violent threats of the husband; or that Mrs. Appleboy had been observed to mail a suspicious letter shortly before the date of the canine assault. They disregarded her. Yet when Tutt upon cross-examination sought to attack her credibility by asking her various pertinent questions they unhesitatingly accepted his implied accusations as true, though under the rules of evidence he was bound by her denials.

Peck 1: "Did you not knock Mrs. Appleboy's flower pots off the piazza?" he demanded significantly.

"Never! I never did!" she declared passionately.

But they knew in their hearts that she had.

Peck 2: "Didn't you steal her milk bottles?"

"What a lie! It's absolutely false!"

Yet they knew that she did. * * *

"I move to dismiss, Your Honor," chirped Tutt blithely at the conclusion of her testimony.

Judge Witherspoon shook his head.

"I want to hear the other side," he remarked. "The mere fact that the defendant put up a sign warning the public against the dog may be taken as some evidence that he had knowledge of the animal's vicious propensities."

"Very well, Your Honor," agreed Tutt, patting himself upon the abdomen. "Mr. Appleboy, take the stand."

Mr. Appleboy heavily rose, and the heart of every fat man upon the jury, particularly that of the Abyssinian brother upon the back row, went out to him. For just as they had known without being told that the new Mrs. Tunnygate was a vixen, they realized that Appleboy was a kind, good-natured man—a little soft, perhaps, like his clams, but no more dangerous. Moreover, it was plain that he had suffered and was, indeed, still suffering, and they had pity for him. Appleboy's voice shook and so did the rest of his person as he recounted his ancient friendship for Tunnygate and their piscatorial association, their common matrimonial experiences, the sudden change in the temperature of the society of Throggs

Neck, the malicious destruction of their property and the unexplained aggressions of Tunnygate upon the lawn. And the jury, believing, understood.

Then like the sword of Damocles the bessemer voice of Pepperill severed the general atmosphere of amiability: "Where did you get that dog?"

Mr. Appleboy looked round helplessly, distress pictured in every feature.

"My wife's aunt lent it to us."

"How did she come to lend it to you?"

"Bashemath wrote and asked for it."

"Oh! Did you know anything about the dog before you sent for it?"

"Of your own knowledge?" interjected Tutt sharply.

"Oh, no!" returned Appleboy.

"Didn't you know it was a vicious beast?" sharply challenged Pepperill.

"Of your own knowledge?" again warned Tutt.

"I'd never seen the dog."

"Didn't your wife tell you about it?"

Tutt sprang to his feet, wildly waving his arms: "I object; on the ground that what passed between husband and wife upon this subject must be regarded as confidential."

"I will so rule," said Judge Witherspoon, smiling.

"Excluded."

Pepperill shrugged his shoulders. * * *

"Mr. Tutt, call your next witness," said the judge.

"Mrs. Appleboy," called out Tutt, "will you kindly take the chair?" And that good lady, looking as if all her adipose existence had been devoted to the production of the sort of pies that mother used to make, placidly made her way to the witness stand.

"Did you know that Andrew was a vicious dog?" inquired Tutt.

"No!" answered Mrs. Appleboy firmly. "I didn't."

"That is all," declared Tutt with a triumphant smile.

"Then," snapped Pepperill, "why did you send for him?"

"I was lonely," answered Bashemath unblushingly.

"Do you mean to tell this jury that you didn't know that that dog was one of the worst biters in Livornia?"

"I do!" she replied. "I only knew Aunt Eliza had a dog. I didn't know anything about the dog personally."

"What did you say to your aunt in your letter?"

"I said I was lonely and wanted protection."

"Didn't you hope the dog would bite Mr. Tunnygate?"

"Why, no!" she declared. "I didn't want him to bite anybody."

Pepperill gave her a last disgusted look and sank back in his seat.

"That is all!" he ejaculated feebly. * * *

"Well, Mr. Tutt," said the judge, "now I will hear what you may wish to say upon the question of whether this issue should be submitted to the jury."

Tutt elegantly rose.

"Your Honor, I shall address myself simply to the question of *scienter*. I might, of course, dwell upon the impropriety of charging the defendant with criminal responsibility for the act of another free agent even if that agent be an animal—but I will leave that, if necessary, for the Court of Appeals. If anybody were to be indicted in this case I hold it should have been the dog Andrew. Nay, I do not jest! But I can see by Your Honor's expression that any argument upon that score would be without avail."

"Entirely," remarked Witherspoon. "Kindly go on!"

"Well," continued Tutt, "the law of this matter needs no elucidation. It has been settled since the time of Moses."

"Of whom?" inquired Witherspoon. "You don't need to go back farther than Chief Justice Marshall so far as I am concerned."

Tutt bowed.

"It is an established doctrine of the common law both of England and America that it is wholly proper for one to keep a domestic animal for his use, pleasure or protection, until, as Dykeman, J., says in Muller vs. McKesson, 10 Hun. 45, 'some vicious propensity is developed and brought out to the knowledge of the owner.' Up to that time the man who keeps a dog or other animal cannot be charged with liability for his acts. This has always been the law. * * *

"In the old English case of Smith vs. Pehal, 2 Strange 1264, it was said by the court: 'If a dog has once bit a man, and the owner having notice thereof keeps the dog, and lets him go about or lie at his door, an action will lie against him at the suit of a person who is bit, though it happened by such person's treading on the dog's toes; for it was owing to his not hanging the dog on the first notice. And the safety of the king's subjects ought not afterwards to be endangered.' That is sound law; but it is equally good law that 'if a person with full knowledge of the evil propensities of an animal wantonly excites him or voluntarily and unnecessarily puts himself in the way of such an animal he would be adjudged to have brought the injury upon himself, and ought not to be entitled to recover. In such a case it cannot be said in a legal sense that the keeping of the animal, which is the gravamen of the offense, produced the injury.'

"Now in the case at bar, first there is clearly no evidence that this defendant knew or ever suspected that the dog Andrew was otherwise than of a mild and gentle disposition. That is, there is no evidence whatever of *scienter*. In fact, except in this single instance there is no evidence that Andrew ever bit anybody. Thus, in the word of Holy Writ the defendant Appleboy should be quit, and in the language of our own courts he must be held harmless. Secondly, moreover, it appears that the complainant deliberately put himself in the way of the dog Andrew, after full warning. I move that the jury be directed to return a verdict of not guilty."

"Motion granted," nodded Judge Witherspoon, burying his nose in his hankerchief. "I hold that every dog is entitled to one bite." * * *

Then he beckoned to Mr. Appleboy. "Come up here!" he directed.

Timidly Mr. Appleboy approached the dais.

"Don't do it again!" remarked His Honor shortly.

"Eh? Beg pardon, Your Honor, I mean——"

"I said: 'Don't do it again!'" repeated the judge with a twinkle in his eye. Then lowering his voice he whispered: "You see I come from Livornia, and I've known Andrew for a long time."

Action. Lawsuit. A term used by lawyers to distract the client from the fact that nothing is happening in his case. —*Daniel R. White*

"Decisions, decisions, decisions!"

THE LAWYER AS JUDGE

H. L. Mencken
THE JUDICIAL ARM*

M Y RECOLLECTION OF JUDGES and my veneration for them
go back a long way before my newspaper days, for I was a
boy not more than eight or nine years old when my father began
taking me on his tours of the more high-toned Washington saloons,
and pointing out for my edification the eminent men who infested
them. Not a few of those dignitaries were ornaments of the Federal
judiciary, and among them were some whose names were almost
household words in the Republic. But it was not their public fame
that most impressed me; it was the lordly and elegant way in which
they did their boozing. Before I really knew what a Congressman
was I was aware that Congressmen were bad actors in barrooms,
and often had to be thrown out, and years before I had heard that
the United States Senate sat in trials of impeachment and formerly
had a say in international treaties I had seen a Senator stricken by
the first acrobatic symptoms of delirium tremens. But though I
search my memory diligently, and it is especially tenacious in
sociological matters, I can't recall a single judge who ever showed
any sign of yielding to the influence. They all drank freely, and with
a majestic spaciousness of style, but they carried their liquor like
gentlemen.

Boy-like, I must have assumed that this gift for the bottle ran
with their high station, and was, in fact, a part of their professional
equipment, for I remember being greatly astonished years later,
when I first encountered, as a young reporter, a judge definitely in
his cups. There was nothing to the story save the bald fact that the

---

* Although known for his insults and condemnations, the author of this piece, H. L.
Mencken, casts a comparatively benign eye upon judges. From *Newspaper Days* by
H.L. Mencken. Copyright 1941 and renewed 1969 by August Mencken and
Mercantile-Safe Deposit and Trust Co. Reprinted by permission of Alfred A. Knopf,
Inc.

poor old man, facing a hard calendar in equity on a morning when he was nursing a hangover from a Bar Association banquet, had thrown in one too many quick ones, and so got himself plastered. When he fell sound asleep in his pulpit, with his feet on the bench, there was a considerable pother, and by the time I wandered upon the scene his bailiffs had evacuated him to his chambers and doused him with ice-water, and he was rapidly resuming rationality, as his loud swearing indicated. Being still innocent, I reported the facts truthfully to Max Ways, and was somewhat puzzled when he ordered me to write a brief piece saying that His Honor had been floored at the post of duty by stomach ulcers, but was happily out of danger. Later on, as my journalistic experience widened, I saw many judges in a more or less rocky state, though I should add at once that I never saw another in that condition on the actual bench or within its purlieus, and that most of those I encountered were very far from their own courts. Indeed, I gradually picked up the impression that judges, like police captains, never really let themselves go until they were away from home. In those days all the police captains of the Eastern seaboard, whenever they felt that they couldn't stand the horrors of their office another minute, went to Atlantic City, and there soused and bellowed incognito, without either public scandal or danger to their jobs. Sometimes as many as a dozen gathered in one saloon—two or three from New York, a couple each from Philadelphia, Baltimore and Washington, and maybe the rest from points as far west as Pittsburgh. In the same way judges commonly sought a hide-away when the impulse to cut loose was on them; in their own archdioceses they kept their thirsts in hand, and so avoided the prying eyes of the vulgar.

At the time I began to find my way about as a reporter there was a rich old fellow in Baltimore who gave a big stag dinner every year at the Maryland Club. He was himself of no prominence, and his dinner had no public significance: it was simply that he loved good eating and enlightened boozing himself, and delighted in getting a group of men of the same mind about him. He had begun long before with a relatively small party, but every year the grateful patients suggested that it would be nice to include this or that recruit, and in the era I speak of the feast had grown to be very large and surpassingly elaborate, with seventy or eighty head of guests at the long table, as many colored waiters toting in the oysters, wild duck and terrapin, a large staff of sommeliers at the wine-buckets, and a battery of bartenders out in the hall. One year a judge was among the delegation of stockbrokers, bank presidents, wine-agents, Tammany leaders and other dignitaries who came down from New York, and the next year he brought another, and the year following there were three, and then six, and so on. They greatly enjoyed the entertainment, and no wonder, for it was in the best Maryland Club manner; and the host, on his side, appreciated having so many men of mark at his board. But in the course of time it began to be hard on the families of some of the judges, and almost as hard on the cops and newspaper reporters of Baltimore.

For every time there was a dinner it launched a drunk in the grand manner, and every time there was such a drunk the job of rounding up the judiciary took two or three days, and was full of

embarrassments and alarms. Many of the other guests, of course, also succumbed to the grape, but no one ever seemed to care what had become of them. A Tammany leader could disappear for two days, and cause no remark; even a bank president would not be posted at Lloyd's until the third day. But judges, it appeared, were missed very quickly, if not by their catchpolls then certainly by their wives and daughters, and by the late afternoon of the day after the dinner inquiries about this or that one would begin to come in from the North. Not infrequently the inquiry would be lodged in person by a frantic daughter, and when she was put off by the cops with weasel words she would tour the newspaper offices, declaring hysterically that her pa must have been murdered, and demanding the immediate production of his carcass.

The cops were indifferent for a plain reason: they always knew where the missing judges were. So, in fact, did everybody know, but it was not etiquette to say so. For aside from a few very ancient men who had gone direct from the dinner to the nervous diseases ward of the Johns Hopkins Hospital, and were there under-going the ammonia cure, all the recreant Pontius Pilates were safely housed in the stews of Baltimore, which were then surpassed in luxury and polish only by the stews of St. Louis. Every such estab-lishment had appropriate accommodations for just such clients. They would be lodged in comfortable rooms, watched over by trustworthy bouncers, entertained with music, dancing and easy female conversation, and supplied with booze until they seemed about to give out, whereupon they would be put on strict rations of milk and soda-water and so prepared for restoration to the world. All the chatêlaines of the Baltimore houses of sin were familiar with that kind of trade, and knew precisely how to handle it, for they got a great deal of it, year in and year out, from Washington. Having handled maniacal Senators and Ambassadors, not to mention even higher dignitaries, they were not daunted by a sudden rush of harmless judges.

Unhappily, it was hard to convince the daughters of the miss-ing jurists that they were comfortable and happy, and under no hazards to either their lives or their morals. Every such inquirer refused violently to be placated with generalizations: she demand-ed to be taken to her father instantly, and allowed to convoy him home. Inasmuch as no one dared to tell her where he was, it became the custom to say that he had gone down to a ducking club on the Eastern Shore of Maryland, and was there engaged in shooting mallards and canvasbacks. But there were always daughters who declared that their fathers were not marksmen, and in fact had a fear of guns, and sometimes it took a good deal of blarney to convince them that duck-shooting could be learned in half an hour, and was done with air-rifles or sling-shots. Even those who swallowed the lie often made trouble, for they usually proposed to proceed to the duck country at once, and I recall one who spent two days and nights roving the Eastern Shore, seeking some trace of a tall old man wearing a heavy white moustache, weighing 220 pounds, and dressed in a broadcloth cutaway and striped pants. It would have done no good to tell this poor lady that her father was still wearing the evening clothes that he had put on for the dinner. All the visitors, in fact, continued in their tails until the time came to wash them up and start them home. The champion in my day went on thus for four days and nights, and when the whistle was blown on him at last his judicial collar, white lawn tie and boiled shirt were in a truly scandalous state. Within the month following his return to duty, so I was told afterward, he sentenced five men to death.

How the old boys accounted for their disappearance to their daughters, once they had got back to their hotels and changed clothes for the journey home, I do not know, and never inquired. I suppose that a daughter is bound in law to believe anything her father tells her, especially if he be a judge, and I assume that judges, having been lawyers, have good imaginations and ready tongues. All I can tell you is that this annual man-hunt was a headache to the city editors of Baltimore, and to their faithful reporters. We had to keep watch on the whole gang for two or three days and nights, ever full of a pardonable hope that this one or that one would fall out of a window, brain a piano-player, drop dead of *mania à potu*, or otherwise qualify for our professional attentions. It would never do to be beaten on such a story—if such a story ever bobbed up. But it never did. The judges all got home safely, and whenever it turned out that one of them had left his watch behind, or his wallet, or his plug hat, the cops always recovered it promptly, and turned it over to the host, who saw that it was restored to its owner.

Art Buchwald
A GREAT HONOR*

THE WORST THING that can happen to any public official in this country is to be mentioned for a top appointment in the government and not get it.

It isn't just the rejection of the job that is hard to swallow—it is that while he is under consideration, the candidate is being subjected to exhaustive investigation by everyone from the FBI to the *Harvard Law Review,* and his reputation can be destroyed forever.

The Supreme Court nomination circus that President Nixon put on is a perfect example of how dangerous it is to be mentioned for one of the highest positions in the land.

Take the case of Judge Chilblain Clamchowder. Judge Clamchowder, who had been appointed to the Fifth Circuit Traffic Court for the work he had done in carrying Tornado County for President Nixon in 1968, found himself listed as one of the "leading" candidates for a Supreme Court seat.

Judge Clamchowder told me in his chambers, "I knew they had just thrown in my name as a smoke screen, and at first I was flattered to see my name in the newspapers.

"But then the Eastern Establishment press started coming down here and asking about me, and my life has become pure hell.

"They talked to my second wife, who said I had cheated not only on her, but also on my bar exam. Even if it's true, it's something you don't like to read about in the newspapers."

Judge Clamchowder continued: "Then some Democratic Senators found out I hadn't paid my income tax for the past five years, and they tried to make a big deal of it just to embarrass the Nixon administration. They made it sound as if I was the first Supreme Court Justice nominee who had ever cheated on his taxes.

"To make matters worse, the FBI discovered that I was a major

---

* Reprinted from Art Buchwald, *I Never Danced at the White House,* Putnam, 1973, by permission of the author.

stockholder in the firm that prints all the traffic tickets for Tornado County. So I had to get rid of the stock at a great financial sacrifice.

"Then Jack Anderson found out about a Christmas party I had last year in my chambers for the meter maids, and while only two of them took off their clothes, he made it sound like an orgy. So now my third wife is suing me for divorce, and it's gonna be damn expensive, particularly since I don't have an interest in the printing firm any more.

"The American Civil Liberties Union then dug up the fact that I had donated a thousand dollars to buy dynamite to blow up all the school buses in Tornado County, and that made the newspaper headlines. Now I believe this was a personal matter and had nothing to do with whether a person would make a good Supreme Court justice or not.

"Finally, some smart-aleck law professor discovered that since I've been ruling on traffic offenses, I have been reversed by higher courts seven hundred and sixty-eight times.

"He also claimed I had fixed the tickets of forty-five members of my country club. It turns out I had only fixed forty tickets since I've been on the traffic court, but the media doesn't seem to be concerned with accuracy as long as it's a good story.

"The American Bar Association rated me as 'less mediocre,' and this certainly hasn't helped me keep any decorum in the courtroom."

"From what I can tell, Judge," I said, "you might have done better by not being mentioned as a possible Supreme Court Justice."

"Frankly," he replied, "if it wasn't for the honor, I would just as soon forget it."

Geoffrey Lincoln
JUDICIAL ETIQUETTE*

A DIFFERENT, and on the whole a less mean approach, is best when dealing with formidable obstacles provided by the Judge. Her Majesty's Judges are, as anyone knows, a race completely apart. Knocking up some eight thousand a year, with a pension of around five thousand, they may seem to the uninformed layman to occupy a somewhat enviable position. In fact, as they are the first to point out, their lot is very hard, they work from 10.30 until 4 p.m. for at least nine months in every year, they pay as they earn and often have to travel on the Tube. As an occupational risk they have to avoid being found drunk in charge of motor-cars or on enclosed premises after dark. For the advocate, the conduct of most cases would be far easier without them. However, as they are there, some sort of approach to them has to be worked out.

Judges can be divided into various categories. There are the plain ghastly, nowadays a dying race, who are rumoured to order double helpings of muffins after death sentences. There are the scholarly, who are inclined to talk Greek at witnesses in factory accident cases, to the complete bewilderment of everyone in Court except one aged solicitor who laughs alone and far too loud. There are bluff, hearty Judges who grow restive after lunch time on Fridays, and there are kindly, courteous Judges who are polite to everyone. Of these the ghastly ones are often the most just, the scholarly the most obtuse, the hearty the least reliable and the courteous the most difficult to deal with.

You are expected to contend with all these types, and what everyone secretly hopes is that you will have a row with them. As you are also expected to win your cases you will rarely do so, but it is true that nothing enhances a barrister's reputation so much as a good row with a Judge. Everyone remembers F. E. Smith because when a Judge said to him "What do you think I am here for?" he replied, "Who am I to question the inscrutable ways of Providence?" No one remembers his opponent, who probably took

---

* Reprinted from Geoffrey Lincoln, *A Moaning of the Bar*, Geoffrey Blés, 1957.

advantage of this regrettable crack to win the case. However, at the slightest sign of truculence at the Bar, at even the smallest edge put to the remark "By now that point should be clear *even* to your Lordship," ancient solicitors' managing clerks quiver like young girls at bull-fights and the ushers are delightedly reminded of the alleged days of Sir Edward Marshall Hall.

On the whole, if you have your client's interests at heart, it is best to deny the onlookers this pleasure and be polite to the Judge. This consists of telling him how you are much obliged to him and asking if he pleases at various intervals and laughing uproariously at his various aimless jokes. The point of a Judge's joke is, of course, not that it should be funny but that it should be there at all. When a Judge leans back with the sad expression of one about to embark on a joke, barristers look nervously at each other in case they should overlook the moment at which they are meant to laugh. There are two sorts of Judge's jokes, the sort that are designed to show his childlike innocence in face of the complexities of modern life, and the sort which start off "I remember when the late Theo Matthew..." Of the two, the second is preferable as having a period charm.

Loud laughter at judicial sallies is desirable and will keep your exchanges with the Judge on a reasonable level of politeness. If he then wants to say something rude and quite unhelpful to you he will at least begin, "It might assist you to know what is passing through my mind," and you can begin your only slightly offended reply: "With the very greatest respect..." If he continues to let you know what is passing through his mind, another telling gambit is to ask him a quite irrelevant question and, just as he opens his mouth to answer it, to say, in a loud voice, "I ask the question, of course, purely rhetorically, my lord," thereby making the most astute Judge gasp for air. The golden rule, however, with any Judge, is to keep your eye firmly on the clock. As soon as the hands reach ten minutes to one it is time to say, even if you are in the middle of a sentence, "I am now passing to another topic. Would your Lordship find that a convenient moment to adjourn?" The look of surprised delight in those hungry eyes is worth another witness. With all Judges it is the hour before lunch that is the most tricky.

By and large, Judges have improved, and many of them are now mild-mannered men. They are no longer scarlet-and-ermined ogres tortured by gout or fired by claret, from whose courts impressionable junior barristers totter green and trembling. They deserve, therefore, and usually get, kindly treatment. Exceptional cases occur. A long while ago someone threw a dead cat at a harmless County Court Judge. After dodging neatly, he uttered the most severe rebuke of which he seemed capable: "I warn you," he said, "should you do that again, the consequences may be extremely serious."

But these are peaceful days in the forensic arena. It is not really necessary to come to Court armed with dead cats. It is sufficient to say, with whatever expression of anger, despair, disgust or plain bewilderment you care to put into it, "If your Lordship pleases..."

Theobald O. Mathew
THE JUDGE WHOSE APPEARANCE
TERRIFIED THE PUBLIC*

O N THE OPENING DAY of the Michaelmas Sittings no Figure in the Judicial Procession was More Awe-Inspiring than that of Mr. Justice Mildew. His Lordship's Grim Countenance Struck Terror into All Beholders. As he Walked up the Central Hall of the Royal Courts of Justice, Barristers, Managing Clerks, Office-Boys, sand Flappers Shook in their Shoes and Thanked their Stars they were not Standing before him in the Dock. It was Clear to All of them that Mr. Justice Mildew had Something of Grave Importance on his Mind, and that he was Thinking Deeply. They were Right. Mr. Justice Mildew was Reflecting, as the Procession Started, that the Champagne at the Lord Chancellor's Breakfast was (for a Light Wine) Uncommonly Good, that it was a Pity he had not Taken a Third Glass, and that he had Better Find Out Where it Came From before he went Circuit. Half-way up the Hall, Mr. Justice Mildew was Wondering whether the Port at Forty-Two Shillings (of which a Considerable Quantity had been Left Over from the Last Circuit) would be Good Enough for the Bar when they Came to Dinner, and was Sincerely Hoping that his Brother Judge would be a Bit more Lively than his Colleague at the Recent Assizes. And during the last Five yards, when his Expression became Particularly Fierce, Mr. Justice Mildew was Internally Debating whether he should Pur-

---

* Reprinted from Theobald O. Mathew, *Further Forensic Fables,* Butterworth & Co., 1928.

chase a "Wilfred" or a "Gollywog" for his Youngest Grand-
Daughter, and Trying Hard to Remember whether her Birthday was
on Tuesday or Wednesday.

MORAL.—*Look Impressive.*

THE JUDGE WHOSE APPEARANCE
TERRIFIED THE PUBLIC

Ambrose Bierce
A DEFECTIVE PETITION*

AN ASSOCIATE JUSTICE of the Supreme Court was sitting by a river when a Traveler approached and said:

"I wish to cross. Will it be lawful to use this boat?"

"It will," was the reply; "it is my boat."

The Traveler thanked him, and pushing the boat into the water embarked and rowed away. But the boat sank and he was drowned.

"Heartless man!" said an Indignant Spectator. "Why did you not tell him that your boat had a hole in it?"

"The matter of the boat's condition," said the great jurist, "was not brought before me."

Sir Carleton Kemp Allen
ONE OF OUR CONQUERORS**

HIS LORDSHIP then summed-up to the jury as follows:

'After a long and, I trust, conscientious hearing of the evidence in this interesting case, it now rests with you to decide an issue the gravity of which I am sure I need not emphasise. It is my duty to direct your attention to the principles which should guide you in arriving at your decision.

'Briefly stated, the case for the prosecution is this: On October 1st last, the accused met the deceased in the street—of course, *before* the deceased was deceased; I hope you will bear that point in mind—and said to him: "If you go messing around with my girl" (there is some conflict of evidence here; according to several witnesses the term used was "skirt" or "bit of stuff"; but the difference is not material), "you will get more than you are looking for." The deceased replied: "Oh, will I?" Stung to fury by this insulting retort, the accused assaulted the deceased in the following manner (as it

* Reprinted from Ambrose Bierce, *Fantastic Fables*, 1899.
**Reprinted from Sir Carleton Kemp Allen, *Law and Disorders: Legal Indiscretions*, Stevens & Sons, 1954.

is alleged): he struck him several times over the head with an iron bar, severed his jugular vein, and emptied the contents of an automatic revolver into his prostrate form. The deceased's condition having given rise to anxiety, Dr. Sawkins was summoned; you have heard his evidence that, on examining the patient, he came to the conclusion that life was extinct. The prosecution contends that this death was due to the behaviour of the accused.

'Twenty-seven witnesses have been called by the Crown to testify that they were on the spot at the time, that they heard the words spoken, and that they saw the alleged assault committed. Their stories substantially coincide, and none of them has been seriously shaken in cross-examination. Now, members of the jury, before considering in detail the evidence of these witnesses, it is my duty to warn you—and I do so very seriously—against certain influences which might dangerously prejudice your minds.

'Counsel for the prosecution has repeatedly reminded you that this is a court of justice. He has referred to you again and again as "judges in a matter of life and death." That is the first thing against which I must warn you. It is most improper to refer to this place as a mere court of justice. It is something far more than that. It is the biggest free entertainment that the State provides for its citizens. I say without hesitation that as a place of entertainment there is not a single cinema *de luxe* which can compare with it. Its audience is the whole population of these islands. It is entirely inconsistent with the dignity of your office to compare you to mere judges in a dull legal dispute. You and I and everybody in this court are providing the public with the biggest thrill it has had for years. I weigh my words carefully when I tell you that this case is an absolute wow. Hollywood has produced nothing like it in a decade. I will not sit here, members of the jury, and hear your high office belittled.

'Counsel has also reminded you time and again of what he was pleased to call your duties. He said a good deal, for example, about your "duty to the public." You do indeed owe a duty to the public. Outside this court at the present moment some thousands of the public are assembled. The deepest emotion sways them. Strong men are trembling with suspense, matrons and maidens are weeping with the tensity of their pent-up feelings. If the accused is acquitted, he will be bathed in the precious tears of these faithful, devoted women; indeed, if he is not very careful, he will be throttled or stunned by the numerous arms which will be passionately flung

round him—a catastrophe which I am sure we should all regret. Assuredly, you must not forget your duty to the thousands—nay, millions—of your fellow-citizens who, not having heard the evidence and not having even read it except in frenzied headlines and garbled gobbets, are obviously in a better position to judge than we can be in the deplorably unimpassioned atmosphere of this court.

'You have other duties, members of the jury, of which the prosecution has made no mention. You have a duty to the Press. You are not to forget that this case has supplied the newspaper Press of this country with better copy than ten wars and fifty earthquakes, and has given it more opportunities of debauching the public mind and stimulating the criminal instincts of the community than any other event in the present century. Those memorable words, "If you go messing around with my girl, you will get more than you are looking for," have stirred the nation to its depths. You would neglect your duty, members of the jury, if you forgot for a moment that a single assassination as sanguinary, as public, and as passionate as this, means large sums of money in the pockets of those wise and public-spirited men who voice the public opinion of this great country, and whose inspiring motto is "Every morn I bring thee violence." It should be present to your minds that since this case began it has occupied four acres of printed matter, most of which doubtless you have read, in order to preserve that strict impartiality of mind which your oath requires of you.

'Above all, you owe a duty to the accused. Need I remind you of the sufferings which this unfortunate man has already endured? For several weeks he had to submit to the unscrupulous persecutions of a coroner. Counsel for the Crown has sought to represent to you that a coroner is an ill-paid and conscientious public officer who, to the best of his ability, endeavours, in a somewhat imperfect state of the law, to discover the causes of violent or suspicious deaths. I do not think you will be deceived by that kind of sophistry. You are as well aware as the really great men of the Press are aware, and the ten thousand people now outside this court are aware, that a coroner is a reptile whose sole object in life is to persecute innocent men and defeat the ends of justice. You will, without any further prompting from me, know how to deal with public pests of that sort.

'The accused has other claims upon you. You will not ignore, in considering your verdict, the very lucrative and well-merited contracts for the films, the music-halls, and the Sunday newspapers which, I must solemnly remind you, depend upon your verdict. You have, in short, members of the jury, to decide whether you will send this fellow-creature of yours—frail perhaps, possibly a little impetuous, but which of us is not frail and impetuous?—to a felon's doom and shame or to the splendour and dignity of A NATIONAL IDOL.'

His Lordship then proceeded to examine the evidence. The jury, without leaving the box, acquitted the accused. The learned judge, when removed from office by an Address of Both Houses and ordered to be confined in a place of safety, expressed extreme surprise and observed: 'Oh, but I was only being ironical!' When questioned about this in the House of Commons, the Attorney-General replied: 'Any judge who indulges in irony with a British jury must be kept under restraint in the public interest.' (*Loud and prolonged cheers.*)

James M. Marsh
MR. DOOLEY DISCOVERS
A UNANIMOUS DISSENT*

"EVERY ONE OF THEM DISSENTED," said Mr. Dooley. "It was unanimous.

"They's nine jedges on that coort, and every one of them dissented—includin' me brother Brennan, who wrote the opinion they're all dissentin' from."

"That don't make sinse," said Mr. Hennessy, "You can't have all the jedges dissentin'—it's impossible."

"Well, it may be impossible, but it happened anyhow," said Mr. Dooley, "And it's printed right here in the Coort's own Joornal of its Proceedings for February 25th.

"Read it for yourself:

"No. 28. James C. Rogers, petitioner *v.* Missouri Pacific Railroad Company, a Corporation. On writ of certiorari to the Supreme Court of Missouri.

"Judgment reversed with costs and case remanded to the Supreme Court of Missouri for proceedings not inconsistent with the opinion of this Court.

"Opinion by Mr. Justice Brennan.

"Mr. Justice Burton concurs in the result.

"Mr. Justice Reed would affirm the judgment of the Supreme Court of Missouri.

"Mr. Justice Harlan, dissenting in Nos. 28, 42, and 59 and concurring in No. 46, filed a separate opinion.

"Mr. Justice Burton concurred in Part I of Mr. Justice Harlan's opinion.

"Mr. Chief Justice Warren, Mr. Justice Black, Mr. Justice Douglas, Mr. Justice Clark, and Mr. Justice Brennan concurred in

---

* Like Edward Bander, whose "On the Case System" appears on p. 83, the author of this piece, James M. Marsh, "borrowed" more than a little from the style of Finley Peter Dunne's "Mr. Dooley" pieces (see, for an example of the original, "Cross-Examinations," p. 146. Reprinted by permission of the *Los Angeles Bar Journal*, for the Los Angeles County Bar Association, from its July issue, 1957.

Part I of Mr. Justice Harlan's opinion except insofar as it disapproves the grant of the writ of certiorari.

"Mr. Justice Frankfurther filed a separate dissenting opinion for Nos. 28, 42, 46, and 50.

"See what I mean," said Mr. Dooley. "Each and ivery one of them dissented in this No. 28, called Rogers varsus the Missouri Pacific. Even Brennan, J., who wrote the opinion for the Court. He signed Harlan's dissent. Me old friend Holmes would've sooner been caught with a spilt writ than to show up on both sides of a case like that."

"But Brennan only signed Part I, and he says 'except insofar as,'" said Mr. Hennessy, "don't that mean anything?"

"Sure it does," said Mr. Dooley. "It means Brennan dissents from Harlan, too. I guess he figgers one good dissent deserves another."

"Where was me friend Burton?" asked Mr. Hennessy.

"He's all over the place," said Mr. Dooley. "As they say, he concurs in the result—which means he likes the answer but he can't stand Brennan's opinion. Thin he concurs in wan part of Harlan, J., but he can't stand the rest of him either."

"How could they git in such a mess?" asked Mr. Hennessy.

"That's what Felix says——in twenty thousand words," said Mr. Dooley.

"Felix who?" asked Mr. Hennessy.

"Frankfurther," said Mr. Dooley. "He's a Havvard, and a perfesser at that; he gave the rest of them a free lecture in this case—and that ain't like most of them Havvards, they come pretty dear."

"Well, what happened to this fellow Rogers anyhow?" asked Mr. Hennessy, "and the Missouri Pacific."

"Plenty," said Mr. Dooley. "Rogers gits his money, wich the supreme coort of Missouri said he couldn't have; and the Missouri Pacific gits to pay it, wich they would probably just as soon not do."

"How's come?" asked Mr. Hennessy.

"Well, pinitratin' all the joodicial gobbley-dook, it's like this: Rogers was workin' on the tracks of the Missouri Pacific and he fell off a culvert; the jury gave him damages but the Supreme Coort of Missouri took them away.

"Then the Supreme Coort of the United States listened to the loiyers' argyments and gave Rogers his money back again. Me brother Brennan is supposed to tell the reasons why—at three hunderd fifty two U.S. five hunderd, which sounds like the odds against anyone but a Philadelphia lawyer understandin' the case.

"But Felix says 'Brennan, me boy, we shoodn't have took this case in the first place, we shoodn't have decided it in the second, and we shoodn't be ladlin' out the railroad's money anyway—it ain't becomin' to this high coort'....

"Then Harlan, J., says 'Ye're half right, Felix, but ye're wrong there where ye say we shoodn't decide the case; but I dissent from me brother Brennan givin' him the money, too.'

"And thin Brennan says 'Ye're half right, too, Harlan, and I agree with your Part I "except insofar as."'

"And so Brennan signed Harlan's dissent from Brennan's own opinion, and so did Warren, Black, Douglas and Clark, JJ., the same ones who signed Brennan's opinion in the first place.

"I tell ye, Hennessy, it's a demoralizin' situation. Here's the highest coort in the land, and they're all half right but none of them are all right, and they're tellin' on each other at that."

"But what about me friend Stanley Reed?" asked Mr. Hennessy, "He didn't sign anybody else's opinion, did he?"

"No, he was the smart wan," said Mr. Dooley. "He quit."

"He *quit?*" said Mr. Hennessy, "Just like *that?*"

"Just like that," said Mr. Dooley, "He voted loud and clear to back up the Supreme Court of Missouri—and then he quit."

"On February 25th he did it, right after they handed down this Rogers case. He walked out of that court that same day and he hasn't been back since."

"Well," said Mr. Hennessy, "I don't blame him, I'd quit too."

"That's the trouble with thim judges, though," said Mr. Dooley.

"What's that?" asked Mr. Hennessy.

"They don't quit often enough," said Mr. Dooley.

Justice Carlin
CORDAS *v.* PEERLESS TRANSPORTATION CO.*

City Court of New York, New York County, 1941.
27 N.Y.S.2d 198.

CARLIN, J. This case presents the ordinary man—that problem child of the law—in a most bizarre setting. As a lonely chauffeur in defendant's employ he became in a trice the protagonist in a breath-bating drama with a denouement almost tragic. It appears that a man, whose identity it would be indelicate to divulge, was feloniously relieved of his portable goods by two nondescript highwaymen in an alley near 26th Street and Third Avenue, Manhattan; they induced him to relinquish his possessions by a strong argument *ad hominem* couched in the convincing cant of the criminal and pressed at the point of a most persuasive pistol. Laden with their loot, but not thereby impeded, they took an abrupt departure, and he, shuffling off the coil of that discretion which enmeshed him in the alley, quickly gave chase through 26th Street toward 2d Avenue, whither they were resorting "with expedition swift as thought" for most obvious reasons. Somewhere on that thoroughfare of escape they indulged the stratagem of separation ostensibly to disconcert their pursuer and allay the ardor of his pursuit. He then centered on for capture the man with the pistol, whom he saw board the defendant's taxicab which quickly veered south toward 25th Street on 2d Avenue, where he saw the chauffeur jump out while the cab, still in motion, continued toward 24th Street; after the chauffeur relieved himself of the cumbersome burden of his fare the latter also is said to have similarly departed from the cab before it reached 24th Street.

The chauffeur's story is substantially the same except that he states that his uninvited guest boarded the cab at 25th Street while it was at a standstill waiting for a less colorful fare; that his "passenger" immediately advised him "to stand not upon the order of his going but go at once," and added finality to his command by an

---

* This case is true. The opinion is set forth as it appears in the official records, except for minor editing.

appropriate gesture with a pistol addressed to his sacroiliac. The chauffeur in reluctant acquiescence proceeded about fifteen feet, when his hair, like unto the quills of the fretful porcupine, was made to stand on end by the hue and cry of the man despoiled, accompanied by a clamorous concourse of the law-abiding who paced him as he ran; the concatenation of "stop thief," to which the patter of persistent feet did maddingly beat time, rang in his ears as the pursuing posse all the while gained on the receding cab with its quarry therein contained. The hold-up man sensing his insecurity suggested to the chauffeur that in the event there was the slightest lapse in obedience to his curt command that he, the chauffeur, would suffer the loss of his brains, a prospect as horrible to an humble chauffeur as it undoubtedly would be to one of the intelligentsia.

The chauffeur, apprehensive of certain dissolution from either Scylla, the pursuers, or Charybdis, the pursued, quickly threw his car out of first speed in which he was proceeding, pulled on the emergency, jammed on his brakes and, although he thinks the motor was still running, swung open the door to his left and jumped out of his car. He confesses that the only act that smacked of intelligence was that by which he jammed the brakes in order to throw off balance the hold-up man, who was half-standing and half-sitting with his pistol menacingly poised. Thus abandoning his car and passenger the chauffeur sped toward 26th Street and then turned to look; he saw the cab proceeding south toward 24th Street, where it mounted the sidewalk. The plaintiff-mother and her two infant children were there injured by the cab, which, at the time, appeared to be also minus its passenger, who, it appears, was apprehended in the cellar of a local hospital where he was pointed out to a police officer by a remnant of the posse, hereinbefore mentioned. He did not appear at the trial. The three aforesaid plaintiffs and the husband-father sue the defendant for damages, predicting their respective causes of action upon the contention that the chauffeur was negligent in abandoning the cab under the aforesaid circumstances. Fortunately the injuries sustained were comparatively slight. * * *

Negligence has been variously defined but the common legal acceptation is the failure to exercise that care and caution which a reasonable and prudent person ordinarily would exercise under like conditions or circumstances. * * * Negligence is "not absolute or intrinsic," but "is always relevant to some circumstances of time,

*"No, I don't think your decisions are too Draconian.
Do you think my decisions are too Draconian?"*

Drawing by Stevenson; © 1988
The New Yorker Magazine, Inc.

place or person." In slight paraphrase of the world's first bard it
may be truly observed that the expedition of the chauffeur's violent
love of his own security outran the pauser, reason, when he was
suddenly confronted with unusual emergency which "took his
reason prisoner." The learned attorney for the plaintiffs concedes
that the chauffeur acted in an emergency, but claims a right to
recovery upon the following proposition taken verbatim from his
brief: "It is respectfully submitted that the value of the interest of
the public at large to be immune from being injured by a dangerous
instrumentality such as a car unattended while in motion is very
superior to the right of a driver to abandon same while it is in
motion, even when acting under the belief that his life is in danger
and by abandoning same he will save his life."

To hold thus under the facts adduced herein would be tantamount to a repeal by implication of the primal law of nature written in indelible characters upon the fleshy tablets of sentient creation by the Almighty Law-giver, "the supernal Judge who sits on high." There are those who stem the turbulent current for bubble fame, or who bridge the yawning chasm with a leap for the leap's sake, or who "outstare the sternest eyes that look, outbrave the heart most daring on the earth, pluck the young sucking cubs from the she-bear, yea, mock the lion when he roars for prey" to win a fair lady, and these are the admiration of the generality of men; but they are made of sterner stuff than the ordinary man upon whom the law places no duty of emulation. The law would indeed be fond if it imposed upon the ordinary man the obligation to so demean himself when suddenly confronted with a danger, not of his creation, disregarding the likelihood that such a contingency may darken the intellect and palsy the will of the common legion of the earth, the fraternity of the ordinary man—whose acts or omissions under certain conditions make the yardstick by which the law measures culpability or innocence, negligence or care. * * *

Returning to our chauffeur. If the philosophic Horatio and the martial companions of his watch were "distilled almost to jelly with the act of fear" when they beheld "in the dead vast and middle of the night" the disembodied spirit of Hamlet's father stalk majestically by "with a countenance more in sorrow than in anger," was not the chauffeur, though unacquainted with the example of these eminent men-at-arms more amply justified in his fearsome reactions when he was more palpably confronted by a thing of flesh and blood bearing in its hand an engine of destruction which depended for its lethal purpose upon the quiver of a hair? When Macbeth was cross-examined by Macduff as to any reason he could advance for his sudden despatch of Duncan's grooms he said in plausible answer, "Who can be wise, amazed, temperate and furious, loyal and neutral in a moment? No man." * * *

The chauffeur—the ordinary man in this case—acted in a split second in a most harrowing experience. To call him negligent would be to brand him coward; the court does not do so in spite of what those swaggering heroes, "whose valor plucks dead lions by the beard," may bluster to the contrary. The court is loathe to see the plaintiffs go without recovery even though their damages were slight, but cannot hold the defendant liable upon the facts adduced at the trial. Motions, upon which decision was reserved, to dismiss the complaint are granted, with exceptions to plaintiffs. Judgment for defendant against plaintiffs dismissing their complaint upon the merits.

Summary Judgment. A dispositive judicial ruling. The term "summary" is ironic, in that it suggests that *other* rulings by a judge are the product of deliberation and care.
                                 —*Daniel R. White*

On All Fours. Descriptive of one's bodily position during an interview with a dean, senior partner, or judge. —*Robert J. Morris*

Supreme Court. The place where the finest legal minds in the country gather—to serve as law clerks to the Justices. —*Daniel R. White*

"... and I ask, gentlemen, if this is the face of
a villain, a cheat, and a parasite?"

JURIES

A. P. Herbert
WHY IS A JURY?*
British Phosphates and Beef-Extract, Ltd. *v.*
The United Alkali and Guano Simplex Association

(Before Mr. Justice Mole)

THIS COMPLICATED ACTION has now lasted thirteen days. Sir Ethelred Rutt, K. C., whose health has recently been causing general concern, made a startling attack upon the jury in his closing speech for the plaintiff to-day. He said:

May it please your Lordship, members of the jury, me learned friend has just completed an eloquent speech which continued for two days, and was at least one day too long. I must confess it wearied me——

Sir Humphrey Codd, K. C. (jumping up): Milord——

The Judge: Be seated, Sir Humphrey. Sir Ethelred no doubt refers to the theme and not to the manner of your remarks.

Sir Ethelred: No, milord, I referred to the whole thing. But the passages which pained me most, members of the jury, were the sickly compliments he paid to you. At fairly regular intervals in his dreary recitations from documents and Law Reports he would break off to tell you that you were intelligent men and women and therefore you would think this; that you were men of the world and so would have noticed that; that you were reasonable, attentive, honourable, and God knows what, and so would certainly conclude the other. Perhaps he thought the only way in which he could hope to keep you awake was to throw bouquets at your heads. *What* a pie-face!

Sir Humphrey: Really, milord, I do protest——

The Judge: Calm yourself, Sir Humphrey. Counsel's language

* Reprinted from *Uncommon Law* by A. P. Herbert, 1935, by permission of A P Watt Limited on behalf of Crystal Hale and Jocelyn Herbert.

is not perhaps 'Parliamentary', but it is not unusual in a court of law. I think that you yourself described his client as a blackmailer and forger.

Sir Humphrey Codd became seated, muttering.

Sir Ethelred (continuing): Now, ladies and gentlemen, I do not propose to slobber insincerities at you, though I too in my time have had occasion to wheedle a jury and drag out the *Vox Humana* stop in a closing speech. Of all the overrated contraptions in the British Constitution I rank highest—I mean lowest—the jury system. It may have been useful in the old days—and may be useful again—to protect the subject against a tyrannical Executive;* and any one who apprehends that he may receive injustice from a judge of the High Court sitting alone—a fantastic conception, milord—should be able to call for a jury to hear his cause. On some broad simple issues too—in libel actions, for example—a jury may help to keep the Courts in touch with modern opinion, though even there, as often as not, the verdict of twelve good men and true is false and wicked, staggering and crazy. But in a case——

The Judge: Sir Ethelred, will there be any charge for your lecture on the jury system?

Sir Ethelred: No, milord. Milord, I was just coming to the present case. Look at it! It's lasted a fortnight. The most complicated dispute in my experience. The documents were a mile high when we began; and they now measure three, for the reports of the proceedings in this Court amount to two (to which the speeches of me learned friend, milord, have contributed about half a mile)——

Sir Humphrey: Milord——

Sir Ethelred: All about debentures and mergers and mortgages and subsidiary companies—twenty-five subsidiary companies on one side alone! Not to mention the expert evidence about the scientific stuff—all that fandango about the magnesium alkaloid and the patent vapour-feed. The chemists on the two sides flatly contradicted each other, and so did the accountants. I don't believe there's an accountant on either side who really knows what some of the figures mean; I don't believe there's a single person in this Court——

* See *Rex* v. *Cochran* (page 253).

The Judge: There is one person in this Court, Sir Ethelred, who has a firm grasp of the whole case.

Sir Ethelred: I beg your Lordship's pardon. Certainly, milord. But, milord, with great respect, that rather bears out—ah—what I was saying—ah—for that one person, milord, as this is a jury case, will not have to answer the important questions in the case. You, milord, have had the advantage at every stage of this protracted bicker of seeing the shorthand reports of the previous day's proceedings, with copies of the material documents, diagrams, maps, schedules, balance-sheets, accounts, and so forth. So, milord, have me learned friend and myself, each of whom is attended by a small cloud of solicitors and junior counsel. We are all three possessed of exceptional intelligence and are equipped by long training and practice for the rapid understanding of complex figures and affairs; and if at any moment we are in doubt we can request each other or our advisers for information and assistance. Yet you will recall, milord, how often we have found ourselves—sometimes all three of us—in an incontestable fog about some vital point, exactly what a witness said or a correspondent wrote, the date of an interview, the amount of a cheque or bribe, the wording of a formula, the position of a building; and how many minutes we have spent each day upon excavating the forgotten facts from the desert of documents with which we are surrounded. And how, milord, can we expect these twelve poor mutts on the jury——

The Judge: What is a mutt?

Sir Ethelred: Milord, a mutt——

The Judge: Sir Ethelred, no doubt you know best the lines of advocacy most likely to advance the interests of your clients; but is it quite wise to describe the jury as 'mutts', which, though I am not familiar with it, I judge instinctively to be a term of depreciation?

Sir Ethelred: Milord, 'mutt' is a relative term. The Prime Minister, if he were requested to transpose a musical composition in A flat major into the key of E minor would readily confess himself a mutt in relation to that particular task.

The Judge: Very well, Sir Ethelred. Proceed.

Sir Ethelred (turning to the jury): How, I say, can you poor mutts be expected to get a grip of this colossal conundrum *without the assistance of any documents at all?* No shorthand notes, no maps, no accounts, except now and then when his Lordship decides it is time you were given a bone to play with, and we let you have a hasty glance at a diagram that doesn't matter. The whole thing's fantastic! There you sit on your hard seats, with scarcely room to wriggle, wondering what it is all about. Decent fellows, I dare say, some of you, but with no particular intelligence or financial training, and wildly divergent in character and opinion. And presently his Lordship will ask you to answer—and answer *unanimously*—about seventeen extremely unanswerable questions: 'Did the defendant knowingly make a false assertion?' and so forth. How the deuce do you know? You don't even know when you've made a false assertion yourselves. And *unanimous!* I look at you, twelve good men and true—or rather, ten good men and true and two women—* and I try to think of any simple subject about which the twelve of you would be likely to agree unanimously if you were assembled together by chance in any place outside this Court; at a dinner-party, on a committee. The simplest questions of fact, morals, ethics, history, arithmetic—and you'd be all over the shop.** And yet when we shut you up in a cold room with nothing to eat you can arrive at unanimous decisions about questions that baffle the wisest brains of the Bench and Bar. I find that highly suspicious. I don't believe——

The Judge: Do the jury wish Sir Ethelred to continue?

The Foreman of the Jury: Yes, milord; we find the gentleman refreshing.

The Judge: Then perhaps Sir Ethelred will make a gradual approach towards the case which is before us?

Sir Ethelred: No, milord, that is just the point. Members of the jury, for the reasons adumbrated I consider it quite idle to discuss this difficult case with you at all. Though I spoke with the tongues of men and of angels and for as long as me learned friend, it would still be a complete gamble which side you came down on. For all I know, the gentleman with the strongest personality in that box may particularly dislike me or have a warm admiration for Sir Humphrey Codd. One of us two is right in this case and represents truth and honesty; the other does not; and all I propose to tell you is that I am the one who is right. But I will fortify that bald assertion

---

* Not, perhaps, a necessary or chivalrous distinction.

**See *Haddock* v. *Mansfield*, where a jury found that it was not defamatory to say that a modern novel was 'objectionable, filthy, and immoral', though they did not think that this was a reasonable description of the book in question. And see Wedderburn on *Women Jurors*.

with the reminder that I have at least, to your knowledge, told the truth about me learned friend, about the jury system, and about yourselves. Which is more than Sir Humphrey can say. And I ask you to argue that if I am demonstrably truthful and right about so much I am probably truthful and right about the rest. Good afternoon.

The Foreman: We find for the plaintiff.

The Judge: But I haven't summed up! This will take three days.

The Foreman: Milord, it is not necessary. We are all sure Sir Ethelred is right. Milord, it is the wish of the jury to give three hearty cheers for Sir Ethelred Rutt!

The Judge: Oh, very well. Judgment for the plaintiff. This jury must not serve again.

NOTE—The learned counsel seems to have left out of account the point of view of the jurors. In a recent case *(Cole* v. *The Chiswick Sewage Farm)* it was found on the third day of the hearing that one of the jury was stone-deaf and had not understood a word of the proceedings. When asked why he had not revealed the fact before, he said that he had enjoyed watching the lawyers and thought he was doing no harm. 'I am sorry to go, because I liked the job,' remarked the juryman as he left the box. 'I have not heard a word, but I liked being here. I am sorry I forgot to say I was deaf.' To serve on a jury is to be free from the telephone, the tax-collector, from noise and other troubles for a much longer period than most citizens ever enjoy in ordinary life. See the *Memoirs of a Dramatist* (Ballock & Co.), where Mr. Athol Fitch records that he wrote two plays during the judge's summing-up in *British Fuel Oil, Ltd.* v. *The University of London* (1926).

When the case is all over, the jury'll pitch th' testimony out'n the window an' consider three questions: Did Lootgert look as though he's kilt his wife? Did his wife look as though she ought to be kilt? Isn't it time we went to supper?
—*Finley Peter Dunne*

Douglas Malloch
QUALIFICATIONS*

I would like to know nothing just for awhile
And quit all this working and scheming,
Just to sit all day with an idiot's smile
With naught to employ me but dreaming.

I would like to know nothing just for a time,
And cease this mad struggle for money;
I would like to forget even reason and rhyme
And have all my sorrows seem funny.

I would like to know nothing just for a day,
With nothing to trouble or worry,
And if all my sense should vanish away
Perhaps I could sit on a jury.

James M. Cain
from THE ADMINISTRATION OF JUSTICE**

THE COURT: Gentlemen of the jury, you have now heard the evidence and the argument of counsel. The court will now instruct you on the law, after which you may retire and consider your verdict. The court instructs you that the defendant Summers is being tried under an indictment which charges murder in the first degree. * * *

The evidence shows that the deceased Brody was a member of an organization known as the Ku Klux Klan, and that he was in the regalia of this organization when he was shot by the defendant

---

* Reprinted from 14 *Green Bag*, 1902.
**This piece consists of the end of Chapter VI and most of Chapter VII of James M. Cain's humorous yet powerful dramatic work, *The Administration of Justice*. Reprinted from *Our Government*, Knopf, © 1930, 1958 James M. Cain, by permission of Harold Ober Associates. Four years later Cain would write *The Postman Always Rings Twice*.

Summers. You are to disregard all allusion in the testimony to the
repute born by this organization, whether favorable or unfavorable,
and confine yourselves strictly to the actions of such members of it
as were present at the time when the acts described in the indictment were committed. You are to disregard all allusions to the
religion of the defendant Summers. As to whether he was an atheist,
or a Disciple of Christ, or anything else, you are not concerned in
the least.

It is the plea of the defendant Summers that he shot in self-
defense and that his act was accordingly justifiable. Such a plea is
permissible under the law, and if supported by the evidence is
ground for acquittal. In view of this plea, then, you must consider
whether the life of the defendant Summers was actually threatened.
To determine this, you must consider the actions of the deceased
Brody and his companions antecedent to the acts described in the
indictment. It is in evidence that the only act which they committed
of which the defendant Summers became aware was their for-
gathering on his front stoop and singing a hymn known as "Nearer,
My God, to Thee," a point on which he satisfied himself by peeping
through the curtains before reaching for his gun. Before his plea can
be allowed, then, you must consider whether the singing of the
hymn "Nearer, My God, to Thee" by Brody and his companions
constituted a threatening act. If you find that it was a threatening
act, then you should acquit him. If you find that it was not a
threatening act, and if you find that his shooting of the deceased
Brody was in no other way justifiable, then you should find him
guilty of whichever of the three crimes are open to you under the
law. Are there any questions, gentlemen?

*   *   *

[The jury room, a few moments later.]

MR. GAIL: Well, men, le's git at it. What I mean, le's git a
verdick quick, so's we can git out in time for supper.

MR. DYER: You said it!

MR. LEE: That suits me!

MR. REDDICK: You're dam tooting!

MR. BASSETT: 'Cepting only that State's attorney tooken away
all my appetite for supper.

MR. REDDICK: Me too. I never seen such a looking sight in my
life.

MR. BASSETT: "For the honor of our fair State, gentlemen, for the honor of your State and my State, I ask to return a verdict of murder in the first degre-e-e-e-e!" And then all that whooping and hollering wasn't enough for him. Oh, no! He had to spit all over you.

MR. GAIL: The spit, it wasn't so good, but what we got to talk about now is the verdict.

MR. WEMPLE: Yeah, the verdict.

MR. GAIL: What we going to do?

MR. PENNELL: I kind of feel like we ought to hear what Mr. Petry thinks about it.

MR. PETRY: This is a hard case. This is an exceptional hard case.

MR. WEMPLE: This is the balled-uppest case I ever hear tell of in my life.

MR. MOON: How come that fellow to git killt?

MR. WEMPLE: What's the matter? Was you deef you couldn't hear what them people was saying out there?

MR. MOON: I heared what they said, but seems like I can't quite git the hang of it.

MR. WEMPLE: Hunh!

MR. MOON: Yes, sir. Scuse me, sir.

MR. WEMPLE: Scuse you? Say, fellow, what ails you, anyhow?

MR. MOON: Yes, sir. I ain't quite got it straight yet, like of that.

MR. WEMPLE: Well, for the love of Mike, quit looking like the police was after you every time I look at you.... Which is the part you don't understand?

MR. MOON: About the singing.

MR. WEMPLE: Why, there wasn't nothing to that. That there was to fill him with the holy fire.

MR. MOON: Oh yeah. Thank you, sir, Mr. Wemple. Oh yeah. The holy fire.

MR. PETRY: I expect you better explain how it was, Mr. Wemple. Anyway, as good as you can. 'Cause this man don't act like he was so bright nohow, and maybe it wouldn't hurt the rest of us none if we was to kind of go over it once more, just to git it all straight.

MR. PENNELL: If Mr. Petry, he feels like he's got to hear it oncet more, then I reckon we all better hear it.

MR. WEMPLE: Well, the way I git it, this here Summers, what they got on trial, he wouldn't never go to church.

MR. FUNK: 'Cepting only he's a Disciples of Christ and there ain't no Disciples church nowhere around here.

MR. WEMPLE: Well, one thing at a time. Whatever the hell he's a disciples of, he wouldn't never go to church. So the Ku Klux got it in their head to go out to his place and try to bring him around.

MR. FUNK: It wasn't no such thing. They was sore at him 'cause he went to work and boughten hisself a disk harrow offen the mail-order house 'stead of down at the store.

MR. WEMPLE: Well then, dam it to hell, you know so much about it, suppose *you* tell it!

MR. REDDICK, MR. BASSETT, MR. ZIEGLER: Let the man talk!

MR. FUNK: All right. But why don't he tell it right?

MR. WEMPLE: I'm trying to tell what them witnesses said. After we git that all straight, why then maybe we can figure the fine points on how much they was lying.

MR. PETRY: I think Mr. Wemple's telling it the way most of us heard it.

MR. WEMPLE: So they went out to his place, this here Brody what got killt and five other of them, all dressed up in them nightgowns.

MR. ZIEGLER: And got it in the neck.

MR. WEMPLE: In the neck and the funny-bone and the seat of the pants and a couple of other places where maybe they're picking the shot out yet. 'Cause this here Summers, he ain't only boughten hisself a disk harrow offen the mail-order house, but a twelve-gauge, single-barrel, six-shot pump-gun too. And when they commence bearing down on the close harmony, what he done to them was a plenty.

MR. LEE: I swear I never heared the beat of that in all my life. Idea of going to a man's house three o'clock in the morning and commence singing right on his front stoop!

MR. DYER: And "Nearer, My God, to Thee"!

MR. REDDICK: They was a hell of a sight nearer than they figured on.

MR. WEMPLE: And Brody, he got it in about all the places there was, and in the middle of the stummick too, and he bled to death. So he come about as near as he's going to git. So that's how come he got killt.

MR. PETRY (*to* MR. MOON): Do you understand now?

MR. MOON: Oh yeah, oh yeah. Anyways, a whole lot better. Thank you, sir. Thank you, Mr. Wemple.

MR. GAIL: Well, men, what are we going to do?

MR. WEMPLE: That there is a question.... Mind, I ain't afraid of the Ku Klux. If this here Brody was in it, and this here Summers what killed him had the right on his side, I'd turn Summers loose just as quick as I would anybody.

MR. GAIL, MR. HAGAR, MR. LEE, MR. DYER, MR. ZIEGLER, MR. REDDICK, MR. FUNK, MR. PENNELL: Me Too! I ain't afraid of no Ku Klux!

MR. PETRY: Mr. Wemple, I don't believe there's a man in this room that's afraid to do his duty on account of the Ku Klux. Unless—

MR. MOON: I ain't afraid of the Ku Klux. Not me.

MR. PETRY: Then I think that's one thing we don't have to worry about. All the same, I think it wouldn't hurt none if all of us was to remember that what goes on in this room ain't to be told outside.

MR. WEMPLE: That's understood. Or dam sight better had be. But what I started to say, we got to be sure this here Summers had the right on his side.

MR. HAGAR: Look to me like he did all right.

MR. FUNK: What I say, when them Ku Klux goes to take a fellow out, why don't they take him out or else stay home?

MR. BASSETT: That's me. I never seen such a mess-around-all-the-time-and-then-never-do-nothing bunch in all my life.

MR. ZIEGLER: And all this "Come to Jesus."

MR. HAGAR: And "Sweet Adeline."

MR. REDDICK: What's the good of that? Everybody knows what they was there for. Then why the hell don't they up and do it thouten all this fooling around?

MR. FUNK: All the time making out they don't never do nothing 'cepting the preacher told them to do it.

MR. DYER: And then, come to find out, when they pick up Brody he had a strap on him looked like a trace off a six-horse harness.

MR. ZIEGLER: I reckon the preacher give them that for to beat time to the singing.

MR. MOON: That was to scare him.

MR. HAGAR: Yeah?

MR. MOON: Anyway, so I hear tell. That's what them Ku Klux said.

MR. HAGAR: Them Ku Klux sure can tell it their own way.

MR. WEMPLE: Wait a minute, wait a minute.... Moon, how come you heared all this what the Ku Klux said?

MR. MOON: They was just talking around.

MR. WEMPLE: I ain't asking you was they talking around. I ask you what the hell you was doing around them?

[MR. MOON *makes no reply. There is a general stir.*]

MR. FUNK: What the hell? ...

MR. WEMPLE: Come on, Moon. Why don't you say something?

MR. PETRY: Why, what's the matter, Mr. Wemple?

MR. WEMPLE: Why, that simple-looking nut, he's in the Ku Klux!

SEVERAL: What!

MR. WEMPLE: Look at him, the lying look he's got on his face! Hell, no wonder he acted like the police was after him! No, he couldn't git it straight about the singing, 'cause they done filled him up with so much talk, he don't know is he going or coming! No, he ain't afraid of no Ku Klux, 'cause he's got a nightgown hisself already.

MR. ZIEGLER: But how about them questions?

MR. WEMPLE: I'm coming to that. Hey, you, why ain't you said something about this when they ask you them questions? When they ask you was you in the Ku Klux, how come you said you wasn't?

MR. MOON: Lemme alone! Lemme alone!

MR. WEMPLE: Quit that crying or I'll bust you one in the jaw. Now answer me what I just now ask you.

MR. PETRY: Let me talk to him, Mr. Wemple. Now, Mr. Moon, when them lawyers ask you was you in the Ku Klux, what made you answer no?

MR. MOON: I tried to tell them how it was, but they wouldn't let me say nothing.... That there man, he kept a-saying. "Answer yes or no." ... I tried to explain it to them, but they wouldn't never give me no chance.

MR. WEMPLE: Chance? What the hell! Couldn't you say yes?

MR. MOON: They ain't tooken me in yet. I ain't never had the money. They won't take me in lessen I give them the ten dollars.

MR. WEMPLE: Well, I'll be damned!

MR. PETRY: I never hear tell of nothing like this in all my life. Why, Mr. Moon, don't you know that was perjury?

MR. MOON: I tried to tell them, but they wouldn't lemme say nothing.

MR. PETRY: Don't you know that when you take oath before the judge to tell the truth, you got to tell the truth else it's against the law? Ain't nobody ever told you that before?

MR. MOON: Lemme alone! Lemme alone!

[There ensues an ominous silence.]

MR. BASSETT: So now every word what's been said in here, the Ku Klux knows it five minutes after we get out.

MR. ZIEGLER: This sure is bad.

MR. HAGAR: Moon, effen a juryman tells what he heared in the jury room, they put him in jail for five year.

MR. LEE: Ten year.

MR. DYER: And the penitentiary, not the jail.

MR. HAGAR: In the penitentiary for ten year. And he don't hardly ever come out. 'Cause before the time comes for him to git out, something generally always happens to him.

MR. MOON: Lemme alone! Lemme alone!

MR. FUNK: Aw hell, what's the use of talking to him? 'Cause that dumb coot, even if you could scare him deef, dumb, and blind, why he'd blab it all around anyhow and never know he done it.

MR. BASSETT: That's the hell of it. And never know he done it.

MR. WEMPLE: What do you think about this, Mr. Petry? Do you think we better report this fellow to the judge?

MR. PETRY: I'm just a-thinking. I'm just a-thinking.

MR. WEMPLE: Well, while we're figuring on that, I reckon we better git up a verdict. This here look like second degree to me.

MR. FUNK: First degree, I say.

MR. REDDICK, MR. DYER, MR. ZIEGLER, MR. GAIL, MR. HAGAR, MR. BASSETT: First degree, I say. Me too. This here is murder.

MR. WEMPLE: Well, I was thinking about first degree myself. 'Cause a Klansman, it stands to reason, he's as good as anybody else.

MR. LEE: He is that. When a man gits killt, something had ought to be done about it and that goes for a Klansman same as anybody else.

MR. HAGAR: Everybody alike, I say.

MR. BASSETT: And another thing, men, what we hadn't ought to forget. Ku Klux is a fine order, when you come right down to it.

MR. FUNK: I know a fellow what he's a kind of a travelling agent for the Red Men. He got something to do with the insurance, I think it is, and believe me he's got it down pat about every kind of a order they is going. And he says to me one time, he says:

"Funk," he says, "you can put it right down, if they'd run it right, the Ku Klux is the best order what they is going. They ain't none of them," he says, "what's got the charter and the constitution and all like of that what the Ku Klux has."

MR. DYER: Why, ain't no better order in the world than the Ku Klux—if they run it right.

MR. REDDICK: That's it. If they run it right.

MR. LEE: I swear, it makes me sick to see how they run a fine order in the ground the way they do around here.

MR. PENNELL: Well, men, I tell you. It's easy enough for us to set here and belly-ache like we're doing about how they run it. But just jump in and try to run it oncet. Just try to run it oncet.

MR. FUNK: And specially a order what's trying to pull off something big, like the Ku Klux is. It's just like this fellow says to me, the one I was just now telling you about. "Funk," he says to me, "there's one thing they can't take away from the Ku Klux. It ain't no steamboat-picnic order. No, sir. When the Ku Klux holds a picnic, they don't sell no round-trip excursion tickets. That they don't."

MR. BASSETT: And another thing: that there singing. You ask me, I say that was a pretty doggone nice way to invite a fellow to church. I hope to git invited that way oncet. I'm here to say I do.

MR. LEE: And this here dirty whelp ain't got no more appreciation than to sock it to them with a pump-gun. Six shots, men. Think of that. Them poor guys didn't have no more chance than a snowball in hell.

MR. HAGAR: Yep. Ku Klux is all right. It sure is.

MR. WEMPLE: You hear that, don't you, Moon?

MR. MOON: Lemme alone. I ain't heared nothing.

MR. WEMPLE: Listen at that! Listen at that! I swear, people that dumb, I don't see how they git put on a jury.

MR. LEE: Why hell, Wemple, that's *why* they git put on a jury. Them lawyers figures the less sense they got, the more lies they believe.

MR. WEMPLE: Now listen at me, Moon. 'Cause if you don't git this straight, you're libel to git Ku Kluxed before you ever git outen this room. Now first off, *effen* you git it straight, we ain't going to tell the judge what you done. Then maybe you won't have to go to jail.

MR. MOON: Oh thank you. Thank you, Mr. Wemple.

MR. WEMPLE: But that ain't all of it. When you go out of here, if you got to do any talking about what you heared in here, we want you to tell what you heared and not no dam lies like some of them does.

MR. MOON: I won't say ary word, Mr. Wemple. I hope my die I won't.

MR. WEMPLE: Well, you might. Now you heared these gentlemen say, didn't you, that the Ku Klux is a fine order, one of the finest orders in the United States?

MR. MOON: I sure did, Mr. Wemple. Ku Klux is a fine order. Yes, Mr. Wemple, I heared them say that. All of them.

MR. WEMPLE: Now—

MR. HAGAR: Wait a minute, Wemple.... You got that all straight, Moon?

MR. MOON: Yep. Ku Klux is a fine order.

MR. HAGAR: Then, Wemple, if he done learned that, why look like to me like he ain't going to learn no more. Not today. Just better let him hang on to that and call it a day.

MR. WEMPLE: I expect you're right at that. Now, Moon, just to show you what a fine order we think the Ku Klux is, we're all going to chip in a dollar so you can git took in. Ain't we, men?

ALL: We sure are.

[There is a brisk digging into pockets. MR WEMPLE collects the money and hands it over to MR. MOON.]

MR. WEMPLE: There you are, Moon. Ten dollars for to git took in the Ku Klux and a dollar to git yourself a pint of corn.

MR. MOON: Thank you, Mr. Wemple. Thank you, everybody. Thank you. Thank you.

MR. GAIL: Well, I reckon that's all there is to it. Look to me like we're done.

MR. PETRY: This ain't no first-degree, men. This here is manslaughter. Fact of the matter, it might be self-defense, 'cepting I always say when a man git killt, why the one that done it had ought to be found guilty of something. There's too many people getting killt lately.

MR. WEMPLE: Well, Mr. Petry, that's all right with me. If it's all right with the rest of them....

[There is a moment of mumbling and nodding, which apparently betokens assent.]

MR. GAIL: Then it's manslaughter.

[He pokes his head out of the door, gives a signal to a bailiff, and in a moment they are filing back to the courtroom.]

MR. WEMPLE: And that's something else I want to bring to your attention, Moon, old man. Up to the last minute, they was all for giving him first degree....

ALL: And fact of the matter, I always did say the Ku Klux was all right, if they'd run it right.... Why sure, Ku Klux is a fine order.... You bet.... Citizenship.... Patriotism.... All like of that....

Welburn Mayock
JURIES*

I

You ask me, my son, were I in your place,
Would I ask for a jury to try my first case?
I know not what facts or what law are involved
But your problem, my lad, can be easily solved.

II.

All jurymen, son, whate'er their vocation,
When called to the box undergo transformation.
Though happy and cheerful a moment ago,
They change to a visage which promises woe.

III.

They all become solemn; they sit there in state,
While litigants tremblingly pass to their fate.
They all are convinced of the height of their tasks
So they tune their souls up to the pitch of their masks.

IV.

While sternly they gaze in a forward direction
The facts pass them by leaving no recollection.
They attend to the judge for all judges demand it
When expounding the law so one can't understand it.

---

* Reprinted from *Docket*, Autumn 1938, by permission of West Publishing Co.

V.

Thus blank as to law and dim as to fact
The jury is called upon now, son, to act.
With faces immobile they pass from the room
While you sit with your client and wait for his doom.

VI.

But don't be dismayed; take some consolation.
Your opponent, my son, 's in the same situation.
No matter how far thru the law you may ramble
A trial by a jury, my son, is a gamble.

VII.

The wisest by far that e'er gladdened my vision
Returned to report the most cock-eyed decision.
Another so stupid I quailed in my fears
Reported a verdict which marked them as seers.

VIII.

Be certain of heaven, be sure of hell's fury,
But never, son, never, be sure of a jury.
Most rules have exceptions—this one's always true,
You never can tell what a jury will do.

Jury Instructions. Instructions given by a judge to a jury prior to the jury's deliberations on a case. These instructions are followed about as closely as you followed the instructions that came with the Erector set or dollhouse you got when you were in the first grade.
—*Daniel R. White*

S. J. Perelman
IF IT PLEASE YOUR HONOR*

Hollywood book dealer Bradley Smith last night was found guilty of violating state obscenity laws by selling a copy of Henry Miller's novel "Tropic of Cancer."

The verdict returned by the jury of three men and nine women ended the six-week Municipal Court trial that followed the arrest of the 31-year-old book dealer last October....

Judge Kenneth A. Holaday, who presided over the lengthy trial, told jurors he would like to give each of them "a medal for public service well and faithfully performed."

At that point, one of the jurors, Mrs. Lillian M. Lake, stood up and told the judge the jury had a gift for him, commenting, "We could not have stood through this for six weeks without your smile."

They presented the jurist with a tie clasp and then gave bailiff Jerome Shapiro and court clerk Richard Key a box of imported chocolate candy, which Mrs. Lake described as her "favorite pep pills." —*Hollywood Citizen-News*

SCENE: *A jury room in the Hall of Justice, in Los Diablos, California. At stage center, a conference table flanked by chairs and littered with scratch pads. Beside door at left stands a coat tree festooned with variegated plastic rainwear. A wall clock bearing an advertisement for a prominent cut-rate mortuary proclaims the time as shortly past two. The stage is deserted at rise. Then door opens to admit a bailiff—whose name, by an extraordinary coincidence, happens to be Morris Bailiff—shepherding a panel of jurors, the majority of them female. While the individual members differ somewhat in age and weight, they are all typical Californians, leathery and exuberant yet plainly moribund. They straggle into place around the table as Bailiff withdraws.*

MRS. PFLAUM (*aggrievedly*): That piece of soup meat they gave me was like rubber. If I served it to my husband, he'd throw it in my face.

MISS FABRICI: All the food there is terrible. Did you see the cottage pie Mr. Robinette ordered? It was nothing but cornstarch—wasn't it, Mr. Robinette?

MR. ROBINETTE (*sepulchrally*): Gastritis. I'd just as soon pour cement in my stomach.

---

* Reprinted from *Chicken Inspector No. 23*, Simon & Schuster, 1966, by permission of the estate of S. J. Perelman.

MRS. TONKONOGY: Well, it's your own fault. I told you to try their special plate, the Yucatan-style chicken.

MR. ROBINETTE: What's the name of it again?

MRS. TONKONOGY: Chicken-Itza. They fry it on hot stones, according to a lost Aztec recipe.

MR. SHUBKIN: Ah, why don't you people stop kidding your-selves? It's one big racket, the restaurants in this neighborhood.

MISS PALMQUIST: There he goes again.

MR. SHUBKIN: I know what I'm talking about—I've been on plenty of juries! No matter where they take you to eat, the judge always gets a rakeoff.

MRS. LATIGO: Not Judge Faulhaber. Judge Faulhaber would not stoop to a petty stunt like that.

MISS FABRICI: No, he certainly would not. He's a very superior type person, and you ought to be ashamed, casting such aspersions. *(All the ladies attest loudly to the Judge's incorruptibility.* ROBINETTE *pounds the table for order.)*

MR. ROBINETTE: Now, let's not fritter away the afternoon, for God's sake. We have to reach a decision on this case.

MISS PALMQUIST: What's there to decide? We heard the evidence—the man's guilty.

MR. SHUBKIN: Says you. I happen to think he's innocent.

MR. ROBINETTE: Please, folks—will you kindly stop squab-bling so I can review the highlights once more? ... All right, here's the background. On January 14th last, the plaintiff, Virgil Chubb, of Pellagra Springs, Colorado, entered a souvenir shop on Hol-lydew Boulevard belonging to Sam Bronislaw, the defendant. Bronislaw sold him a postcard that showed a young woman buried up to her neck in oranges spilling out of a cornucopia, with the caption "Lotsa goodies out here in the Southland."

MR. SHUBKIN: One minor detail before you proceed. This, er, babe on the postcard—was it established that she was naked under the oranges?

MR. ROBINETTE: What's that got to do with it?

MR. SHUBKIN: I was just trying to clarify the scene in my mind's eye.

MR. ROBINETTE: Well, the prosecution didn't stress the point other than to say that the card had an adverse effect on Chubb. It inspired him with lustful thoughts, causing him to visit a massage parlor on South Hermosa Avenue, where he was rolled. Bronislaw,

"Being hopelessly confused by your instructions, we have voted to have nothing further to do with this case."

when taken into custody, denied he was the instigator of the affair. In hundreds of similar sales, he asserted, no customer had ever had their libido aroused nor their wallet glommed. He contended that besides being visibly ginned up on entering the store, Chubb wore an unmistakable leer. As for criminal responsibility, Bronislaw added, he himself was merely a retailer; if there was any onus, it rested on the manufacturer of the cards, the Thomas Peeping Corporation, of Chicago.

MRS. PFLAUM *(with a snort):* Excuses—he's trying to wriggle out of it.

MISS FABRICI: What are we shilly-shallying around for? Judge Faulhaber as much as told us to bring in a guilty verdict.

MRS. TONKONOGY: A fair-minded man like he couldn't do anything else. I hope he gives that smut merchant a good stiff sentence. At least twenty years.

MRS. LATIGO: He should get life, the no-good.

MR. SHUBKIN: Hold on a minute, everybody. I've got a right to my opinion, and I still say the Court is prejudiced.

MR. ROBINETTE: Why? Simply because His Honor owns a shoe store next to the defendant's place of business?

MR. SHUBKIN *(doggedly):* Well, you heard Bronislaw's testimony. He claimed that the Judge was using pressure to squeeze him out so he could expand. He tried to cancel his lease, he engaged hoodlums to throw acid on the stock, he even came in personally and threatened to break Bronislaw's arm.

MISS FABRICI: So what? You want to prevent someone from using up-to-date methods on account of he's a jurist?

MISS PALMQUIST: Look, Shubkin, you're in California now, not back East.

MRS. LATIGO: Mr. Foreman, I move that Mr. Shubkin's remark be stricken from the record and that we hear a report from the Gift Committee.

MR. ROBINETTE: I agree. All in favor? *(Resounding approbation)* Very well—I call on Mrs. Tonkonogy.

MRS. TONKONOGY *(reading from notebook):* A total of $24.70 was collected from the panel to buy presents for Judge Faulhaber and the court attendants. Everybody contributed but Mr. Shubkin. *(All heads swivel toward the malcontent, who reddens in embarrassment.)* Our chief problem, though, was to select appropriate gifts.

MISS PALMQUIST: I thought we decided on a briefcase and hankerchiefs.

MRS. TONKONOGY: So you did, but the Committee felt we needed something with more verve—something to fit the personalities of the recipients. Well, we finally found a perfect remembrance for the Judge at a rummage sale in Altadena. A genuine, handmade Russian knout.

MISS FABRICI: That'll make a lovely ornament for his chambers.

MRS. TONKONOGY: Yes, and practical, too—he can use it on witnesses with sluggish memories. Now, for the clerk and bailiff we chose a more traditional gift, but also full of pep and spice. We bought them each a box of those imported licorice chewies, Afro-Dizzies.

MRS. LATIGO: Well, then, I guess we're about ready to bring in our verdict. How do we stand?

MR. ROBINETTE: Unanimous for conviction, all but Shubkin.

MRS. PFLAUM: Who cares what he thinks? A tightwad that begrudges two dollars shouldn't be allowed a vote.

MISS PALMQUIST: No, that's unfair. After all, he is a juryman, even if he is a louse.

MR. ROBINETTE: All right, let's have a show of hands. Those for guilty? *(A dozen hands are raised.)* Twelve. Those opposed? (SHUBKIN *timidly signifies his dissent.)*

MISS FABRICI: Wait a minute—something's wrong. Isn't there

an extra person in our midst? *(Sensation. Suddenly, as the panel members gape at each other,* ROBINETTE *peels off a putty nose and false whiskers, revealing the lineaments of* JUDGE FAULHABER.*)*

MRS. TONKONOGY: Why, Judge Faulhaber, whatever are you doing here?

JUDGE FAULHABER: Your astonishment is understandable, dear lady. I owe you all a profound apology for my little masquerade. Had it not been for certain special circumstances of this case, I should never have interfered in your deliberations.

MRS. PFLAUM: You mean you possess evidence which you dared not disclose it from the bench?

JUDGE FAULHABER: Precisely. Being as how my shoe store was contiguous to Sam Bronislaw's mart, I naturally sought to bust up his traffic in lascivious postals, but that was only a tithe of the chap's infamy. He was an inveterate wife-beater. *(The ladies buzz indignantly.)* Yes, many was the sound drubbing I overheard him administer on occasion through the walls. It took iron self-control not to rush in there and cane the ruffian.

MISS FABRICI: Small wonder you strove to abrogate his lease.

JUDGE FAULHABER: In vain, as you know, so that I was forced to resort to subterfuge. Being as how I have a modest talent for makeup, I assumed the guise of Virgil Chubb, a putative Coloradan, and framed Bronislaw on a bum rap. I think that if you take the trouble to visit South Hermosa Avenue, you will find no massage parlor at that address.

MRS. TONKONOGY: Well, this *has* been a day packed with surprises, and judging from his nonplussed expression, to nobody more than our colleague Shubkin.

MR. SHUBKIN *(sheepishly):* Your Honor, I'm not very good at flowery speeches, but if there were more people like you, this community would be a better place to live in.

JUDGE FAULHABER *(rounding on him):* What's wrong with this community?

MR. SHUBKIN: Uh—nothing, nothing. My last shred of recalcitrance is gone. I find Bronislaw guilty as charged, and here's the two dollars I owe the kitty.

JUDGE FAULHABER: That's more like it. O.K., gang—got those presents you spoke of?

MRS. TONKONOGY: All wrapped up and ready to go, Judge.

JUDGE FAULHABER: Then let's file in and hand 'em to the old buzzard.

MRS. TONKONOGY: But, er, pardon me, sir—aren't *you* the old buzzard?

MISS FABRICI: You're practically the whole works around here, outside of the defendant.

JUDGE FAULHABER: Damn tooting I am. Just give me a second to don my judicial robes and I'll show you. (*He exits, as the jurors fall into step and march after him to the strains of "For He's a Jolly Good Fellow."*)

CURTAIN

Art Buchwald
INSIDE THE JURY ROOM*

THE JUSTICE SYSTEM in this country seems as loused up as everything else. One of the reasons for this is that the law provides that anyone who has a legal dispute involving more than $50 is entitled to a jury. Most jurors can deal with personal injury and liability cases. But you have to have an MBA from Harvard, a law degree from Stanford and an accounting diploma from the Wharton School to be able to follow the complicated suits that ordinary citizens are required to adjudicate these days.

How can the average jury understand the issues in a multi-billion dollar corporation lawsuit?

A well-known trial lawyer told me they can't. Most juries involved with any business litigation make their decisions based on things other than the thousands of pieces of evidence and months of testimony that neither they nor the judge understand.

This is how it goes in the jury room, he told me.

"I think we should find for the plaintiffs."

"Why?"

"Their chief lawyer always looks so fresh and neat no matter how hot it is in the courtroom."

"I'm for throwing out all the charges. The defense has a woman lawyer on the staff, and I think if we voted for the defen-

---

* Reprinted from a syndicated newspaper column originally published in 1980, by permission of the author.

dants, it would encourage large corporations to hire more women lawyers."

"That's the stupidest reason I ever heard for judging a case. If we're going to play by those rules, we have to take into consideration that one of the plaintiffs' executives has a bad limp. Why not give the billion dollars to them for hiring the handicapped?"

"Wait, we're getting away from the evidence. Let's go over it again."

"Are you crazy? No one in this room knows what anyone out there was talking about."

"Okay. Let's *not* go over the evidence. How do we arrive at a decision?"

"I'm for giving the nod to the plaintiffs. Their backup lawyer always came over to us when he wanted to make a point. The defendants' lawyer preferred to address his remarks to the judge. If he wanted to win, the defense counsel should have paid more attention to us."

"You're too sensitive. Only the fat defendants' lawyer ignored us. The cute one with the horn-rimmed glasses spent a lot of time leaning against the jury box. He had beautiful eyes."

"But he had a beard. I'd never trust a person who sports a beard."

"My son has a beard."

"I thought as much, and while we're on the subject—I don't trust you either."

"Hold it. We've been together five months. Let's get a decision so we can all go home. How do you vote?

"How is she voting?"

"I'm voting for the plaintiffs."

"Then I'm voting for the defendants."

"We're never going to see our loved ones again. There has to be a compromise. I suggest we give the plaintiffs half of what they are asking."

"Why?"

"Do you remember when the president of the injured company testified? His entire family sat in the first row for five days. I thought that was very loyal of them. You don't see families that close any more."

"Are you planning to give the plaintiffs half a billion dollars because their chief executive officer has a nice family? How do we know what goes on behind closed doors?"

"I agree. Besides, the defendant company's chairman of the board wore his Shriner's pin when he took the stand. I happen to be a Shriner, and I'll take a lodge brother's word against anyone who drags his kids out of school to sit at a trial."

"We appear to be split on a verdict. Shall I report to the judge that we can't come to a decision?"

"Don't do that. He'll make us read the court transcript again. I say we flip a coin. Heads we find for the plaintiffs—tails for the defendants."

"Okay, as long as she takes back what she said about men with beards."

"I take it back, but only because I believe justice should be served."

Hay
JURY DUTY*

HE TOOK HIS SEAT sadly and wistfully in the jury box. He was a meek, rather undersized man whose watery blue eyes peered timidly out at the courtroom through a pair of thick-lensed spectacles. The leonine counsel for the plaintiff arose to examine him.

"What is your name?" asked the lawyer.

"Peebles," he replied meekly.

"Ha," exclaimed the lawyer. "Just Peebles?"

"Alonzo T. Peebles," he explained. "I was named after my great-uncle Zachary."

"I beg your pardon?" said the lawyer.

"He was in the hay and feed business," said Mr. Peebles. "Old Ironsides, they used to call him in those days, because of his indomitable will. He was practically the first man in the hay and feed business who could tear a deck of cards with his fingers and sing tenor with the other."

"With the other what?" interrupted the judge, who was busily taking notes. Mr. Peebles looked up at him sadly.

"That's what everyone used to ask," he replied. "It's funny you

* Reprinted by permission; © 1928, 1956 The New Yorker Magazine, Inc.

should have thought of it. It ruined his life. After the Spanish-American War—"

"One minute," exclaimed the lawyer. "I object! I object on the grounds..."

"Overruled," murmured the judge.

"Are you acquainted with my friend Mr. Beazle, counsel for the defence?" asked the lawyer.

"Now, that all depends," replied Mr. Peebles. "My great-uncle used to say..."

"Never mind your great-uncle," said the lawyer. "Will Your Honor tell this man to answer my questions? What we're trying to find out is whether you can serve as a fair and impartial juror in this case. You don't know me, do you?"

Mr. Peebles looked at him intently for a moment. "Take off your glasses," he said. The lawyer removed his glasses. "Now turn your head just a little this way—just a little more. That's right. No, I never saw you before in my life."

"And are you acquainted...?"

"One minute," said Mr. Peebles. "Did you ever live in Syracuse?"

"No!" said the lawyer. "Answer my question! Are you..."

"Lots of people live in Syracuse," said Mr. Peebles in a pained voice. "I used to have a cousin who lived there. He was a fellow with a wen."

"A yen?" inquired the Judge.

"A wen, Your Honor," said Mr. Peebles. "His name was Howe. They used to call him Wen and Howe, or Tubby for short."

"Will Your Honor instruct the talesman to answer my questions and not to argue with me?" exclaimed the exasperated lawyer.

"Don't argue with counsel," said the judge.

"My cousin in Syracuse was a great one for arguing," said Mr. Peebles. "I used to say that he was quite a card, although many people said he was a case. We used to have great arguments about it."

"Did you really?" said the judge.

"Please answer my question," pleaded the lawyer. "Do you know of any reason why you can't serve as a fair and impartial juror in this case?"

"I'm opposed to capital punishment," said Mr. Peebles.

"This case has nothing to do with capital punishment," said the lawyer.

"I'm sorry," said Mr. Peebles politely, "but I'm opposed to it anyway—and tapioca pudding."

"I beg your pardon," said the judge. "I didn't get that."

"There are two things I don't like, Your Honor," said Mr. Peebles. "Capital punishment and tapioca pudding."

"But this case is an action for breach of contract," said the lawyer. "What has capital punishment...?"

"You never can tell," said Mr. Peebles. "Now my great-uncle Alonzo..."

"Your Honor," exclaimed the lawyer, "I'm afraid this man hasn't sufficient intelligence to serve as a juror in this case. I challenge him."

As Mr. Peebles walked out of court the shadow of a smile played about his meek, wistful countenance.

Parke Cummings
TWELVE GOOD MEN AND TRUE*

Juror Five appears a little
Set in favor of acquittal.
Number One, in contradiction,
Leans to swift and sure conviction.
Three (a shipping clerk) is rather
Bored with all the fuss and bother.
Number Ten, a dapper fellow,
Notes the plaintiff's shoes are yellow.
Six (Augustus Miller, tanner)
Doesn't like the judge's manner.
Seven, weary-eyed, unfeeling,
Counts the fissures in the ceiling.
Twelve, who's quite unused to collars,
Wonders how he'll spend four dollars.
Number Eight, old hand at trying,
Thinks the witnesses are lying,
And Eleven, dozing, nodding,
Is a mark for constant prodding.

Number Two (bricklayer, married)
Thinks the County's point is carried.
Nine, who's bound for Queens for dinner,
Hopes his horse came in a winner.
Juror Four (three sons, one daughter)
Only wants a glass of water.

Trial. A formal inquiry designed to prove and put upon record the blameless characters of judges, advocates and jurors. In order to effect this purpose it is necessary to supply a contrast in the person of one who is called the defendant, the prisoner, or the accused. If the contrast is made sufficiently clear, this person is made to undergo such an affliction as will give the virtuous gentlemen a comfortable sense of their immunity, added to that of their worth.

—*Ambrose Bierce*

"Oh, I know how they made the perjury charge stick; it's because I'm black."

LEGAL REASONING

H. Pomerantz and S. Breslin
REGINA v. OJIBWAY*

BLUE, J.:—This is an appeal by the Crown by way of the stated case from a decision of the magistrate acquitting the accused of a charge under the Small Birds Act, R.S.O., 1960, c.724, s.2. The facts are not in dispute. Fred Ojibway, an Indian, was riding his pony through Queen's Park on January 2, 1965. Being impoverished, and having been forced to pledge his saddle, he substituted a downy pillow in lieu of the said saddle. On this particular day the accused's misfortune was further heightened by the circumstance of his pony breaking its right foreleg. In accord with Indian custom, the accused then shot the pony to relieve it of its awkwardness.

The accused was then charged with having breached the Small Birds Act, s.2 of which states:

> 2. Anyone maiming, injuring or killing small birds is guilty of an offence and subject to a fine not in excess of two hundred dollars.

The learned magistrate acquitted the accused holding, in fact, that he had killed his horse and not a small bird. With respect, I cannot agree.

In light of the definition section my course is quite clear. Section 1 defines "bird" as "a two legged animal covered with feathers". There can be no doubt that this case is covered by this section.

Counsel for the accused made several ingenious arguments to which, in fairness, I must address myself. He submitted that the evidence of the expert clearly concluded that the animal in question was a pony and not a bird, but this is not the issue. We are not interested in whether the animal in question is a bird or not in fact,

* Reprinted from 8 *Criminal Law Quarterly* 137-9 (1965) by permission of Mr. Hart Pomerantz and Canada Law Book, Inc., 240 Edward Street, Aurora, Ontario, Canada L4G 3S9.

but whether it is one in law. Statutory interpretation has forced many a horse to eat birdseed for the rest of its life.

Counsel also contended that the neighing noise emitted by the animal could not possibly be produced by a bird. With respect, the sounds emitted by an animal are irrelevant to its nature, for a bird is no less a bird because it is silent.

Counsel for the accused also argued that since there was evidence to show accused had ridden the animal, this pointed to the fact that it could not be a bird but was actually a pony. Obviously, this avoids the issue. The issue is not whether the animal was ridden or not, but whether it was shot or not, for to ride a pony or a bird is of no offence at all. I believe counsel now sees his mistake.

Counsel contends that the iron shoes found on the animal decisively disqualify it from being a bird. I must inform counsel, however, that how an animal dresses is of no concern to this court.

Counsel relied on the decision in *Re Chicadee*, where he contends that in similar circumstances the accused was acquitted. However, this is a horse of a different colour. A close reading of that case indicates that the animal in question there was not a small bird, but, in fact, a midget of a much larger species. Therefore, that case is inapplicable to our facts.

Counsel finally submits that the word "small" in the title Small Birds Act refers not to "Birds" but to "Act", making it The Small Act relating to Birds. With respect, counsel did not do his homework very well, for the Large Birds Act, R.S.O. 1960, c. 725, is just as small. If pressed, I need only refer to the Small Loans Act R.S.O. 1960, c. 727 which is twice as large as the Large Birds Act.

It remains then to state my reason for judgment which, simply, is as follows: Different things may take on the same meaning for different purposes. For the purpose of the Small Birds Act, all two legged, feather-covered animals are birds. This, of course, does not imply that only two-legged animals qualify, for the legislative intent is to make two legs merely the minimum requirement. The statute therefore contemplated multi-legged animals with feathers as well. Counsel submits that having regard to the purpose of the statute only small animals "naturally covered" with feathers could have been contemplated. However, had this been the intention of the legislature, I am certain that the phrase "naturally covered" would have been expressly inserted just as 'Long' was inserted in the Longshoreman's Act.

Therefore, a horse with feathers on its back must be deemed

for the purposes of this Act to be a bird, and *a fortiori*, a pony with feathers on its back is a small bird.

Counsel posed the following rhetorical question: If the pillow had been removed prior to the shooting, would the animal still be a bird? To this let me answer rhetorically: Is a bird any less of a bird without its feathers?

Appeal allowed.

Bernard Levin
THE MAN WHO MISSED THE
CLAPHAM OMNIBUS?*

IT IS A LITTLE EARLY to be sure, but I think that we may have recently witnessed the birth of one of the great representative fictional characters of the law. The "reasonable man" has long been familiar—at least, the idea has, though whether the beast has ever been tracked to his lair is another matter; I suspect we can say of him what Don Alfonso says of the fidelity of women—that, like the phoenix, everybody has heard of it but nobody has seen it. But whether the reasonable man exists or not, he is often found in the company of the man in the street, a figure no less reasonable than his brother, but with the added advantage of being able to speak on behalf of a vast throng of other men in other streets, he being generally recognized as always holding the average view, no doubt with average firmness. The man in the street, incidentally, has come down in the world; he used to be "the man on the Clapham omnibus," but none the less representative for that. Apparently, however, he can no longer afford the fare, for I have not for many years heard him cited as an example of all that is sensible, reasonable and widely believed.

Anyway, the point is that a new star has risen to join this particular constellation. He made his first appearance in the judgment of Mr. Justice Foster in the case brought by the Communist Party's newspaper, the *Morning Star*, against Express Newspapers, in which an injunction was sought to prevent the former Beaverbrook group from launching a new newspaper called the *Daily Star*;

* Reprinted from *The Times* of London, 1978.

the comrades argued that the opportunities for confusion were too great.

I take it that the *Morning Star*'s action was designed for publicity purposes; if so, it was a hugely successful stunt; for days on end the paper's name and nature featured in every other paper's pages, to register on the consciousness of millions who had never previously heard of it at all. (It only sells about 25,000 copies a day, and many of those are bought, by way of tactful subsidy, by the authorities in Eastern Europe.) If it is true, as reports suggest, that the action (which the *Morning Star* lost) cost about £10,000, it was money well spent; ten times that sum would not have bought in the form of advertising the column inches the case provided. An eminently sensible and practical application of the principles of capitalism.

In the course of the judgment, however, the judge wished to reject as vehemently as possible the claim, advanced on behalf of the *Morning Star*, that people wishing to buy the Communists' newspaper might find themselves, through error on the part of the newsagent, provided instead with its near-namesake, thus getting not stirring articles on the democratic character of the Soviet Union and the immense popularity of the Berlin Wall among East Berliners grateful for the defence it provides against capitalist invasion but pictures of ladies with bulgy chests and inviting expressions—which, it seems, is what the *Daily Star* proposes to offer its readers, though perhaps "lookers" would be a more exact description of them.

Not so, said Mr. Justice Foster, clearly a man who can tell at a glance the difference between the Dnepropetrovsk Dam and a pair of titties; the two papers could not be confused "even by a moron in a hurry".

I do not think we have heard the last of this gentleman. Indeed, I suspect that in years to come juries not yet born will hear counsel urge them to reject evidence that would not impose on a moron in a hurry, and future generations of judges will cite their learned brother Foster with approval whenever they need an illustration of a figure possessing slightly less than the absolute minimum of perspicuity. ("The doubt, members of the jury, must be a *reasonable* one; one that would occur only to a moron in a hurry would not be sufficient". Or: "Apply the old test, members of the jury: would the missing stair have been noticed by a moron in a hurry?" Or even: "Note, members of the jury, that a man may be a moron without being in a hurry, or in a hurry and yet no moron. Only if you are satisfied that the plaintiff was both...")

There is something about the *obiter dicta* of judges (though I think that the particular remark under discussion was not *obiter* at all, but a central pillar of Mr. Justice Foster's judgment, and therefore now binding as a test of the limits of confusion) which seems to give them a head start in the race for immortality. (Mind you, they know that as well as I do, and one or two of them are not above asking "What is a Beatle?" or "Who is Mr. Healey?" at the best moment of the day for getting into the afternoon newspapers, just like those dreadful dial-a-quote MPs.) And the idea of a distinction so great that it could not be missed even by a moron in a hurry is so striking, and potentially so useful, that I am convinced that it will eventually take its place in the dictionaries of legal maxims.

Of course, whether Mr. Justice Foster was correct in his decision that not even a moron in a hurry could confuse the *Morning Star* with the *Daily Star* remains to be seen; that confusions no less great have been made, and in newsagents, at that, I can myself testify, for some years ago, I went into a shop to ask for the *New Statesman* (I can no longer remember why), and the assistant behind the counter began to search through the shelves of cigarettes for this mysterious and hauntingly named brand. But the usefulness of the concept of a moron in a hurry is independent of its application in any particular case, just as, indeed, the concept of a reasonable man is useful whether one exists or not.

True, there is a pejorative ring about a moron in a hurry that does not sound for the man in the street; I dare say there have been occasions when an example of clumsiness combined with unseemly haste has provoked a complaint (perhaps from the man with the soup in his lap) that somebody has been behaving like a moron in a hurry, whereas I do not think anyone has ever addressed a passer-by who has stepped on his foot as a stupid man-in-the-street, let alone as a wall-eyed man on a Clapham omnibus. Judges and counsel, therefore, may be chary of using the new test except in purely theoretical circumstances (as Mr. Justice Foster did), or when they have before them a particularly obtuse witness or party. ("Would you not describe your behaviour on that occasion as that of a moron in a hurry?") They will be even more chary, of course, of trying to define it, or even of letting anybody in a case before them try to. When it comes to hurry, *tot homines, quot sententide*, and no mistake; as for a definition of moron in its colloquial sense, wild horses on their bended knees (the phrase is Mr. Alan Bennett's, and is scarcely less useful than the ones we have been discussing) would not induce me to attempt one.

Of course, Mr. Justice Foster might only have been trying to head off the possibility of an appeal, assuming, reasonably enough, that few counsel would care to open an address to the Court of Appeal with the words "My lords, I have here 58 affidavits from morons in a hurry, none of whom can tell the difference between the *Morning Star* and the *Daily Star*". But on the whole, I think it likely that he was only trying to make clear, in a striking manner, his conviction that the danger of confusion was too remote to be entertained, and in this very reasonable aim he not only succeeded, but gained the additional and unforeseen bonus of a place in legal history. A place, I may add, that will be begrudged him only by a moron in a hurry.

Cephas
PRECEDENTS*

> A wabbly calf walked through the wood,
> But why, it never understood;
> And as it wandered in and out,
> Its trail would turn and twist about;
> The mother cow, with anxious mind,
> Its footsteps trailed right close behind;
> A boy, with joyous care-free laugh,
> Too, tramped along behind that calf;
> And other folks, ere since that day
> Have trudged along that crooked way.
> For though that calf has long been dead,
> Folks blindly follow where it led.
>
> An Olden Judge in wig and gown,
> With solemn tones the law laid down,
> And by the wagging of his jaw
> Decreed that thus and so was law;

---

* There are several versions of this classic poem. This one was reprinted from *Docket*, Spring 1928, by permission of West Publishing Co.

Reporters printed what he said,
And now in legal tomes 't is read.
His words we lawyers glibly quote
And cram them down the Judge's throat,
For courts are loath to break away
From that which was decreed that day,
But meekly follow precedent
And go the way that ancient went.
Yet lawyers have the nerve to laugh
At those who trail that wabbly calf.

George R. Craig
THE KNOWNE CERTAINTIE OF THE LAW*

"The Knowne Certaintie of the Law is the Safetie of All"
—Coke (c.1600)

Oh come now, m'lord, take a second look—
'Cause your platitude has now been forsook.
Chucking principles of every sort
Has become routine with each changing court.
And the only certaintie, so it seems,
Is the certaintie of reams and reams
Of loose-leaf pages which lawyers must face
In attempting to keep up with the pace.
We pull up the ring or we slide the slide
We spring out those claw-teeth extremely wide
We place new inserts before us neatlie
We read the instruction sheet compleatlie
We discard the old and insert the new
We work ourselves into an awful stew
We curse that careless instruction-drafter
For the missing sheet that this comes after
And before we have finished, sad to state,
This stuff may already be out of date.
With courts at *stare decisis* winking
Your platitude was wishful thinking.

* Reprinted from 7 *Duquesne Law Review* 553 (1969) by permission of the Law Review.

A. P. Herbert
IS A GOLFER A GENTLEMAN?*
Rex v. Haddock

THIS CASE, which raised an interesting point of law upon the meaning of the world "gentleman," was concluded at the Truro Assizes today.

Mr. Justice Trout (giving judgment): In this case the defendant, Mr. Albert Haddock, is charged under the Profane Oaths Act, 1745, with swearing and cursing on a Cornish golf-course. The penalty under the Act is a fine of one shilling for every day-labourer, soldier, or seaman, two shillings for every person of or above the degree of gentleman—a remarkable but not unique example of a statute which lays down one law for the rich and another (more lenient) for the poor. The fine, it is clear, is leviable not upon the string or succession of oaths, but upon each individual malediction (see *Reg.* v. *Scott* (1863) 33 L.J.M. 15). The curses charged, and admitted, in this case, are over four hundred in number, and we are asked by the prosecution to inflict a fine of one hundred pounds, assessed on the highest or gentleman's rate at five shillings a swear. The defendant admits the offences, but contends that the fine is excessive and wrongly calculated, on the curious ground that he is not a gentleman when he is playing golf.

He has reminded us in a brilliant argument that the law takes notice, in many cases, of such exceptional circumstances as will break down the normal restraint of a civilised citizen and so powerfully inflame his passions that it would be unjust and idle to apply to his conduct the ordinary standards of the law; as, for example, where without warning or preparation he discovers another man in the act of molesting his wife or family. Under such provocation the law recognises that a reasonable man ceases for the time being to be a reasonable man; and the defendant maintains that in the special circumstances of his offence a gentleman ceases to be a gentleman and should not be judged or punished as such.

* Reprinted from *Uncommon Law* by A. P. Herbert (1935) by permission of A P Watt Limited on behalf of Crystal Hale and Jocelyn Herbert.

Now, what were these circumstances? Broadly speaking, they were the 12th hole on the Mullion golf-course, with which most of us in this Court are familiar. At that hole the player drives (or does not drive) over an inlet of the sea which is enclosed by cliffs some sixty feet high. The defendant has told us that he never drives over, but always into, this inlet, or Chasm, as it is locally named. A steady but not sensational player on other sections of the course, he says that before this obstacle his normal powers invariably desert him. This has preyed upon his mind; he has registered, it appears, a kind of vow, and year after year, at Easter and in August, he returns to this county determined ultimately to overcome the Chasm.

Meanwhile, unfortunately, his tenacity has become notorious. The normal procedure, it appears, if a ball is struck into the Chasm, is to strike a second, and, if that should have no better fate, to abandon the hole. The defendant tells us that in the past he has struck no fewer than six or seven balls in this way, some rolling gently over the cliff and some flying far and high out to sea. But recently, grown fatalistic, he has not thought it worth while to make even a second attempt, but has immediately followed his first ball into the Chasm and there, among the rocks, small stones, and shingle, has hacked at his ball with the appropriate instrument until some lucky blow has lofted it onto the turf above, or in the alternative, until he has broken his instruments or suffered some injury from flying fragments of rock. On one or two occasions a crowd of holiday-makers and local residents have gathered on the cliff and foreshore to watch the defendant's indomitable struggles and to hear the verbal observations which have accompanied them. On the date of the alleged offences a crowd of unprecedented dimensions collected, but so intense was the defendant's concentration that he did not, he tells us, observe their presence. His ball had more nearly traversed the gulf than ever before; it struck the opposing cliff but a few feet from the summit; and nothing but an adverse gale of exceptional ferocity prevented success. The defendant therefore, as he conducted his customary excavations among the boulders of the Chasm, was possessed, he tells us, by a more than customary fury. Oblivious of his surroundings, conscious only of the will to win, for fifteen or twenty minutes he lashed his battered ball against the stubborn cliffs, until at last it triumphantly escaped. And before, during, and after every stroke he uttered a number of imprecations of a complex character which were carefully recorded by an assiduous caddie and by one or two of the spectators. The defendant says that he recalls with shame a few of the expressions which he used, that he has never used them before, and that it was a shock to him to hear them issuing from his own lips; and he says quite frankly that no gentleman would use such language.

Now, this ingenious defence, whatever may be its legal value, has at least some support in the facts of human experience. I am a golf-player myself—*(laughter)*—but, apart from that, evidence has been called to show the subversive effect of this exercise upon the ethical and moral systems of the mildest of mankind. Elderly gentlemen, gentle in all respects, kind to animals, beloved by children, and fond of music, are found in lonely corners of the downs, hacking at sandpits or tussocks of grass, and muttering in a blind, ungovernable fury elaborate maledictions which could not be extracted from them by robbery or murder. Men who would face torture without a word become blasphemous at the short fourteenth. It is clear that the game of golf may well be included in that category of intolerable provocations which may legally excuse or mitigate behaviour not otherwise excusable, and that under that provocation the reasonable or gentle man may reasonably act like a lunatic or lout respectively, and should legally be judged as such.

But then I have to ask myself, What does the Act intend by the words "of or above the degree of gentleman"? Does it intend a fixed social rank or a general habit of behaviour? In other words, is a gentleman legally always a gentleman, as a duke or solicitor remains unalterably a duke or solicitor? For if this is the case the defendant's argument must fail. The prosecution says that the word "degree" is used in the sense

"See for yourself. There's only room for ten."

Cartoon by Frank Tyger, © 1970; reprinted by permission of *New Jersey Lawyer*.

of "rank." Mr. Haddock argues that it is used in the sense of a university examination, and that, like the examiners, the Legislature divides the human race, for the purpose of swearing, into three vague intellectual or moral categories, of which they give certain rough but not infallible examples. Many a first-class man has "taken a third," and many a day-labourer, according to Mr. Haddock, is of so high a character that under the Act he should rightly be included in the first "degree." There is certainly abundant judicial and literary authority for the view that by "gentleman" we mean a personal quality and not a social status. We have all heard of "Nature's gentlemen." "Clothes do not make the gentleman," said Lord Mildew in Cook v. The Mersey Docks and Harbour Board (1896) 2 A.C., meaning that a true gentleman might be clad in the foul rags of an author. In the old maxim "Manners makyth man" (see Charles v. The Great Western Railway) there is no doubt that by "man" is meant "gentleman," and that "manners" is contrasted with wealth or station. Mr. Thomas, for the prosecution, has quoted against these authorities an observation of the poet Shakespeare that

"The Prince of Darkness is a gentleman,"

but quotations from Shakespeare (in Court) are generally meaningless and always unsound. This one, in my judgment, is both. I am more impressed by the saying of another author (whose name I forget) that the King can make a nobleman, but he cannot make a gentleman.

I am satisfied therefore that the argument of the defendant has substance. Just as the reasonable man who discovers his consort in the embraces of the supplanter becomes for the moment a raving maniac, so the habitually gentle man may become in a bunker a violent, unmannerly oaf. In each case the ordinary sanctions of the law are suspended; and while it is right that a normally gentle person should in normal circumstances suffer a heavier penalty for needless imprecations than a common seaman or cattle-driver, for whom they are part of the tools of his trade, he must not be judged by the standards of the gentle in such special circumstances as provoked the defendant.

That provocation was so exceptional that I cannot think that it was contemplated by the framers of the Act; and had golf at that date been a popular exercise I have no doubt that it would have been dealt with under a special section. I find therefore that this case is not governed by the Act. I find that the defendant at the time

was not in law responsible for his actions or his speech and I am
unable to punish him in any way. For this conduct in the Chasm he
will be formally convicted of Attempted Suicide while Temporarily
Insane, but he leaves the court without a stain upon his character.

(Applause)

James Roy Calhoun
In re PLEASURE VEHICLES*

*A state Supreme Court held recently that a hearse could be classed
as a pleasure vehicle.*

A forward move of great purport struck Sleepytown at last
The Council woke from lethargy and countless measures passed;
A great White Way provided they, and paved streets without
    number.
The civic pride so newly born removed the age-old slumber.
Then Boulevards were specified, and Stop Signs were in order;
Soon maple trees and stately elms grew on each broad street
    border.
On Boulevard no one could ride, according to a measure,
Except that he, while traveling same, be solely bent on pleasure.

A portly man, named Berium Wright, the city's chief mortician,
On Boulevard did place his hearse at head of long procession.
The last sad rites at church were o'er and everything in place;
The sad and mournful 'customed look did show on every face.
But when the three-block funeral train had scarcely put in action,
A City Father saw the sight, and great was his distraction.
To Mr. Wright a summons came, within which it was stated
That he appear in City Court for Ordinance violated.

And in this court the case was tried, on facts that were agreed to.
Defendant then appealed the fine, to see what it would lead to.
To Circuit court the case now went, and counsel selves bestirred
To ascertain the Leading Case—to find the latest word.
The Ordinance first was introduced—its words were rather terse:
"On Boulevard just pleasure cars," but not one word of "hearse."

---

* Reprinted from *Docket*, Fall 1928, by permission of West Publishing Co.

"Did pleasure cars include a hearse?" On such the answer
    hinged.
On this the lawyers fumed and roared, and one another singed.

"Facetious," said the plaintiff, "No one enjoys a hearse;
What other means of travel can one name that's any worse?
When one has ridden in a hearse, he never rides again.
This clearly proves, beyond a doubt, a hearse gives only pain."
Defense attorney rose and spoke, "In all this broad domain,
Show just one rider in a hearse who ever did complain.
On you is placed the burden, a well-fixed point of law,
To prove beyond a single doubt conclusions that you draw."

By Writ of Error then did go the case to highest court.
And, after careful study, the same did make report:
"To us the Ordinance indicates, the way that it is stated,
That banning hearse from Boulevard was never contemplated."
And then the Judge spoke *obiter*, "I think that in a measure
The greater part of heirs at law regard a hearse with pleasure."
And so, my friends, it came to pass, no city could retard
The snail-like gait of mournful hearse upon a boulevard.

Thurman Arnold
CONFLICT OF LAWS*

Conflict of laws with its peppery seasoning,
Of pliable, scarcely reliable reasoning,
Dealing with weird and impossible things,
Such as marriage and domicil, bastards and kings,
All about courts without jurisdiction,
Handing out misery, pain and affliction,
Making defendant, for reasons confusing,
Unfounded, ill-grounded, but always amusing,
Liable one place but not in another,
Son of his father, but not of his mother,
Married in Sweden, but only a lover in
Pious dominions of Great Britain's sovereign.
Blithely upsetting all we've been taught,

---

* This little ditty was written while Thurman Arnold was a budding humorist at the
Harvard Law School.

Rendering futile our methods of thought,
Till Reason, tottering down from her throne,
And Common Sense, sitting, neglected, alone,
Cry out despairingly, "Why do you hate us?
Give us once more our legitimate status."
Ah, Students, bewildered, don't grasp at such straws.
But join in the chorus of Conflict of Laws.

M. C. Dillon
DESIGN BY REGULATION*

If the Pharaohs had planning boards, it would explain a lot

GIZA, 2650 B.C. The applicant is asking for a permit to construct a mausoleum on land clearly zoned for residential uses and it would appear that the application should fail. However, the plans call for a mortuary chamber fully furnished and supplied with food, utensils and clothing and, on further enquiry, I found that it appears to be the custom for several of the deceased's retainers to follow him to the tomb. The tomb is sealed and thereafter, according to tradition, they live on to serve him in the next life. In my opinion, a structure, the only room of which is furnished and supplied as a dwelling house and will be occupied, however briefly, as a dwelling house, is a dwelling house as defined by law and is not excluded from the residential zone.

This does not settle the matter and, in fact, it posed additional problems for the builder. If the tomb is considered a dwelling for the purposes of this application, it must be so treated throughout. The builder has, therefore, ceased excavation below ground level and submitted a revised design with the so-called living quarters above ground level.

An insurmountable difficulty arose when the residents objected to the bulk of the building. It is true that the cupola and minarets would have obstructed the sight lines above 52 degrees as viewed from the lot line. The architect refused to alter the design or reduce the scale to comply with the restrictions. He has severed

---

* Reprinted from *Gazette of the Law Society of Upper Canada*, 1976, by permission of the Gazette.

relations with the builder and is trying to arrange private financing to construct the tomb in white marble at Agra where land use controls are primitive.

By tradition, the proposed structure must be impressive, if not in design at least in size. Having lost his architect, the builder now proposed to simplify the design and build the largest structure permitted on the land available. This is accomplished by starting the walls at the limits of the lot and sloping them towards the centre at an angle of 51 ½ degress to keep them within the sight line limits and extending them to the point where they meet. The appropriate setback from the street line is achieved by locating the main entrance some fifty-five feet above ground level and entering the building by way of a descending shaft.

The residents now object that the new design is even more massive than the one rejected and less pleasing to the eye. That may be so, but we cannot consider it an objection to this application. These regulations are necessary for the protection of the residents. This new design complies with them and the other one didn't.

There was another minor infringement resulting from the new design. If the tomb is regarded as living quarters, its area is measured to the outside of the walls. Although the room measures only 17 feet by 34 feet, its area, for the purposes of this application, is more than 13 acres. Fortunately, the design of the building permits the infraction to be cured by further raising the chamber to the level where the area to the outside of the walls will not exceed fifty per cent of the lot area.

On this application, we had the usual conservationist presentation. This time the theory seemed to be that in some way the level of the water table is related to the amount of vegetation and, if we continue to cover this oasis with sphinxes, pyramids and temples, we are risking desert conditions. It is not necessary for me to decide if there is any substance to this theory because we are dealing with only one application for a building permit and not with a proposal to pave a substantial part of the Nile Valley. There seems to be no reason to suppose that the surrounding land will not remain fertile for at least the next 5,000 years.

The increase in traffic in the area will be enormous, but it will occur on only one occasion. The date cannot be predicted but it will almost certainly be declared a public holiday, and the residents have no cause for complaint because they will be participating. My decision may have been otherwise had the statute permitted us to consider traffic generated by the building process and not confined it to the completed building. The hazards of some half million workers and slaves hauling huge slabs of stone across peoples' front yards for the next 20 or 30 years with no decibel limit on their activities may inspire legislation to gradually limit the size of these structures, which contribute nothing to the economy except full employment.

In the result, the application as amended will be allowed. The two chambers, one at ground level and the other below it, incautiously commenced by the builder while these proceedings were in progress, will be blocked off and remain unused.

Since both sides seem to have lost, I order them each to pay my costs.

Karel Capek
MR. HAVLENA'S VERDICT*

"AS FOR NEWSPAPERS," said Mr. Beran, "this is what I think: Most people turn first of all to the crime reports. It's hard to say whether they're so keen on reading them because of a suppressed desire to commit crime, or for their moral satisfaction and their increased knowledge of the law. What's certain is that they simply gloat over them. That's why the papers have to publish crime reports every day. But now suppose that the courts are on vacation. Even though the courts aren't sitting, there's got to be a column about them just the same. And often there aren't any sensational cases at any of the courts, but the crime reporter has got to have a sensational case, by hook or by crook. When things are like that, the reporters somehow have to lay their hands on a sensational case. They're bought, lent, or exchanged at the rate of twenty cigarettes or so per item. I know all about it, because I used to share an apartment with a crime reporter. He was fond of booze and a slacker, but apart from that he was a talented and poorly paid young man.

---

* The author of this piece, Karel Capek, is the preeminent Czech author of the first half of the twentieth century. Reprinted from *Tales from Two Pockets*, translated from the Czech by Paul Selver, Faber & Faber, 1932. The translation has been edited by Robert Wechsler.

"One day a strange sort of fellow, down on his luck, dirty and bloated, turned up at the café where the crime reporters used to meet. His name was Havlena; he'd studied law but never finished school, and he'd gone completely to the dogs. Nobody knew exactly how he made a living—in fact, he didn't quite know himself. Well, this fellow Havlena, this loafer, was quite well-versed on criminal and legal matters. When this pressman I knew gave him a cigar and some beer, he would close his eyes, take a few puffs, and begin to give the details of the finest and strangest criminal cases you could imagine. Then he'd mention the chief points for the defense and quote the prosecutor's speech in reply, after which he'd pass sentence in the name of the Republic. Then he'd open his eyes, as if he had just woken up, and growl, 'Lend me five crowns.'

"Once they put him to the test: At one sitting he invented twenty-one criminal cases, each one better than the one before it; but when he got to the twenty-second, he stopped short and said: 'Wait, this isn't a case for the lower courts; it'd have to go before a jury, and I don't do juries.' You see, he was opposed to juries on principle. But to be fair to him, I must say that the sentences he passed, though a bit severe, were models of their kind from a legal point of view; he prided himself on that.

"When the reporters discovered Havlena and saw that the cases he supplied them with were not hackneyed and dull as those which actually came up before the courts, they formed a sort of trust. For every case which he thought up, Havlena got what they called a court fee, consisting of ten crowns and a cigar, and in addition, two crowns for every month's imprisonment which he imposed. You see, the heavier the sentence, the more difficult the case. Newspaper readers had never before got such a kick out of the crime reports as when Havlena was supplying his sham criminal cases. No, sir, and now the papers aren't nearly as good as they were in his day; now it's nothing but politics and lawsuits—only Heaven knows who reads the stuff.

"Now one day Havlena thought up a case, which wasn't at all one of his best, and though up till then none of them had ever caused any trouble, this time they were caught red-handed. Reduced to its most basic facts, the case was like this: An old bachelor had a row with a respectable widow who lived across the courtyard from him; so he got a parrot and trained it so that whenever the lady appeared on her balcony, it screeched out at the top of its voice: 'You slut!' The widow brought an action against him for defamation of character. The district court decided that the defendant, through the agency of his parrot, had made a public laughing-stock of the prosecutrix, and in the name of the Republic sentenced him to fourteen days' imprisonment with costs. 'Eleven crowns and a cigar, please,' said Havlena to conclude the proceedings.

"This particular case appeared in about six newspapers, although it was written up in a variety of ways. In one paper the headline was: 'In a Quiet Building.' In another: 'Bachelor and Poor Widow.' A third paper called it: 'Accusation Against Parrot.' And so on. But suddenly all these papers received a communication from the Ministry of Justice asking for particulars of the district court before which the charge of defamation of character, reported in number so-and-so of your esteemed journal, had been tried; the verdict and sentence should be appealed against, since the incriminating words had been uttered not by the defendant, but by the parrot. It could not be regarded as proven that the words uttered by the said parrot indubitably referred to the prosecutrix; therefore, the words in question could not be regarded as defamation of character, but at the very utmost as disorderly conduct or a breach of the peace, which could have been dealt with by taking the defendant into custody, by duly imposing a fine, or by issuing a court order for the removal of the bird in question. The Ministry of Justice accordingly desired to know which district court had dealt with the case, in order that it might institute appropriate inquiries and so forth. In fact, it was a regular official rumpus.

"'Good Lord, Havlena, you've really gotten us into a mess,' the reporters protested to their retailer. 'Look here, that sentence you passed in the parrot case is illegal.'

"Havlena went as white as a sheet. 'What!' he shouted, 'The sentence I passed is illegal? Holy Moses, the Ministry of Justice has got the nerve to tell me that? Me, Havlena?' The reporters said they'd never seen a man so offended and angry. 'I'll give them what for,' shouted Havlena, flying into a temper. 'I'll show them whether my verdict's illegal or not! I'm not going to take this lying down.' In his vexation and excitement he got terribly drunk; then he took a sheet of paper and for the benefit of the Ministry of Justice drew up a detailed legal statement to vindicate the verdict. In it he said that by teaching his parrot to insult the lady the defendant had manifested his deliberate intention to insult and disparage her; that hence this was a clear case of unlawful intent; that the parrot was not the perpetrator of, but only the instrument for, the offense in question; and so forth. As a matter of fact, it was the most subtle and brilliant piece of legal reasoning the reporters had ever seen. Whereupon he signed it with his full name, Vaclav Havlena, and sent it to the Ministry of Justice. 'That's that,' he said, 'and until the matter's dealt with, I'm not going to hand down any more judgments; I must get satisfaction first.'

"As you can well imagine, the Ministry of Justice took no notice whatever of Havlena's communication. In the meantime, Havlena went about looking disgruntled and down at the mouth; he looked seedier than ever and he got very thin. When he saw that he had no chance of getting an answer from the Ministry, he lost heart; he would spit silently or talk treason, and at last he declared: 'Just you wait, I'll show 'em yet who's in the right.'

"For two months they didn't see a sign of him; then he turned up again, beaming and smirking, and announced: 'Well, I've been served with a writ at last! Whew! Damn that old lady! I had the deuce of a time persuading her to do it. You wouldn't believe that an old girl like that could be so hard to offend; she made me sign a paper that whatever happened I'd foot the bill for her. Anyhow, boys, now it's going to be settled in court.'

"'What is?' the reporters asked."

"'Why, that affair with the parrot,' said Havlena. 'I told you I wouldn't let it slide. You see, I bought a parrot and taught it to say: "You slut! you wicked old hag!" And the devil of a job it was, I tell you. For six weeks I didn't set foot outside the house and never uttered a word but: "You slut!" Anyway, now the parrot says it very well; the only thing is that the damned idiot bird keeps on shouting it the whole damned day. It just couldn't manage to limit its shouting to the old lady across the courtyard. She's an old music teacher; she's seen better days, quite a nice lady, but as there aren't any other females in that building, I had to pick on her for the defamation of character. I tell you, it's easy enough to think up an offense like that, but, holy Moses, when it comes to committing it, that's a different thing altogether. I just couldn't teach that brute of a parrot to limit its name-calling. It calls everyone names. If you ask me, it does it out of sheer cussedness.'

"Havlena had a long drink and then continued: 'So I tried a different scheme. Whenever the old lady showed her face at the window I rushed the parrot to the window so it could shout at her: "You slut! You wicked old hag!" And I'll be damned if the old girl didn't start laughing and call over to me: "Well I never, Mr. Havlena! What a nice little bird you've got there!" Damn old lady,' Mr. Havlena growled. 'I had to keep at her for weeks before she'd bring an action against me; but I've got witnesses from all over the house. Yes, and now it's going to be settled in court,' and Havlena rubbed his hands. 'I'll eat my hat if I'm not convicted for defamation of character. Those "Your Excellencies" down at the ministry won't get much change out of me!'

"Until the day the case came on, Mr. Havlena drank like a fish; he was nervous and restless. In court he was quite the little gentleman. He made a biting speech against himself, referring to the evidence of all the people in the house that the insult was a disgraceful and flagrant one, and demanded the most exemplary penalty. The judge, quite a decent old fellow, stroked his beard and said that he would like to hear the parrot. So he adjourned the proceedings and instructed the defendant at the next hearing to bring the bird with him as an exhibit or, should the need arise, as a witness.

"Mr. Havlena appeared at the next hearing with the parrot in a cage. The parrot goggled its eyes at the frightened lady clerk and began to shriek with all its might: 'You slut! You wicked old hag!'

"'That's enough,' said the judge. 'The evidence of the parrot Lora makes it plain that the expression it used did not refer directly and unequivocally to the prosecutrix.'

"The parrot looked at him and yelled: 'You slut!'— 'But it is obvious,' continued his honor, 'that it makes use of the expression in question toward all persons, irrespective of their gender. Accordingly, there is an absence of contumelious intent, Mr. Havlena.'

"Havlena jumped up as if he'd been stung. 'Your worship,' he protested excitedly, 'the unlawful intent to cause annoyance is shown by the fact that I was in the habit of opening the window which gave access to the prosecutrix for the purpose of causing the parrot to bring her into contempt.'

"'That's a moot point,' said his worship. 'The opening of the window possibly indicates some degree of unlawful intent, but in itself it is not a contumelious action. I cannot convict you for opening the window from time to time. You cannot prove that your parrot had the prosecutrix in mind, Mr. Havlena.'

"'But I had her in mind,' urged Havlena in self-defense.

"'We have no evidence as to that,' demurred the judge.

Reprinted from George Price,
Is It Anyone We Know?, 1944.

'Nobody heard you utter the incriminating expression. It's no use, Mr. Havlena, I shall have to acquit you.' Whereupon he pronounced judgment accordingly.

"'Then I beg to give notice of appeal against the acquittal,' Havlena exclaimed. He snatched up the cage containing the bird and rushed out of court, nearly weeping with rage.

"After that, they used to come across him here and there, all muddled and withdrawn. 'You call that justice?' he would scream. 'Is there any chance for a man to get his rights anywhere at all? But I won't let matters rest. I'll have it brought up before the highest court in the land. I've got to get back for the way I've been made a fool of, even if I have to spend the rest of my life bringing actions. I'm not fighting for my own cause, but for justice.'

"I don't exactly know what happened in the the court of appeals; all I know is that Mr. Havlena's appeal against his acquittal was dismissed. Then Havlena vanished into thin air. There were people who said they'd seen him loitering about the streets like a lost soul and muttering something to himself. I have also heard that to this very day the Ministry of Justice still receives, several times a year, a long and furious petition headed: *Defamation of Character Committed by a Parrot*. But Mr. Havlena has stopped supplying crime reporters with cases; most likely because his faith in law and order has been rudely shaken."

Alan M. Dershowitz
THE EYES OF THE BEHOLDERS*

THERE CAN NEVER BE OBJECTIVE STANDARDS of obscenity. Obscenity is truly in the eye of the beholder, or—as Justice Douglas once quipped—"in the crotch of the beholder." One person's obscenity is another's art, and yet another's comedy.

Former Justice Potter Stewart of the United States Supreme Court once admitted that he could not define obscenity, but he assured us that "I know it when I see it." But other judges, who also claim to know it, see it quite differently. Each Justice has his or her own personal definition of obscenity, which is rarely written into opinions. Justice Byron White's law clerks say that their boss looks for a sufficient degree of erection and penetration before he classifies a film as obscene; they refer to this as the "angle of the dangle" rule. Justice Brennan's clerks label his criterion, which permits anything short of a full erection, the "limp dick" standard. The late Chief Justice Earl Warren used to regard the portrayal of "normal" sex—no matter how graphic—as constitutionally protected; but when "abnormal" sex was even hinted at, he would fly into a rage. "Would my daughters be offended?" was his personal test. The late Justice Hugo Black believed that dirty pictures were absolutely

* Reprinted from Alan M. Dershowitz, *The Best Defense*, Random House, 1983, by permission of the author.

protected by the First Amendment, but that dirty words—such as "Fuck the Draft"—were not. Justice John Paul Stevens, on the other hand, believes that dirty words deserve more protection than dirty pictures. Every Justice has his own standards, and they are just as likely to reflect individual tastes, hang-ups, and upbringing as they do constitutional doctrine or precedent.

A. Laurence Polak
MEPHISTOPHELES v. FAUST*

Contract—Rejuvenation of Defendant by Plaintiff—Consideration— Delivery up of defendant's "soul"—Undisclosed principal—Statute of Frauds, 1677, s.4—Application of lex fori—"Soul"—Whether personal property of reversionary nature—Whether chose in action—Subject-matter of contract insufficiently defined.

IMPORTANT QUESTIONS of contract law fell to be decided in this case, in which Mr. Justice Gounod delivered the following considered judgment:

"This is an action brought by Mr. Mephistopheles, of Gehenna, described as a Fuel Contractor, against Dr. Faust, a German scientist resident in the United Kingdom under the licence of the Crown. The Plaintiff claims (1) specific performance of an oral contract alleged to have been made, within the German Reich, between himself of the one part and the Defendant of the other part, (2) delivery up of the subject-matter of the said contract, namely, the 'soul' of the Defendant, to the Plaintiff or such person or persons as he may nominate, or in the alternative (3) the execution by the Defendant of a deed (to be settled by Counsel nominated by the Court) transferring all the Defendant's property in and title to the said 'soul' to the Plaintiff or to such person or persons as aforesaid.

"The Defendant raises a number of defences with which I shall deal in due course. The facts disclosed by the evidence are as follows:—

---

* The author of this piece, A. Laurence Polak, a Briton, has written several books of legal humor, most of them consisting of cases based on mythical and literary figures. Reprinted from *Final Legal Fictions: A Series of Cases from Folk-Lore and Opera*, Stevens & Sons, 1948.

"The parties met in 1930 in Germany, where the Defendant was at that time residing and where he was engaged in scientific and psychic research. He was then a man of some seventy years of age. His lifelong studies and researches were about to come to fruition. He was, as I understand, on the verge of an important discovery connected with the release of atomic power. His great regret was that, at his advanced age, he feared he would not live to put the results of his discoveries to practical application.

"The Defendant discussed his problem with the Plaintiff, who represented to him that he (the Plaintiff) was in possession of the secret of a medical or surgical process which would have a thoroughly rejuvenating effect and would give the Defendant a further thirty or forty years of vigorous life. On the basis of these representations the Defendant orally agreed with the Plaintiff that, in consideration of the Plaintiff's giving him the appropriate treatment by the process described, the Defendant would, if the treatment was successful, surrender, transfer and assign all the Defendant's property in and title to his 'soul' to the Plaintiff or to such person or persons as aforesaid.

"In pursuance of this agreement the Plaintiff gave the Defendant the required treatment, which appears to have been entirely successful in its rejuvenating effect. Having seen the Defendant in the witness-box, where he admitted that he is now in his eighty-eighth year, I have been able to form my own conclusions, and I have no hesitation in finding that he has the physique and vitality of a man of forty.

"The Defendant has not denied that his physical rejuvenation has been brought about by the intervention of the Plaintiff, or that the agreement between the parties was substantially in the terms alleged. Nor has he attempted to deny that he has so far failed to carry out his part of the contract. He has, however, put forward in his defence a number of procedural and legal arguments, the validity of which it is now incumbent upon me to examine.

"The first of these is that the Plaintiff entered into this oral contract merely as agent for a principal who should have been made a party to these proceedings, but who has not appeared therein, though his identity was disclosed at the time when the contract was made. This mysterious personage, whom the Defendant admits he has never seen, and whose address he does not know, is said to have been mentioned under a variety of aliases which are so numerous as to leave in my mind a most vague and ambiguous impression.

The Defendant alleges that the Plaintiff referred to him at different times under the names of Satan, Lucifer, Beelzebub, 'Der Teufel,' 'The Evil One,' and even 'Old Nick.' His residence, he says, was at no time disclosed and, except that he was alleged to be engaged in some occupation connected with central heating, no hint of his profession was vouchsafed. In the absence of some more definite evidence of the existence and activities of this alleged principal, I regret that I am driven to the conclusion that he exists only in the Defendant's imagination, and on this part of the defence I hold that the Defendant was contracting and intended to contract with the person (the Plaintiff) present and identified by sight and hearing (*Phillips* v. *Brooks*). I am fortified in this conclusion by the fact (which the Defendant does not deny) that it was the Plaintiff solely who conducted the negotiations throughout and who personally carried out the rejuvenating treatment which I have described. In the circumstances this part of the defence must fail.

"The second line of defence may be equally shortly disposed of. The Defendant pleads that, whatever may be the proper law of the contract (a matter to which I will revert), no action thereon can be entertained by the Courts of England in view of the provisions of sec. 4 of the Statute of Frauds, which provides (*inter alia*):

> No action shall be brought whereby to charge any person..........upon any agreement that is not to be performed within the space of one year from the making thereof.........unless the agreement........or some memorandum or note thereof shall be in writing and signed by the party to be charged therewith or some other person thereto by him lawfully authorised.

"I will admit that the Defendant is right to this extent—that the matters dealt with by the Statute of Frauds are matters of evidence and procedure and must be governed by the *lex fori* (the Law of England) of which the Plaintiff is seeking to avail himself. But, that being said, I am by no means convinced that this oral contract falls within the statutory words 'not to be performed within the space of one year from the making thereof,' as interpreted by the decided cases. These words have been limited by authority to such contracts as appear by their terms to be incapable of complete performance within the statutory period (*Boydell* v. *Drummond*); had the parties stipulated that the treatment to be given by the Plaintiff, the successful outcome of which was a condition precedent to the performance by the Defendant of his part of the contract, must continue for more than one year, there might have been more merit in the Defendant's contention. But no such stipulation was made. The further argument of the Defendant—that the term of the contract for the delivery up of his 'soul' contemplated, by the very nature of the transaction, that performance must be postponed until the end of his life (of which I shall have more to say anon) cannot avail him either. For even if the Defendant is right in his allegation that performance was to be so postponed, yet the promise of the Plaintiff to carry out the rejuvenating process amounted only to this—that it would confer upon him the vigour and vitality of a man in the prime of his life, *capable* of living for another thirty or forty years; it implied no warranty or guarantee that his life would unquestionably be so prolonged and that he would assuredly escape those risks of sudden death from accident or disease which are inevitably associated with human life—'what he may have to pass through—its normal vicissitudes, with all its joys, all its sorrows, with its hardships and its various burdens and duties' *(Rose* v. *Ford)*. For these reasons I cannot hold that the Defendant has made out his plea under this Statute. It thus becomes unnecessary for me to deal with the argument of the Plaintiff's Counsel putting up the doctrine of part performance—the carrying out by the Plaintiff of his side of the bargain—or to consider whether the acts done by the Plaintiff were or were not unequivocally referable to the terms of the contract in issue. On this matter I have grave doubts, but fortunately I am not called upon to express a final opinion thereon.

"The only merit that I can observe in the Defendant's pleas is to be found in his third line of defence—that the subject-matter of the contract is of an ambiguous and unidentifiable nature, and that the acts which he is required by the contract to perform are not defined with sufficient accuracy. Here the Defendant is on surer ground. The evidence of Dr. Goethe has established only that the contract is not illegal or invalid by the *lex loci contractus*—the law of Germany; but neither this careful witness nor any of the other experts have succeeded in making clear to me under what class of property the 'soul' of the Defendant can be said to fall, or whether, indeed, it can be described as 'property' in any sense of the word.

"The difficulty is this. The remedy of specific performance—the delivery up of the Defendant's 'soul', or the execution of a document purporting to transfer to the Plaintiff the title thereto—is sought from the English Court, the forum where the action is being tried. I will assume in the Plaintiff's favour that the proper law of the contract is the law of Germany. I have it on the authority of the experts that the contract is valid and legal by that law. But the grant of a decree of specific performance by the English Court is limited to the case where the Court is in a position to enforce its decree. That is not this case.

"Whether the oral contract in its original terms was for the Defendant to perform forthwith after the Plaintiff had performed his part, or whether performance was intended to be postponed until after his death (as the Defendant contends) and to be binding upon his legal personal representatives, makes little difference to the elucidation of the main difficulty. It is clear that the Defendant's 'soul' is not a chattel, to be transferred by manual delivery. It has not been produced for inspection, and no description thereof by form or substance, size, weight or colour has been given. It is clearly not a *chose* in possession. I am not therefore in a position to make an order for delivery up of the Defendant's soul as the statement of claim requires.

"As to the alternative claim, Counsel has suggested that the subject-matter of the contract is a *chose* in action, analogous to a share in a joint stock company, conferring on the owner certain rights and duties during his lifetime and certain benefits and liabilities on his death or dissolution, and that I should order the Defendant to execute a deed of transfer. This argument, ingenious as it was, left me profoundly unconvinced. There are, it is true, certain similarities between a natural person and a legal or artificial *persona*, such as a corporation, but the analogy, if pressed too far, breaks down. The rights and duties of the Defendant in respect of his 'soul' are not dependant upon any documents in the nature of a company's Articles of Association, which are susceptible of legal construction, either while he remains (if I may be permitted the metaphor) a going concern or upon his winding-up, whether compulsory or voluntary; and I have yet to learn that the conduct of his affairs is regulated by ordinary, extraordinary or special resolutions, or that he can effect a transfer of his 'soul' by writing under seal.

"Counsel's endeavours to bring the subject-matter of this contract within other classes of property recognised by the law of England were equally unsuccessful. Can the Defendant's 'soul' be classed as a species of reversionary interest? I have the gravest doubts. In what sense can it be said to be vested in him in reversion rather than in possession, and under what recognised type of interest can it be classed? Counsel was unable to enlighten me, and could only suggest that it was an equitable interest in the nature of a trust. This, however, takes us no further. For a trust implies a trustee and a *cestui que trust*, and if it be said that the Defendant stands in both capacities there is no trust subsisting, and consequently no equity to be enforced.

"I am therefore unable to make the alternative order asked for, that the Defendant do execute a deed of transfer, surrender or assignment. I was not impressed by the evidence that a writing by the Defendant on a piece of human skin, signed in his own blood, would be valid to effect the necessary transfer by the *lex loci solutionis*. This Court, as the appropriate *forum*, can do no more than order the execution of documents recognised by the *lex fori*, viz., simple contracts or specialities under seal. The law of England does not recognise any special validity as attaching to a further class of documents which are alleged to depend for their validity upon the material with which, or upon which, they may be inscribed.

"In all the circumstances I am bound to hold that the subject-matter of the contract is of a nature not recognised by the law of England; that in consequence the contract is void for ambiguity and that this action for specific performance must fail. There will be judgment for the Defendant, with costs."

Went down and spoke at some Lawyers' meeting
last night. They dident think much of my little
squib yesterday about driving the shysters out of
the profession. They seemed to kinder doubt just
who would have to leave. —*Will Rogers*

How did I happen to go to Harvard Law School?
One day I started to go to Morningside Heights
to matriculate at Columbia...on a nice spring day
with ten dollars in my pocket. On the way up I
ran into a buddy of mine. I told him what I was
doing. "Oh," he said, "you can do that some
other day. Let's go to Coney Island." So we went
to Coney Island. —*Justice Felix Frankfurter*

Normalcy is when you run out of money.
Insolvency is when you run out of excuses.
Bankruptcy is when you run out of town.
                    —*Martin J. Yudkowitz*

turtlenecks
HE'S LEADING THE WITNESS, YOUR HONOR!
© 1978 Fincher

LEGAL LANGUAGE

Fred Rodell
GOODBYE TO LAW REVIEWS*

THERE ARE TWO THINGS wrong with almost all legal writing. One is its style. The other is its content. That, I think, about covers the ground. And though it is in the law reviews that the most highly regarded legal literature—and I by no means except those fancy rationalizations of legal action called judicial opinions—is regularly embalmed, it is in the law reviews that a pennyworth of content is most frequently concealed beneath a pound of so-called style. The average law review writer is peculiarly able to say nothing with an air of great importance. When I used to read law reviews, I used constantly to be reminded of an elephant trying to swat a fly.

Now the antediluvian or mock-heroic style in which most law review material is written has, as I am well aware, been panned before. That panning has had no effect, just as this panning will have no effect. Remember that it is by request that I am bleating my private bleat about legal literature.

To go into the question of style then, it seems to be a cardinal principle of law review writing and editing that nothing may be said forcefully and nothing may be said amusingly. This, I take it, is in the interest of something called dignity. It does not matter that most people—and even lawyers come into this category—read either to be convinced or to be entertained. It does not matter that even in the comparatively rare instances when people read to be informed, they like a dash of pepper or a dash of salt along with

* This is an excerpt from *the* classic essay on the law review article. Reprinted from 23 *Virginia Law Review* 38-41 (1936) by permission of the Virginia Law Review Association and Fred B. Rothman & Co. Twenty-five years later, Professor Rodell published a follow-up article, noting that little had changed in the world of law review writing since his first critique. See 48 *Virginia Law Review* 286-90 (March 1962).

their information. They won't get any seasoning if the law reviews can help it. The law reviews would rather be dignified and ignored.

Suppose a law review writer wants to criticize a court decision. Does he say "Justice Fussbudget, in a long-winded and vacuous opinion, managed to twist his logic and mangle his history so as to reach a result which is not only reactionary but ridiculous"? He may think exactly that but he does not say it. He does not even say "It was a thoroughly stupid decision." What he says is—"It would seem that a contrary conclusion might perhaps have been better justified." "It would seem—," the matriarch of mollycoddle phrases, still revered by the law reviews in the dull name of dignity.

One of the style quirks that inevitably detracts from the force-fulness and clarity of law review writing is the taboo on pronouns of the first person. An "I" or a "me" is regarded as a rather shocking form of disrobing in print. To avoid nudity, the back-handed pas-sive is almost obligatory: "It is suggested—," "It is proposed—," "It would seem—." Whether the writers really suppose that such con-structions clothe them in anonymity so that people can not guess who is suggesting and who is proposing, I do not know. I do know that such forms frequently lead to the kind of sentence that looks as though it had been translated from the German by someone with a rather meager knowledge of English.

Long sentences, awkward constructions, and fuzzy-wuzzy words that seem to apologize for daring to venture an opinion are part of the price the law reviews pay for their precious dignity. And circumlocution does not make for strong writing. I grant that a rapier in capable hands can be just as effective as a bludgeon. But the average law review writer, scorning the common bludgeon and reaching into his style for a rapier, finds himself trying to wield a barn door.

Moreover, the explosive touch of humor is considered just as bad taste as the hard sock of condemnation. I know no field of learning so vulnerable to burlesque, satire, or occasional pokes in the ribs as the bombastic pomposity of legal dialectic. Perhaps that is the very reason why there are no jesters or gag men in legal literature and why law review editors knit their brows overtime to purge their publications of every crack that might produce a real laugh. The law is a fat man walking down the street in a high hat. And far be it from the law reviews to be any party to the chucking of a snowball or the judicious placing of a banana-peel.

Occasionally, very occasionally, a bit of heavy humor does get into print. But it must be the sort of humor that tends to produce, at best, a cracked smile rather than a guffaw. And most law review writers, trying to produce a cracked smile, come out with one of those pedantic wheezes that get an uncomfortably forced response when professors use them in a classroom. The best way to get a laugh out of a law review is to take a couple of drinks and then read an article, any article, aloud. That can be really funny.

Then there is this business of footnotes, the flaunted Phi Beta Kappa keys of legal writing, and the pet peeve of everyone who has ever read a law review piece for any other reason than that he was too lazy to look up his own cases. So far as I can make out, there are two distinct types of footnote. There is the explanatory or if-you-didn't-understand-what-I-said-in-the-text-this-may-help you type. And there is the probative or if-you're-from-Missouri-just-take-a-look-at-all-this type.

The explanatory footnote is an excuse to let the law review writer be obscure and befuddled in the body of his article and then say the same thing at the bottom of the page the way he should have said it in the first place. But talking around the bush is not an easy habit to get rid of and so occasionally a reader has to use reverse English and hop back to the text to try to find out what the footnote means. It is true, however, that a wee bit more of informality is permitted in small type. Thus "It is suggested" in the body of an article might carry an explanatory footnote to the effect that "This is the author's own suggestion."

It is the probative footnote that is so often made up of nothing but a long list of names of cases that the writer has had some stooge look up and throw together for him. These huge chunks of small type, so welcome to the student who turns the page and finds only two or three lines of text above them, are what make a legal article very, very learned. They also show the suspicious twist of the legal mind. The idea seems to be that a man can not be trusted to make a straight statement unless he takes his readers by the paw and leads them to chapter and verse. Every legal writer is presumed to be a liar until he proves himself otherwise with a flock of footnotes.

In any case, the footnote foible breeds nothing but sloppy thinking, clumsy writing, and bad eyes. Any article that has to be explained or proved by being cluttered up with little numbers until it looks like the Acrosses and Downs of a cross-word puzzle has no business being written. And if a writer does not really need footnotes and tacks them on just because they look pretty or because it is the thing to do, then he ought to be tried for wilful murder of his reader's (all three of them) eyesight and patience.

Exceptions to the traditions of dumpy dignity and fake learnedness in law review writing are as rare as they are beautiful. Once in a while a Thomas Reed Powell gets away with an imaginary judicial opinion that gives a real twist to the lion's tail. Once in a while a Thurman Arnold forgets his footnotes as though to say that if people do not believe or understand him that is their worry and not his. But even such mild breaches of etiquette as these are tolerated gingerly and seldom, and are likely to be looked at a little askance by the writers' more pious brethren.

In the main, the strait-jacket of law review style has killed what might have been a lively literature. It has maimed even those few pieces of legal writing that actually have something to say. I am the last one to suppose that a piece about the law could be made to read like a juicy sex novel or a detective story, but I can not see why it has to resemble a cross between a nineteenth century sermon and a treatise on higher mathematics. A man who writes a law review article should be able to attract for it a slightly larger audience than a few of his colleagues who skim through it out of courtesy and a few of his students who sweat through it because he has assigned it.

Daniel R. White
THE SKY IS BLUE*

EVERY LAW PARTNER FANCIES HIMSELF a grammarian. He would edit Strunk and White. There is no sentence so straightforward and simple that he will not happily torture it beyond recognition.

Take the sentence "The sky is blue."

No junior associate would be so naïve as to think this proposition could pass muster in a big firm. If he made it through law school, he knows enough to say, "The sky is *generally* blue."

Better yet, "The sky generally *appears* blue."

---

* Reprinted from D. Robert White, *The Official Lawyer's Handbook,* Simon & Schuster, 1983.

For extra syllables, "The sky generally appears *to be* blue."

A senior associate seeing this sentence might take pity on the junior associate and explain that before showing it to a partner the junior associate should put it in a more "lawyerly" form. At the very least the sentence should be revised to say, "In some parts of the world, what is generally thought of as the sky sometimes appears to be blue."

Armed with these qualifiers, the junior associate thinks himself protected.

His conversation with the reviewing partner will proceed thus:

Partner Carter: You say here that in some parts of the world, what is generally thought of as the sky sometimes appears to be blue. I assume this is just an early draft. Could I see the final version?

Associate Williams: Uh, that's all I have right now ... what exactly do you mean?

Partner Carter: Well, it's a bit bald, don't you think? I mean, just to come right out and assert it as fact.

Associate Williams: I beg your pardon? Are we talking about the same thing?

Partner Carter: Well, this business about "the sky"—what did you mean by "the sky"?

Associate Williams: Well, I meant what I see when I look up ... at least, when I'm outside. Isn't that what everyone sees?

Partner Carter: Okay, if you mean *only* when you're outside, you have to say so. Our opponents in this case would love to rip us apart on that kind of error. And what about at night? Even at night? I see stars at night—are they blue? Do you mean everything *but* stars, or do you mean when there are no stars out?

Associate Williams: I meant during the day, I guess.

Partner Carter: You *guess.* Williams, this is serious business. We can't go around guessing at things. Besides, what about the sun? If it's daytime, the sun will be out—or do you know something I don't?

Associate Williams: Well, sure ... I mean, no, I don't.... But no one in his right mind looks at the sun. You'd go blind.

Partner Carter: What support do you have for this comment about "some parts of the world?" *Which* parts? Do we need to state it so broadly? Can't we just say "in Cleveland" or wherever we mean?

Associate Williams: That sounds fine to me. I just never thought anyone would challenge ... that is, who would disagree with...

Partner Carter: And what do you mean by "generally thought of?" Thought of by whom? Lawyers? Scientists? Morticians? Dammit, Williams, this piece has more holes in it than Swiss cheese. I haven't seen such sloppiness in all my years at Cavil, Quibble & Quiver. Take it back and see if you can't do a little better this time around.

Principles of Legal Writing

1. Never use one word where ten will do.
2. Never use a small word where a big one will ~~do~~ suffice.
3. Never use a simple statement where it appears that one of substantially greater complexity will achieve comparable goals.
4. Never use English where Latin, *mutatis mutandis,* will do.
5. Qualify virtually everything.
6. Do not be embarrassed about repeating yourself. Do not be embarrassed about repeating yourself.
7. Worry about the difference between "which" and "that."
8. In pleadings and briefs, that which is defensible should be stated. That which is indefensible, but which you wish were true, should merely be suggested.
9. Never refer to your opponent's "arguments;" he only makes "assertions," and his assertions are always "bald."
10. If a layperson can read a document from beginning to end without falling asleep, it needs work.

Anonymous
THE LITTLE LAWYER MAN*

It was a little lawyer man
Who softly blushed as he began
Her poor, dead husband's will to scan.

He smiled while thinking of his fee,
Then said to her, so tenderly,
"You have a nice, fat legacy."

And when, next day, he lay in bed
With bandages upon his head,
He wondered what on earth he'd said.

Michael A. Musmanno
HOW STRAIGHT DOES A CROW FLY?**

AN APPLICATION was filed with the Pennsylvania liquor control board on February 7, 1938, by Theodore Somach for a restaurant liquor license for premises at No. 1802 Crafton Boulevard, in the city of Pittsburgh, Allegheny county, Pennsylvania. Subsequently on March 30, 1938, the application was refused, because the establishment was located less than three hundred feet from the Crafton high school. * * *

It is argued by the appellant, *inter alia,* that the distance between his establishment and the school building should be measured, not on a straight line, but along such a route as would normally be traversed by a pedestrian travelling between the two points. He claims that it should be measured not "as a crow flies," but as a man walks.

We are here called upon to construe that part of section 403 of

---

* Reprinted from *The Green Bag.*
**Reprinted from *Docket,* Spring 1939, by permission of West Publishing Co.

the Pennsylvania liquor control act, 47 P.S. ¶744-403, which reads
as follows:

> Provided, however, that, in the case of any new license or the
> transfer of any license to a new location, the board may, in its
> discretion, grant or refuse such new license or transfer if such
> place, proposed to be licensed, is within three hundred feet of
> any church, hospital, charitable institution, school or public
> playground.

It seems fundamental to us that in measuring distances, there
can be only one method employed—and that is straight linear
measure. Geographical measurements have no regard for streets,
curbs or walking lanes. They are direct, undeviating and absolute.
Distances referred to in statutes can only be measured in the same
way. Three hundred feet can not contract or stretch according to the
view of the particular person doing the measuring. It is not a matter
of deciding which street or route to follow. * * *

There is a popular notion that the most direct route is that one
which is expressed by the phrase, "as a crow flies." This is a
fallacious notion. A crow does not always fly straight. In fact, he
rarely does. Indeed, he is a rather unreliable bird. When he sets out
on a journey he seldom proceeds with bullet precision to his des-
tination. He must alight from time to time to sample worms, cater-
pillars and grasshoppers; he can never soar directly over a corn
field, he must circle over it several times and then swoop down to
dine on newly planted corn, not infrequently glutting himself to the
extent that his navigational sense of direction is considerably
dulled.

The crow is wary and cautious, which are points in his favor,
self-preservation being the first law of nature, but his caution is
often carried to a foolish extreme. He is, with reason, afraid of the
farmer who stands ready with a shotgun to give him a warm
welcome for uprooting his corn field, but in his (the crow's) fright,
he cannot tell the difference between a farmer and a scarecrow.
Thus he will always fly pell mell away from the latter, which in its
shapeless bundle of rags looks no more like a farmer than an Eskimo
harpooning a fish.

To use "as a crow flies" as a simile for bullet directness is
incorrect. "As a crow flies" is a phrase that should be eliminated
from the lexicon of accurate speech and writing. A crow sent out on
a direction and distance-marking expedition would come back with
a report whose accuracy could only be conjectured at, after making
allowances and deduction for the time and effort expended by him

in the pursuit of grasshoppers, in the visits to cornfields, and in the fluttering flights away from scarecrows.

We do not intend by this opinion to proscribe the crow. He is really not a bad bird and can (and does) give plenty of "caws" to show his friendliness. We only say that he is not accurate and cannot be utilized, in the interpretation of a liquor statute, as a surveyor to draw a straight line. If a bird must be used in charting a direct course to a liquor establishment, it would appear that the swallow would more instinctively find the direct route than a crow. However, we are firmly of the opinion that the nomenclature of birds has no place in legal language, not dealing strictly with an ornithological subject. So far as we are concerned, "as a crow flies" to suggest a straight line is here banned, both in the popular and juristic use. Nor would we suggest for a substitute, "as a airplane flies," or "as a bullet is projected." It is our opinion that in describing a straight line it is quite sufficient simply to say "in a straight line."

Euclid and Einstein are sufficient authorities for what we have here stated.

We thus decide that since the Somach establishment is within three hundred feet, on a straight line, of the Crafton high school, the application for a liquor license must be refused.

Gerald Abrahams
CONVEYANCER'S LOVE STORY*

THE OLD CHANCERY JUNIOR brushed an accumulation of tobacco ash from his threadbare black coat and ordered further and better coffee.

"Women," he said, "resemble property. I don't complain that they in particular are no longer chattels, as they were in Blackstone's time. I complain of that tendency reflected in the law (the law being said, in more than one case, to express society, whatever that is) by which private property tends to become public property." He paid the waitress for his coffee, and then looked at

---

* Reprinted from Gerald Abrahams, *Lunatics and Lawyers*, Home and Val Thal, 1951.

the bill that she left him as if trying to work out whether it was a form of account stated or valid as a receipt.

"Besides," he added, "they've become too important—they're realty now." He sighed, as if he were a poet, and he looked shaggy as a bear does in the Bear Garden. In truth, there was little conventional poetry in the man. Shelley, to him, was a rule in Conveyancing: Keats a Probate Case: Shakespeare a decision on a deed. From time to time in the Law Reports he found snatches of song quoted by Law Lords and Justices of Appeal in order to illustrate the meaning of ambiguous or vague phrases like "for ever". For the rest, Beauty was to him a "term of art". His knowledge of literature began with Williams Saunders and ended with the modern Reports. Yet, as he spoke now, one felt that there was a poet in him, gone mouldy among the parchment.

"The lunatic, the lover, and the lawyer..." meditated his companion.

"I started life," the Chancery man said, "desirous of a pleasant unencumbered freehold; uncultivated yet fertile; undeveloped, so to speak, yet a site for a home."

"Were you in the market?" inquired the much younger Common Law man, knowing how slow progress is at the Chancery Bar.

"Yes," the older man replied—and one almost detected a reminiscent gleam in his sunken eyes. "I gave her a handbag by way of deposit. It was the product of a small Application to Foreclose with Consent." He paused, "Was that ominous, I wonder? However, like so many deposits, my deposit was lost. Unknown to me, the estate was mortgaged. I was young enough to be worried about that. I was angry at the non-disclosure of a material fact in a contract which I erroneously thought was 'in the best faith.' I did not know then that the rule in matrimony is Caveat Emptor—and glad of it. I told myself that I was afraid of a subsequent foreclosure, or entry into possession by the encumbrancer. So I called the deal off."

"And you did not recover the deposit," completed the other, facetiously.

The old conveyancer's answer was so candid and serious that his interlocutor immediately felt ashamed of the interruption. "I expect that on the cases I could have recovered it, because she was in the position of a stakeholder, rather than the receiver of part payment. Or else she had deceived me (there was evidence of misrepresentation, if necessary) but I was too upset to press the point." He seemed distrait for a moment, as if wondering whether he had overstated his view of the contract.

"Well," encouraged the Common Law man, "I suppose you looked elsewhere."

"Yes, I looked elsewhere, but that piece of realty"—the word sounded almost like "reality"—"continued to attract me. After much heart-searching, and reading a lot of divorce cases ... Unhappy stuff, that," he added, with a melancholy unusual in those who rejoice in perpetuity among the contingent remainders—"I decided that I had been asking for too much. After all, what I wanted was only a lease for life; and what matter the existence of a landlord or encumbrancer, provided the ground rent and interest weren't exorbitant?"

"You didn't go to the auction again?" The Common Lawyer was horrified at the idea of a conveyancer wandering round what amounted to a casual sale-room.

"Yes, an attempt is being made to destitute this orphan, whom I will not characterize as a young orphan, since he is fifty-seven years old, but an orphan nonetheless ... but I am confident, gentlemen, in any case, for the eyes of justice are constantly open to all such culpable manoeuvres!" —Honoré Daumier, *Men of Justice*, 1845.

"No," he replied, in a way that again made the interrupter regret his facetiousness, "it was by private treaty. And, as I had expressed myself from time to time on the subject, with a freedom that a Chancery Master would not have approved, you may imagine that I had difficulty entering into negotiations. I had to pay a further deposit of a diamond ring which took away all the benefit of a rather good settlement we had been construing."

"Well, that should have led to a quick conveyance."

The other waved a melancholy hand. "Unfortunately, it didn't. I suspect now that there were rival bidders, even after contract. I had no such suspicion then." His tone was pathetically naïve, for all the pedantry of his words. "What thwarted the completion was her failure to give undertakings, on which I insisted having regard to the history of the estate."

"Couldn't you, so to speak, 'curtain' the past?" asked the Common Law man, rather proud of his ability to throw in a good equity term.

The Chancery man shook his head patiently.

"No, my young friend. You must appreciate that this was before the legislation of 1925." He spoke the words sadly, as one pronounces a *Labuntur Anni*. "And," he added, speculatively, "I apprehend that even 1925, which turned realty into something like Chattels with a market overt title, couldn't have defeated the kind of encumbrancers that had attached themselves to my 'baggage'."

The metaphor of the left-luggage office was suddenly so strong in the Common Law man's mind as to reduce him to a compassionate silence. The other resumed, a trifle petulantly.

"However, you interrupted me. The fact is, I was losing my bargaining power. It was a case of a willing buyer and an unwilling seller. At least, that's what she made me think. I had believed that I would be in a position to demand something pretty good about sole user. Instead, after some mysterious process which I forget now, it's all so long ago, I found myself being told that in certain eventualities the demise would only be for a term of years—a term of years uncertain, moreover. And, as you know, that's anathema to the practice."

"Until death, remarriage or desertion, whichever shall be the earlier," ventured the other, *sotto voce*.

"Yes," replied the narrator sombrely, "and, as one has so often told the court, that can mean anything."

"So the deal was off?"

"Yes, and another tenant—yes, a lessee, not the original mortgagee—entered into possession."

The Common Lawyer couldn't bring himself to ask about the second deposit, but the Chancery man relieved the other's curiosity.

"Of course, there was no question of recovering the part-payment—it was definitely that—but I went into the market a bit impoverished, and couldn't find anything. So I continued to hang round the same site. I may say that, under cultivation and development, it looked more desirable than ever."

"Didn't the tenant object?"

"Well, no. As a matter of fact, his tenure didn't last very long. After some years a Will of mine ended up the right way in the House of Lords, and I got well paid out of the estate—Solicitor and Client costs. So I invested a rope of pearls on a rather vague agreement that gave me something—not exactly the reversion, because that was a bit encumbered, and there was no way of negotiating for the equity, but I thought I got something. I sort of arranged, on a probably contingency, to take over what was left of the term of years, subject to paramount rights that I hoped would not be too rigorously enforced."

"A thoroughly bad contract," remarked the listener, boldly. "Even a Common Lawyer can see that."

"Yes," he replied, "and it was probably against public policy. And it wasn't even in writing. But," he added, as if in extenuation, "there was something that a Court of Lunacy might have interpreted as part performance." For a moment he almost looked pleased at the recollection.

"Well, did you complete?" The listener was getting fascinated as the tale proceeded.

"No." His tone was sad again now, "A woman, unlike a messuage or hereditament, has a mind to change. And, applying the Interpretation Act 1889 to a famous *obiter dictum*, one can say that 'the devil knoweth not the heart of woman'." He paused, drank his now cold coffee, and resumed more strongly. "Having, then, got rid of the first tenant, she was not anxious for the regularity of occupation that a second tenant implied. By that time I was getting on in years. I couldn't ask for the pearls back, because they'd been sold—and the proceeds applied for decorations that I had approved. I decided to give up in disgust."

"Didn't you?"

"The answer to that, my dear sir, is, as they say in the King's Bench, 'Yes and No.' I had learnt my lesson. I was no longer anxious for a freehold or a leasehold. The obligations and the anxieties seemed too great. But there was no point in abandoning my contacts with that particular estate. At the time in question, and subsequently for some years, my practice was not too bad. The property needed more decoration from time to time, not to mention repairs. Perhaps the original mortgagee was losing interest. So, with the aid of a necklace or two, less easily given, I secured for myself what has amounted to a reasonably convenient licence or right of way."

It could not be said that he smiled at this recollection, but in a melancholy way he looked almost satisfied, as one who, notwithstanding the difficulties of the market, has ultimately achieved a conveyance of sorts. The story was obviously ended.

"But if you had your time over again," ventured the younger man, in a not unkindly spirit, "you would surely not allow yourself to enter the same market in the same way."

The old man rose. In a determined voice, he said, "If I had my time over again I'd be a solicitor, or a stockbroker, or one of those other property dealing gentry who seem to be able to get hold of the best mortgages in the first instance." The tone was of one who had never been entirely unpractical, however ill-advised. "I think," he added, with a gleam that may have had something to do with the passing of the waitress, "I would become a slum landlord, constantly insisting on possession."

As he went away in order to make application at the counter for particulars of lunch, the Common Law man, reflecting on his own bitter experiences, decided not to tell the old boy about the Rent Act.

Charles R. Maher
THE[1] [*1]INFERNAL FOOTNOTE[2]*

[*4]Countless[3] [*5]law students and legal researchers have been afflicted with Ping-Pong Ocular Syndrome,[4] [*6]and several with Brightoncliffe's Phenomenon,[5] [*7]because of the apparently incurable addiction of legal writers to the footnote.[6]

[*8]You've doubtless seen scores[7] [*9]of illustrations of this addiction in *Corpus Juris Secundum*,[8] [*10]Kluptpfester's *Negligence in the Operation of Funicular Railways*[9] [*11]and other celebrated works. At the top of a page will be two or three lines of text, the balance of the page being covered by a Himalayan heap of footnotes, some of which have probably spilled over from the previous page, at the top of which was one line of text. Assuming, arguendo,[10] [*12]that people who do things like that should not be publicly flogged, the question arises: How otherwise to combat the footnote menace?[11] [*13]The answer, of course, is to expose it, and this article has been prepared in easy-to-read fashion to do precisely that.[12]

[*14]In the case of encyclopedic works, perhaps, authors may be excused if their footnotes happen to occupy only slightly less space than the surface of Saturn. It must be admitted that case citations are at least occasionally useful to the legal practitioner.[13] [*15]Similarly, authors of law review articles may be pardoned for their footnotational extravagances. When you've got too much junk to fit in the house, the cellar may be about the only place to put it.

Not to be forgiven, however, are three other breeds of footnote artists: the Exhibitionist,[14] [*16]the Obsessive Annotator[15] [*18]and the Midsentence Dislocationist.[16] [*20]All such footnotefeasors are guilty (as the jury will be instructed to find before their trial begins) of an unspeakable offense.[17]

Footnotes

1. **Warning to reader:** This article contains compound footnotes and reciprocal reference marks, either of which may cause dizziness or split vision unless handled according to directions.

* Reprinted from 70 *American Bar Association Journal* 92-94 (1984).

Reciprocal reference marks are asterisks followed by numbers (*e.g:* ***10).** These symbols, revolutionary in concept, are found in the footnotes and direct the reader to *preceding* rather than to subsequent points in the article. They are introduced by an arrow symbol, →, meaning "Kindly go back to the point indicated by the reciprocal reference mark, and be quick about it." You will encounter the first such symbol at the end of this paragraph and will be directed to the reciprocal mark ***1,** suspended just before the second word in the title of the article. Once there, begin reading at that word and continue until you encounter a conventional, asterisk-free footnote mark directing you elsewhere. Repeat this procedure each time you arrive at a raised reciprocal mark in response to an arrow command. Caution: When finished reading, do not operate forklifts or other heavy machinery for at least three or four hours, whichever occurs sooner. → ***1, title.**

2. Welcome back. A footnote is "a note of reference, explanation or comment placed below the text on a printed page or underneath a table or chart...."[a] [*2]Abbrev.: fn.[b] [*3]*Webster's Third New International Dictionary of the English Language,* at 885 (abbrev. at 880).[c]

3. countless: "of such great number as to defy counting...." *Ibid.,* at 521. Sometimes also used to describe the status of a widowed countess, as in "The countess is countless."

(You are approaching another reciprocal reference mark and are entitled to know that for purposes of brevity, as well as confusion, the abbreviation **t** will be used hereinafter for **text.**) → ***5, t.**

4. So called because the reader's eye, jumping from text to footnote and back to text, resembles that of a spectator at a Ping-Pong match. The difference being that the spectator at least knows what the score is → ***6, t.**

5. Named for the renowned Lord Justice Percival Brighton-cliffe, whose practice it was to keep his left forefinger pointed at footnote numbers in the text while tracing the footnotes themselves with his right forefinger. Alas, he panicked one day while trying to follow a particularly treacherous footfootnote. This triggered a convulsive reaction known as "forefinger recoil," the lamentable result of which was that the good justice poked out both of his eyes. And thus was born the expression "justice is blind." → ***7, t.**

6. See **fn 2** and its progeny. Then → ***8, t.**

7. Of which the following are merely a few examples:

Green Bay 17, Chicago 16
St. Louis 14, Philadelphia 10
Houston 3

(Because of an oversight by the schedulemakers, Houston played this particular week without an opponent. After failing to cross midfield for more than three periods, the Oilers finally won the game when one of their backs muffed a pitchout, swung his foot at the ball in disgust and inadvertently kicked a field goal.) → *9.t.

8. West Publishing Co. (St. Paul: 1963). Watch for the gripping sequel, *Corpus Juris Thirdum*. Sorry, but we're sworn not to reveal the electrifying ending. → *10, t.

9. Symon & Shyster (Ober Grafendorf: 1839). Translated from the Tyrolean by O. d'Laeheehu. → *11, t.

10. This word is a corruption of R. Guendeaux, the name of an infamous 16th-century Transylvanian war minister known for his disputatious manner and loud neckties. → *12, t.

11. The runaway growth of the footnote industry is thought by many to rank right up there with the skateboard craze among the great perils faced by Western society since World War II.[d]

12. To be sure, easy reading like this can wear you out. You may feel free at this point to take a break, the time for which has just expired. And now, as a reward for having come this far, you may proceed to any footnote or footfootnote of your choice.[e]

13. See Dimwitty's *Advanced Legal Research and Other Parlor Tricks*. Tragically, the author died at a rather early age (11) and left only one copy of this masterpiece, in handwritten manuscript form done entirely in crayon. But legal scholars will find it readily available at his mother's house, just up the street from the 7-Eleven. → *15, t.

14. His byword: "If you don't think that was a great article I wrote, just count the footnotes." →*16, t.

15. Some writers annotate excessively not to show off but simply because they can't help it.[f] [*17]Perhaps the most irredeemable of this class was Prof. S. Llewellyn Screed, author of an unpublished treatise (*The Dry Well and Its Place in Riparian Law*), containing 39 words of text and 78,853 words of footnotes, some of which were so extended they had to be broken into chapters. → *18, t.

16. This is the writer who plants a footnote number in a long sentence, sending the reader scurrying to a note the length of the Palsgraf case.[g] [*19]Having returned from that note after hacking

THE STATE OF THE NATION

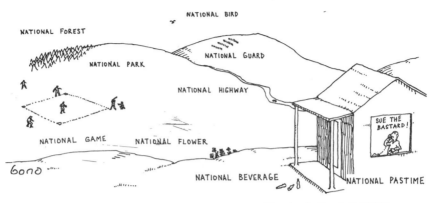

Drawing by Bond; © 1988 The
New Yorker Magazine, Inc.

through a half acre of typographical underbrush, the reader apparently is expected to resume reading the text at midsentence as though not the slightest distraction had intervened.[h]

17. Gross abuse of footnation, for which the minimum penalty is amputation of both feet, above the wrists. Although footnotes are at best rather hard-to-reach subterranean storage vaults that should be used as little as possible, if that often, they have been used by these defendants knowingly, wilfully, intentionally, consciously, deliberately and more or less on purpose for misplacement of two common types of material: (1) that which properly belongs only in the custody of a licensed trash collector, and (2) that which is worth preserving but which could just as easily be worked into the text.[i]

Footfootnotes

a. Hi. The origin of the footnote is lost in antiquity. One legend is that it was introduced circa 3777 B.C. by the Abalonian writer Hammerknocker. Composing a love verse in stone one day, Hammerknocker committed a transpositional blunder, chiseling out "moon harvest" instead of "harvest moon." This, of course, was before the development of erasable stone. Not wishing to discard an otherwise flawless work, Hammerknocker invented the asterisk, inserted a specimen of his invention after "moon harvest" and, in history's first footnote, chiseled at the bottom of the stone: "*Sometimes also called 'harvest moon.'"

What you are reading now, by the way, is called a footfootnote (ffn) or footnotenote (fnn). For a penetrating study of this device, see Fleishbender's *The Pathology of the Footfootnote and Related Disorders of the Lower Extremities.* Pathological Press (Skittsafrenia, N.Y.: 1937). → ***2, footnote 2** (and, in case you still haven't got the hang of it, begin reading at "Abbrev.," the word following the raised symbol ***2** appears).

b. The abbreviation **n** is more common in legal texts and other whimsical works. But the more formal **fn** is better suited to serious writing and accordingly will be used hereinafter. → ***3,fn2.**

c. G. & C. Merriam Co. (Springfield, Mass.: 1966). This volume also contains an excellent full-page color illustration of butterflies and moths (facing page 297). Note particularly the sinister Pipevine Swallowtail butterfly. How'd you like to meet one of these in a dark meadow?

(You are about to receive an arrow command directing you to the first raised reciprocal mark in the text. Remember, whenever sent in search of such a mark, to look first for an asterisk, so as to avoid confusing a reciprocal mark with a like-numbered footnote mark that may be hovering nearby.) → ***4, text.**

d. For the benefit of younger readers, World War II was a rather drawn-out and at times impolite confrontation in which the Allies finally prevailed after the intervention of John Wayne. → ***13, t.**

e. Except this one, which is none of your business. → ***14, t.**

f. Their inability to restrain themselves makes them no less detestable. → ***17,fn15.**

g. *Palsgraf* v. *Long Island R.R. Co.*, 162 N.E. 99 (1928). By the way, while this overrated case is fresh in mind, can anyone explain how on earth the explosion of a small package of firecrackers at one end of a railway platform "threw down some scales" clear at the other end, causing injury to the estimable Mrs. Palsgraf? After 55 years, it's high time we got an answer to this question—and it better be good. → ***19,fn16.**

h. California's best-known legal writer, Bernard E. Witkin, touches on the problem of reader dislocation in his *Manual on Appellate Court Opinions.* West Publishing Co. (St. Paul: 1977), at 78-80:

> 'If judicial opinions had Blue Cross, they could go to the hospital and have their footnotes removed.' (Gordon, August 1974 *ABA Journal,* page 952.) A converted former 'ardent footnoter,' Justice Gordon directs his main attack at the placement in footnotes of holdings on points of law, but he also complains of the difficulties facing 'the reader of the footnote-bedecked

decision,' *who must deal with the physically separated pieces of the opinion.* [Emphasis supplied.]

...[E]ven where footnoting is appropriate, it ought to be reasonable in size and scope....

One commentator (Simonett, December 1969 *ABA Journal*, page 1141) has a few words of tongue-in-cheek praise for '[t]he essay footnote, the commentary that competes with the main text, where the author undertakes an excursion on some tangential point, interesting in itself if not essential to the text....'

Simonett (as quoted by Witkin) then excavates an abyss into which to hurl himself: "Legal writing is reasoned writing and tends to be taut."

One could readily argue, in response, that legal writing not only doesn't tend to be taut but often doesn't even tend to be taught.

Simonett continues: "[A]nd yet there must be some flexibility, some room. The excursionary footnote provides this extra space, a kind of necessary extravagance. Tea need not be served in a cup with a saucer, but the saucer does add a touch of elegance and catches the spillage."

Which spillage is poured down the sink, where it belongs. →
*20, t.

i. Where it could be read with less irritation and more comprehension. Reason: Continuity is to understanding what Simon was to Garfunkel, and footnotes are the enemies of continuity. In fact, when used indiscriminately, rather than in the judicious manner employed here, footnotes may leave readers hopelessly disoriented, so that they will never get to the point you will have reached with no difficulty in just two more words.[1]

_____

(1) The end.

Legalese. An obscure language, based on Latin (and hopefully destined for the same fate), which lawyers use to prevent laymen from understanding what they're being charged with and for. —*Daniel R. White*

Lex
There once was a lawyer named Rex
Whose organ was small for his sex.
When charged with exposure,
He said with composure,
"De minimis non curat lex."
> —*Men's Room, Columbia*
> *Law Library, 1979*

Last Clear Chance. *1.* In the law of torts, the doctrine that liability should rest with the person who had the last opportunity to avoid the collision. *2.* For people who aspire to happiness in life, the moment before taking the LSATs.
> —*Daniel R. White*

*"It is further agreed by both parties
that the bride shall retain her name
and her Southern drawl."*

MARRIAGE AT LAW

Corey Ford
SEAT OF JUSTICE*

JUDGE PARKER'S BROW was beaded as he shouldered hastily into his judicial robes. His August court session had fallen on the very afternoon that the Lower Forty Shooting, Angling and Inside Straight Club was planning its annual bass-fishing excursion and cookout at Beaver Meadow, and only the Judge's heartfelt pleas had persuaded his fellow members to postpone their departure until his official duties were over.

"I won't be long," he assured them, pulling the loose black gown over his canvas fishing jacket and hooking the collar to conceal the red bandanna at his neck. "All I've got to do is pass sentence on Hentracks Hennessy."

"What's Hentracks up for?" asked Doc Hall.

"Assault and battery and creating a disturbance of the peace and driving his poor wife out into the rain." The Judge gathered his lawbooks under an arm, slung his creel over his shoulder and led the way out of his private chambers. "If there's anything I hate, it's a wife beater," he said grimly, "particularly in bass season."

He clumped across the courtroom, the long robe flapping around his rubber boots, and dumped the lawbooks on the bench and stowed his fishing gear carefully behind it. The other members of the Lower Forty seated themselves at the rear of the room, and the Judge rapped for order. "Now then, Hentracks," he said briskly, "you got anything to say in your own defense?"

"He ain't got any defense, Judge," Mrs. Hennessy interrupted from the other side of the courtroom. "He hit me with a canoe paddle and..."

Judge Parker held up his hand. "The court sympathizes with

* Reprinted from *Minutes of the Lower Forty* by Corey Ford, © 1962 Corey Ford, by permission of Henry Holt & Co. and Harold Ober Associates.

you, Myra," he said gently, "but in all justice we must let this lowdown, good-for-nothing husband of yours speak for himself." He glowered at the culprit over his spectacles. "I intend to give you a fair trial before I jail you. Just wotinell did you hit your wife for?"

"Wal, your honor," Hentracks sighed, "it's a long story."

"Cut it short," the Judge ordered, glancing at the clock on the wall. "This court has some very important business as soon as I've finished sentencing you."

The defendant licked his lips nervously. "The way it all started," he began, "I was rummaging through my freezer down in the cellar the other day, and I come acrost one last package of venison that was left over from my two hundred-pound buck I got last fall. Natchally I re'lized I didn't have no legal right to keep the meat this late in the year," he explained with a guilty look at Owl Eyes Osborn, the conservation officer, "so I decided to make a venison stew, because they ain't nothing I like better than a good stew, except I like to make it myself, because you know how it is, your honor, a woman don't know how to make a venison stew right."

"That's true," Judge Parker admitted. "They never put in enough onions."

"You need lots of onions," Hentracks agreed, "and butter, of course, and flour, and some beef stock, and peppercorns, and bay leaf..."

"And half a cup of lemon juice," Cousin Sid suggested from the rear of the room. "That makes all the difference."

"And a few cloves," Colonel Cobb offered. "I always put cloves in mine."

"I got to remember that," Hentracks said appreciatively and resumed. "So I mixed everything all together, and cooked it a couple of hours, and I added jes' a mite of wine to the gravy, and then at the last minute I dropped in some potato dumplings, and I tell you, Judge, it would have made your mouth drool. My wife Myra don't like venison, so she'd made herself an omelet, which meant I had the whole stew for myself, and we was really a happy family and the very pitcher of domestic bliss as we sat down to the table together. Wal, I took a little taste of the stew, and I decided it needed another dash of pepper and mebbe jes' a soopson more salt, so I reached for a pair of salt and pepper shakers I always use that are made up to look like shotgun shells..."

"I've got a pair just like them," Judge Parker said with growing interest. "They never plug up."

"That's why I always use 'em," Hentracks said. "The holes are big enough for the salt to come out when you want salt, so I reached for 'em, your honor, and—" he paused a moment—"and they wa'n't there. No, sir, my wife she'd threw them out, and in place of them she had a pair of antique cut-glass salt and pepper shakers she'd bought at an antique show. You know those little dinky kind?"

The Judge nodded. "My wife goes in for antiques too," he sighed, and gazed at Mrs. Hennessy reprovingly.

"So I picked up this little cut-glass saltcellar and I shook it, but nothing come out, so I shook it harder and still nothing come, so I turned it upside down and hit it with the palm of my hand, and the top come off and dumped the whole shakerful into my lovely stew and ruint it, and they wa'n't no more venison till next fall. And with that I jumped up from the table and grabbed my .410, and I opened the front door and threw the cut-glass saltcellar as high as I could into the air, and I nailed it with the right barrel as it come down, and then I threw the pepper shaker into the air and unlatched the left barrel and ground it into powdered glass—"

Judge Parker cocked his ears. "How is your .410 bored?"

"Full and full, your honor. It's the last of them wonderful old Parkers that they stopped production on after the war. It was rigged on special order with semibeavertail fore end and single trigger."

"What load were you using?" Cousin Sid inquired.

"Wal, I started to load with 7½, and then I decided if I really wanted to dust that goldang saltcellar I'd better use No. 6 chilled."

"Very sound," the Judge beamed. "Very sound."

"Look here," Mrs. Hennessy broke in impatiently, "I come to this court to get justice, not to hear a lot of silly talk about guns."

Judge Parker stiffened. "Woman, guard your tongue," he warned, "or your name will be a byword and a hissing." He turned to the defendant. "Go on, Hentracks."

"Wal, with that my wife let out a bellow like a bull with a hot pitchfork stuck in its rear, and she run upstairs to my gun room and grabbed my favorite four-ounce, split-bamboo rod that's got jes' the right action, your honor, that rod would put a dry fly clear acrost a brook and lay it onto the water slick as you'd want to see—"

"That's the kind I like," Doc Hall agreed enthusiastically. "Stiff enough but not too stiff."

"—and she took it in her both hands and laid the tip acrost her knee, and she smashed it to smithereens." His voice broke, and he controlled himself with an effort. "So with that I run up to the gun room and got my canoe paddle, and my wife seen me coming and started for the door, and I made one big swipe and caught her on the rump and boosted her halfway down the front walk."

The courtroom was silent as he finished. "Lemme see that paddle," said Owl Eyes, picking up the evidence and examining it with a professional eye. "Yessir, Judge, there's a split right here in the blade where it collided with her fanny." He handed the paddle to Judge Parker. "Why, if Hentracks was to use that paddle in fast water and mebbe hit a rock, it would bust clean in two and prob'ly upset the canoe."

The Judge leveled an accusing forefinger at Mrs. Hennessy. "Do you realize that your carelessness might have caused your husband to get drowned or suffer even more serious injury?"

"Carelessness!" Mrs. Hennessy gasped, springing to her feet. "Why, that brute deliberately assaulted me. I got bruises and welts all over me to prove it."

"This court does not admit evidence by testimony when it is available for direct visual examination," Judge Parker announced, "and you needn't use any false plea of modesty with me, either, because what the females are wearing for bathing suits these days has destroyed modesty and damn near ruined the textile industry. If you've got any bruises, you can show them here and now, or I'll have to render a verdict of not guilty for the defendant."

"I'll do no such thing," Mrs. Hennessy bristled, her cheeks reddening, "and you can render any verdict you've a mind to."

"In that case," said the Judge, "I hereby sentence the complainant to pay for damages to the canoe paddle. And what's more," he added quickly as Mrs. Hennessy opened her mouth to protest, "the complainant is warned to depart quietly, because it would be just as easy for me to say ten days for contempt." He rapped the gavel. "This setting of court is hereby adjourned."

Judge Parker waited until the courtroom door slammed behind Mrs. Hennessy. He yanked off his black robe with relief, gathered up his fishing gear and beckoned to the other members to follow him. Hentracks Hennessy was lingering in the doorway.

"By the way, Hentracks," the Judge suggested, "why don't you come along to Beaver Meadow this afternoon for our cookout? We've got some venison meat we've been saving up all year, and maybe you could show us how you made that stew."

Anonymous
CORN ON THE COB*

M Y BUSY SEASON IS OVER. I am a lawyer, but my busy season is while green corn is in market.

This may seem strange, but there is an explanation. I am a specialist in obtaining divorces for husbands or wives who can no longer stand the sight of the other gnawing at an ear of green corn.

Your heart would ache at some of the stories I hear, of the callousness with which some men reach for ear after ear of corn, of the greediness with which they gnaw away at it until their plates are piled with cobs, of the glistening and disgusting smear of butter about their mouths, while the poor wife sits by, her nerves a-quiver. Or perhaps the addict is the wife, whose bared teeth, as she attacks an ear of corn, remind her husband of some small rodent—a woodchuck, or a squirrel.

At last the breaking-point is reached. The wronged spouse abruptly leaves the table, seeks me out, and begs me to undertake the case.

I do so, and with all the eloquence at my command I ask the court how ordinary respect, to say nothing of affection, can continue to exist in such an atmosphere. I point out that my client's health is being impaired; that his or her sanity is at stake; and I ask that a divorce be granted on the ground of extreme cruelty. Nor do I ask in vain; the Judge, with tears in his eyes, always signs the decree which I lay before him.

As I have said, I am known as a specialist in this field, and earn a very nice income.

What do I do with my money? I have invested in a farm where I grow green corn for the market. I see no good reason why those who like green corn should not have it. Besides, I like corn on the cob myself, although my wife does not care for it, and she dislikes watching me eat it.

* Reprinted from 61 *Case & Comment* 8 (Summer 1956) by permission of *Case & Comment*.

O. Henry
THE HYPOTHESES OF FAILURE*

LAWYER GOOCH bestowed his undivided attention upon the engrossing arts of his profession. But one flight of fancy did he allow his mind to entertain. He was fond of likening his suite of office rooms to the bottom of a ship. The rooms were three in number, with a door opening from one to another. These doors could also be closed.

"Ships," Lawyer Gooch would say, "are constructed for safety, with separate, water-tight compartments in their bottoms. If one compartment springs a leak it fills with water; but the good ship goes on unhurt. Were it not for the separating bulkheads one leak would sink the vessel. Now it often happens that while I am occupied with clients, other clients with conflicting interests call. With the assistance of Archibald—an office boy with a future—I cause the dangerous influx to be diverted into separate compartments, while I sound with my legal plummet the depth of each. If necessary, they may be baled into the hallway and permitted to escape by way of the stairs, which we may term the lee scuppers. Thus the good ship of business is kept afloat; whereas if the element that supports her were allowed to mingle freely in her hold we might be swamped—ha, ha, ha!"

The law is dry. Good jokes are few. Surely it might be permitted Lawyer Gooch to mitigate the bore of briefs, the tedium of torts and the prosiness of processes with even so light a levy upon the good property of humour.

Lawyer Gooch's practice leaned largely to the settlement of marital infelicities. Did matrimony languish through complications, he mediated, soothed and arbitrated. Did it suffer from implications, he readjusted, defended and championed. Did it arrive at the extremity of duplications, he always got light sentences for his clients.

But not always was Lawyer Gooch the keen, armed, wily belligerent, ready with his two-edged sword to lop off the shackles

---

* Reprinted from O. Henry, *Whirligigs,* Doubleday, Page, 1916.

of Hymen. He had been known to build up instead of demolishing, to reunite instead of severing, to lead erring and foolish ones back into the fold instead of scattering the flock. Often had he by his eloquent and moving appeals sent husband and wife, weeping, back into each other's arms. Frequently he had coached childhood so successfully that, at the psychological moment (and at a given signal) the plaintive pipe of "Papa, won't you tum home adain to me and muvver?" had won the day and upheld the pillars of a tottering home.

Unprejudiced persons admitted that Lawyer Gooch received as big fees from these reyoked clients as would have been paid him had the cases been contested in court. Prejudiced ones intimated that his fees were doubled because the penitent couples always came back later for the divorce, anyhow.

There came a season in June when the legal ship of Lawyer Gooch (to borrow his own figure) was nearly becalmed. The divorce mill grinds slowly in June. It is the month of Cupid and Hymen.

Lawyer Gooch, then, sat idle in the middle room of his client-less suite. A small anteroom connected—or rather separated—this apartment from the hallway. Here was stationed Archibald, who wrested from visitors their cards or oral nomenclature which he bore to his master while they waited.

Suddenly, on this day, there came a great knocking at the outermost door.

Archibald, opening it, was thrust aside as superfluous by the visitor, who without due reverence at once penetrated to the office of Lawyer Gooch and threw himself with good-natured insolence into a comfortable chair facing that gentlemen.

"You are Phineas C. Gooch, attorney-at-law?" said the visitor, his tone of voice and inflection making his words at once a question, an assertion and an accusation.

Before committing himself by a reply, the lawyer estimated his possible client in one of his brief but shrewd and calculating glances.

The man was of the emphatic type—large-sized, active, bold and debonair in demeanour, vain beyond a doubt, slightly swaggering, ready and at ease. He was well-clothed, but with a shade too much ornateness. He was seeking a lawyer; but if that fact would seem to saddle him with troubles they were not patent in his beaming eye and courageous air.

"My name is Gooch," at length the lawyer admitted. Upon

pressure he would also have confessed to the Phineas C. But he did not consider it good practice to volunteer information. "I did not receive your card," he continued, by way of rebuke, "so I——"

"I know you didn't," remarked the visitor, coolly; "and you won't just yet. Light up?" He threw a leg over an arm of his chair, and tossed a handful of rich-hued cigars upon the table. Lawyer Gooch knew the brand. He thawed just enough to accept the invitation to smoke.

"You are a divorce lawyer," said the cardless visitor. This time there was no interrogation in his voice. Nor did his words constitute a simple assertion. They formed a charge—a denunciation—as one would say to a dog: "You are a dog." Lawyer Gooch was silent under the imputation.

"You handle," continued the visitor, "all the various ramifications of busted-up connubiality. You are a surgeon, we might say, who extracts Cupid's darts when he shoots 'em into the wrong parties. You furnish patent, incandescent lights for premises where the torch of Hymen has burned so low you can't light a cigar at it. Am I right, Mr. Gooch?"

"I have undertaken cases," said the lawyer, guardedly, "in the line to which your figurative speech seems to refer. Do you wish to consult me professionally, Mr.——" The lawyer paused, with significance.

"Not yet," said the other, with an arch wave of his cigar, "not just yet. Let us approach the subject with the caution that should have been used in the original act that makes this pow-wow necessary. There exists a matrimonial jumble to be straightened out. But before I give you names I want your honest—well, anyhow, your professional opinion on the merits of the mix-up. I want you to size up the catastrophe—abstractly—you understand? I'm Mr. Nobody; and I've got a story to tell you. Then you say what's what. Do you get my wireless?"

"You want to state a hypothetical case?" suggested Lawyer Gooch.

"That's the word I was after. 'Apothecary' was the best shot I could make at it in my mind. The hypothetical goes. I'll state the case. Suppose there's a woman—a deuced fine-looking woman— who has run away from her husband and home? She's badly mashed on another man who went to her town to work up some real estate business. Now, we may as well call his name. I'm giving you straight tips on the cognomens. The Lothario chap is Henry K.

Jessup. The Billingses lived in a little town called Susanville—a good many miles from here. Now, Jessup leaves Susanville two weeks ago. The next day Mrs. Billings follows him. She's dead gone on this man Jessup; you can bet your law library on that."

Lawyer Gooch's client said this with such unctuous satisfaction that even the callous lawyer experienced a slight ripple of repulsion. He now saw clearly in his fatuous visitor the conceit of the lady-killer, the egoistic complacency of the successful trifler.

"Now," continued the visitor, "suppose this Mrs. Billings wasn't happy at home? We'll say she and her husband didn't gee worth a cent. They've got incompatibility to burn. The things she likes, Billings wouldn't have as a gift with trading-stamps. It's Tabby and Rover with them all the time. She's an educated woman in science and culture, and she reads things out loud at meetings. Billings is not on. He don't appreciate progress and obelisks and ethics, and things of that sort. Old Billings is simply a blink when it comes to such things. The lady is out and out above his class. Now, lawyer, don't it look like a fair equalization of rights and wrongs that a woman like that should be allowed to throw down Billings and take the man that can appreciate her?"

"Incompatibility," said Lawyer Gooch, "is undoubtedly the source of much marital discord and unhappiness. Where it is positively proved, divorce would seem to be the equitable remedy. Are you—excuse me—is the man Jessup one to whom the lady may safely trust her future?"

"Oh, you can bet on Jessup," said the client, with a confident wag of his head. "Jessup's all right. He'll do the square thing. Why, he left Susanville just to keep people from talking about Mrs. Billings. But she followed him up, and now, of course, he'll stick to her. When she gets a divorce, all legal and proper, Jessup will do the proper thing."

"And now," said Lawyer Gooch, "continuing the hypothesis, if you prefer, and supposing that my services should be desired in the case, what——"

The client rose impulsively to his feet.

"Oh, dang the hypothetical business," he exclaimed, impatiently. "Let's let her drop, and get down to straight talk. You ought to know who I am by this time. I want that woman to have her divorce. I'll pay for it. The day you set Mrs. Billings free I'll pay you five hundred dollars."

Lawyer Gooch's client banged his fist upon the table to punctuate his generosity.

"If that is the case—" began the lawyer.

"Lady to see you, sir," bawled Archibald, bouncing in from his anteroom. He had orders to always announce immediately any client that might come. There was no sense in turning business away.

Lawyer Gooch took client number one by the arm and led him suavely into one of the adjoining rooms. "Favour me by remaining here a few minutes, sir," said he. "I will return and resume our consultation with the least possible delay. I am rather expecting a visit from a very wealthy old lady in connection with a will. I will not keep you waiting long."

The breezy gentleman seated himself with obliging acquiescence, and took up a magazine. The lawyer returned to the middle office, carefully closing behind him the connecting door.

"Show the lady in, Archibald," he said to the office boy, who was waiting the order.

A tall lady, of commanding presence and sternly handsome, entered the room. She wore robes—robes; not clothes—ample and fluent. In her eye could be perceived the lambent flame of genius and soul. In her hand was a green bag of the capacity of a bushel, and an umbrella that also seemed to wear a robe, ample and fluent. She accepted a chair.

"Are you Mr. Phineas C. Gooch, the lawyer?" she asked, in formal and unconciliatory tones.

"I am," answered Lawyer Gooch, without circumlocution. He never circumlocuted when dealing with a woman. Women circumlocute. Time is wasted when both sides in debate employ the same tactics.

"As a lawyer, sir," began the lady, "you may have acquired some knowledge of the human heart. Do you believe that the pusillanimous and petty conventions of our artificial social life should stand as an obstacle in the way of a noble and affectionate heart when it finds its true mate among the miserable and worthless wretches in the world that are called men?"

"Madam," said Lawyer Gooch, in the tone that he used in curbing his female clients, "this is an office for conducting the practice of law. I am a lawyer, not a philosopher, nor the editor of an 'Answers to the Lovelorn' column of a newspaper. I have other clients waiting. I will ask you kindly to come to the point."

"Well, you needn't get so stiff around the gills about it," said the lady, with a snap of her luminous eyes and a startling gyration of her umbrella. "Business is what I've come for. I want your opinion in the matter of a suit for divorce, as the vulgar would call it, but which is really only the readjustment of the false and ignoble conditions that the short-sighted laws of man have interposed between a loving——"

"I beg your pardon, madam," interrupted Lawyer Gooch, with some impatience, "for reminding you again that this is a law office. Perhaps Mrs. Wilcox—"

"Mrs. Wilcox is all right," cut in the lady, with a hint of asperity. "And so are Tolstoi, and Mrs. Gertrude Atherton, and Omar Khayyam, and Mr. Edward Bok. I've read 'em all. I would like to discuss with you the divine right of the soul as opposed to the freedom-destroying restrictions of a bigoted and narrow-minded society. But I will proceed to business. I would prefer to lay the matter before you in an impersonal way until you pass upon its merits. That is to describe it as a supposable instance, without—"

"You wish to state a hypothetical case?" said Lawyer Gooch.

"I was going to say that," said the lady, sharply. "Now, suppose there is a woman who is all soul and heart and aspirations for a complete existence. This woman has a husband who is far below

"It won't take long. I just wanted my attorneys to go over the exact wording of the ceremony."

her in intellect, in taste—in everything. Bah! he is a brute. He despises literature. He sneers at the lofty thoughts of the world's great thinkers. He thinks only of real estate and such sordid things. He is no mate for a woman with soul. We will say that this unfortunate wife one day meets with her ideal—a man with brain and heart and force. She loves him. Although this man feels the thrill of a new-found affinity he is too noble, too honourable to declare himself. He flies from the presence of his beloved. She flies after him, trampling, with superb indifference, upon the fetters with which an unenlightened social system would bind her. Now, what will a divorce cost? Eliza Ann Timmins, the poetess of Sycamore Gap, got one for three hundred and forty dollars. Can I—I mean can this lady I speak of get one that cheap?"

"Madam," said Lawyer Gooch, "your last two or three sentences delight me with their intelligence and clearness. Can we not now abandon the hypothetical and come down to names and business?"

"I should say so," exclaimed the lady, adopting the practical with admirable readiness. "Thomas R. Billings is the name of the low brute who stands between the happiness of his legal—his legal, but not his spiritual—wife and Henry K. Jessup, the noble man whom nature intended for her mate. I," concluded the client, with an air of dramatic revelation, "am Mrs. Billings!"

"Gentleman to see you, sir," shouted Archibald, invading the room almost at a handspring. Lawyer Gooch arose from his chair.

"Mrs. Billings," he said courteously, "allow me to conduct you into the adjoining office apartment for a few minutes. I am expecting a very wealthy old gentleman on business connected with a will. In a very short while I will join you, and continue our consultation."

With his accustomed chivalrous manner, Lawyer Gooch ushered his soulful client into the remaining unoccupied room, and came out, closing the door with circumspection.

The next visitor introduced by Archibald was a thin, nervous, irritable-looking man of middle age, with a worried and apprehensive expression of countenance. He carried in one hand a small satchel, which he set down upon the floor beside the chair which the lawyer placed for him. His clothing was of good quality, but it was worn without regard to neatness or style, and appeared to be covered with the dust of travel.

"You make a specialty of divorce cases," he said, in an agitated but business-like tone.

"I may say," began Lawyer Gooch, "that my practice has not altogether avoided——"

"I know you do," interrupted client number three. "You needn't tell me. I've heard all about you. I have a case to lay before you without necessarily disclosing any connection that I might have with it—that is—"

"You wish," said Lawyer Gooch, "to state a hypothetical case."

"You may call it that. I am a plain man of business. I will be as brief as possible. We will first take up the hypothetical woman. We will say she is married uncongenially. In many ways she is a superior woman. Physically she is considered to be handsome. She is devoted to what she calls literature—poetry and prose, and such stuff. Her husband is a plain man in the business walks of life. Their home has not been happy, although the husband has tried to make it so. Some time ago a man—a stranger—came to the peaceful town in which they lived and engaged in some real estate operations. This woman met him, and became unaccountably infatuated with him. Her attentions became so open that the man felt the community to be no safe place for him, so he left it. She abandoned husband and home, and followed him. She forsook her home, where she was provided with every comfort, to follow this man who had inspired her with such a strange affection. Is there anything more to be deplored," concluded the client, in a trembling voice, "than the wrecking of a home by a woman's uncalculating folly?"

Lawyer Gooch delivered the cautious opinion that there was not.

"This man she has gone to join," resumed the visitor, "is not the man to make her happy. It is a wild and foolish self-deception that makes her think he will. Her husband, in spite of their many disagreements, is the only one capable of dealing with her sensitive and peculiar nature. But this she does not realize now."

"Would you consider a divorce the logical cure in the case you present?" asked Lawyer Gooch, who felt that the conversation was wandering too far from the field of business.

"A divorce!" exclaimed the client, feelingly—almost tearfully. "No, no—not that. I have read, Mr. Gooch, of many instances where your sympathy and kindly interest led you to act as a mediator between estranged husband and wife, and brought them together again. Let us drop the hypothetical case—I need conceal no longer that it is I who am the sufferer in this sad affair—the names you shall have—Thomas R. Billings and wife—and Henry K. Jessup, the man with whom she is infatuated."

Client number three laid his hand upon Mr. Gooch's arm. Deep emotion was written upon his careworn face. "For Heaven's sake," he said fervently, "help me in this hour of trouble. Seek out Mrs. Billings, and persuade her to abandon this distressing pursuit of her lamentable folly. Tell her, Mr. Gooch, that her husband is willing to receive her back to his heart and home—promise her anything that will induce her to return. I have heard of your success in these matters. Mrs. Billings cannot be very far away. I am worn out with travel and weariness. Twice during the pursuit I saw her, but various circumstances prevented our having an interview. Will you undertake this mission for me, Mr. Gooch, and earn my ever-lasting gratitude?"

"It is true," said Lawyer Gooch, frowning slightly at the other's last words, but immediately calling up an expression of virtuous benevolence, "that on a number of occasions I have been successful in persuading couples who sought the severing of their matrimonial bonds to think better of their rash intentions and return to their homes reconciled. But I assure you that the work is often exceedingly difficult. The amount of argument, perseverance, and, if I may be allowed to say it, eloquence that it requires would astonish you. But this is a case in which my sympathies would be wholly enlisted. I feel deeply for you sir, and I would be most happy to see husband and wife reunited. But my time," concluded the lawyer, looking at his watch as if suddenly reminded of the fact, "is valuable."

"I am aware of that," said the client, "and if you will take the case and persuade Mrs. Billings to return home and leave the man alone that she is following—on that day I will pay you the sum of one thousand dollars. I have made a little money in real estate during the recent boom in Susanville, and I will not begrudge that amount."

"Retain your seat for a few moments, please," said Lawyer Gooch, arising, and again consulting his watch. "I have another client waiting in an adjoining room whom I had very nearly forgotten. I will return in the briefest possible space."

The situation was now one that fully satisfied Lawyer Gooch's love of intricacy and complication. He revelled in cases that presented such subtle problems and possibilities. It pleased him to think that he was master of the happiness and fate of the three individuals who sat, unconscious of one another's presence, within his reach. His old figure of the ship glided into his mind. But now the figure failed, for to have filled every compartment of an actual vessel would have been to endanger her safety; while here, with his compartments full, his ship of affairs could but sail on to the advantageous port of a fine, fat fee. The thing for him to do, of course, was to wring the best bargain he could from some one of his anxious cargo.

First he called to the office boy: "Lock the outer door, Archibald, and admit no one." Then he moved, with long, silent strides into the room in which client number one waited. That gentleman sat, patiently scanning the pictures in the magazine, with a cigar in his mouth and his feet upon a table.

"Well," he remarked, cheerfully, as the lawyer entered, "have you made up your mind? Does five hundred dollars go for getting the fair lady a divorce?"

"You mean that as a retainer?" asked Lawyer Gooch, softly interrogative.

"Hey? No; for the whole job. It's enough, ain't it?"

"My fee," said Lawyer Gooch, "would be one thousand five hundred dollars. Five hundred dollars down, and the remainder upon issuance of the divorce."

A loud whistle came from client number one. His feet descended to the floor.

"Guess we can't close the deal," he said, arising. "I cleaned up five hundred dollars in a little real estate dicker down in Susanville. I'd do anything I could to free the lady, but it out-sizes my pile."

"Could you stand one thousand two hundred dollars?" asked the lawyer, insinuatingly.

"Five hundred is my limit, I tell you. Guess I'll have to hunt up a cheaper lawyer." The client put on his hat.

"Out this way, please," said Lawyer Gooch, opening the door that led into the hallway.

As the gentleman flowed out of the compartment and down the stairs, Lawyer Gooch smiled to himself. "Exit Mr. Jessup," he murmured, as he fingered the Henry Clay tuft of hair at his ear. "And now for the forsaken husband." He returned to the middle office, and assumed a businesslike manner.

"I understand," he said to client number three, "that you agree to pay one thousand dollars if I bring about, or am instrumental in bringing about, the return of Mrs. Billings to her home, and her abandonment of her infatuated pursuit of the man for whom she has conceived such a violent fancy. Also that the case is now unreservedly in my hands on that basis. Is that correct?"

"Entirely," said the other, eagerly. "And I can produce the cash any time at two hours' notice."

Lawyer Gooch stood up at his full height. His thin figure seemed to expand. His thumbs sought the armholes of his vest. Upon his face was a look of sympathetic benignity that he always wore during such undertakings.

"Then sir," he said, in kindly tones, "I think I can promise you an early relief from your troubles. I have that much confidence in my powers of argument and persuasion, in the natural impulses of the human heart toward good, and in the strong influence of a husband's unfaltering love. Mrs. Billings, sir, is here—in that room—" the lawyer's long arm pointed to the door. "I will call her in at once; and our united pleadings—"

Lawyer Gooch paused, for client number three had leaped from his chair as if propelled by steel springs, and clutched his satchel.

"What the devil," he exclaimed, harshly, "do you mean? That woman in there! I thought I shook her off forty miles back."

He ran to the open window, looked out below, and threw one leg over the sill.

"Stop!" cried Lawyer Gooch, in amazement. "What would you do? Come, Mr. Billings, and face your erring but innocent wife. Our combined entreaties cannot fail to—"

"Billings!" shouted the now thoroughly moved client; "I'll Billings you, you old idiot!"

Turning, he hurled his satchel with fury at the lawyer's head. It struck that astounded peacemaker between the eyes, causing him to stagger backward a pace or two. When Lawyer Gooch recovered his wits he saw that his client had disappeared. Rushing to the window, he leaned out, and saw the recreant gathering himself up from the top of a shed upon which he dropped from the second-story window. Without stopping to collect his hat he then plunged downward the remaining ten feet to the alley, up which he flew with prodigious celerity until the surrounding building swallowed him up from view.

Lawyer Gooch passed his hand tremblingly across his brow. It was an habitual act with him, serving to clear his thoughts. Perhaps also it now seemed to soothe the spot where a very hard alligator-hide satchel had struck.

The satchel lay upon the floor, wide open, with its contents spilled about. Mechanically Lawyer Gooch stooped to gather up the articles. The first was a collar; and the omniscient eye of the man of law perceived, wonderingly, the initials H. K. J. marked upon it. Then came a comb, a brush, a folded map and a piece of soap. Lastly, a handful of old business letters, addressed—every one of them—to "Henry K. Jessup, Esq."

Lawyer Gooch closed the satchel, and set it upon the table. He hesitated for a moment, and then put on his hat and walked into the office boy's anteroom.

"Archibald," he said mildly, as he opened the hall door, "I am going around to the Supreme Court rooms. In five minutes you may step into the inner office, and inform the lady who is waiting there that"—here Lawyer Gooch made use of the vernacular—"that there's nothing doing."

James M. Rose
ANTI-NUPTIAL AGREEMENT*

Unmarried clients who are desirous of remaining in that status have begun to consult lawyers about how to protect themselves from palimony suits. The California Supreme Court has added a new twist to the age old question "My place or yours?", which is now a fact question to be determined by equitable distribution laws (i.e., The Accountant and Appraiser Full Employment Act). There's a new definition to "good housekeeper"—it's someone who, following a divorce, gets to keep the house.

Law blank publisher Julius Humbug has devised an anti-nuptial agreement and matrimonial release to be signed before dating begins. It will be particularly helpful if your client double dates with a notary.

* Reprinted from *Westchester County Bar Journal*, Spring 1985, by permisson of the *Westchester Bar Journal* and James M. Rose.

X0xx-090—Anti-Nuptial Agreements©
and Matrimonial Release 4/80's

LAYMEN:
ATTENTION: DO NOT SIGN THIS FORM WITH-
OUT CONSULTING A MATRIMONIAL BOMBER

[Void where prohibited by General Obligations Law—In N.Y.C. consult Administrative Code for varying provisions and regulations of Dept. of Consumer Affairs of the heart]

TO ALL TO WHOM THESE PRESENTS SHALL COME OR MAY CONCERN OR ARE JUST NOSEY, KNOW THAT:

WHEREAS the party of the first part_____and the party of the second part_____are desirous of partying with each other;

WHEREAS the parties' partying is not intended by either party to constitute a binding agreement, commitment, emotional attachment, legal attachment, liaison, pseudo-marriage, encumbrance, lien or security agreement in or with one another, and they wish to be upfront and totally open;

WHEREAS the parties intend to fully retain all of their inalienable rights as free and independent citizens to life, liberty, and the happiness of pursuit and do not intend their connection to be a permanent connection leading to responsibilities of a financial or emotional nature or a hereditament either corporeal, incorporeal or otherwise, nor to impinge upon one another's space;

AND in the absence of any consideration in hand, nor delivered and with very little consideration for one another's feelings, or their obligations to society in general which is generally ignored and unacknowledged, and with a knowledge of the vagaries of equitable distribution, and in an effort to teach the bottom line;

IT IS HEREBY STIPULATED AND AGREED by and between the undersigned and the attorneys of record for all the parties that all parties hereto are not infants and are relatively competent, have their heads together and are in touch with their feelings, and understand where each other is coming from, and can relate to it, and be totally upfront with their feelings;

THAT they have not agreed to any commitments one to the other of any financial, emotional, physical, spiritual, paranormal, biological, existential, psychological, physiological, philosophical, sociological, or subliminal of any kind or nature whatsoever, that they acknowledge and respect one another's right to his or her own space, to do their own thing, and to do whatever their heads are into, and accept one another for what they are, and hereby mutually

RELEASE one another, their heirs, executors, administrators, successors, assigns, next of kin, next door neighbors, best friends and former roommates unto the 20th generation yet unborn of ANY commitments real or imagined, expressed or implied, as recited above and including but not limited to obligations for financial, emotional or physical support, or alimony, palimony, maintenance or the like, due from one another to one another from any interpersonal relationship, pseudo-marriage, arrangement, contract, whether express, oral, written or imagined, and HEREBY forgive any trespasses (as ours are forgiven), damages, judgments (moral, ethical or legal), variances (from the original text), covenants (spiritual or temporal), suits, dues, accounts, reckonings, bonds (including but not limited to pseudo-matrimonial or municipal), bills, extents in law, equity, admiralty or ecclesiastical courts from the first day of creation (hereinafter the "BIG BANG") through and including the parties splitting up (hereinafter the "LITTLE BANG") up to and including the day after tomorrow.

ANTEDATED: , 19_____

_____
Party of the first part in blood

_____
Party of the second part in blood

On   19   before me personally came
                     and known to me to be the individuals who
were previously possessed of 25 cents and who stopped fighting long enough to execute the foregoing release and anti-nuptial agreement and while swearing at and to one another swore to this agreement and executed the same.

_____
Notary Public
I expire_____if not sooner.

Marcel Strigberger
OF EDEN *v.* OF EDEN*

GABRIEL, L. J. S. C.:—This is a petition for divorce presented by Adam Of Eden. It is urged that the respondent Of Eden has treated the petitioner with physical and mental cruelty of such a kind as to render intolerable the continued cohabitation of the spouses.

The parties assert that they are husband and wife but neither remembers much about the facts surrounding their marriage. The respondent says that "it's all basically a blank" to her. She believes, however, that the period of courtship for the couple was brief. The petitioner testified that all that he could remember is that he was alone for quite a while. One day he went into a deep sleep and when he woke up, "there she was". He swears that since that day his ribs have felt "different". It is a first marriage for both parties.

There are two children of the marriage, Cain, son of Adam, and Abel, son of Adam.

The relief asked, in addition to a decree of divorce, is custody of the children and costs.

The parties are presently living with their children next to the Euphrates River, just outside of the Garden of Eden. They resided previously in the Garden in a jointly owned matrimonial home until a recent misfortune befell them.

The petitioner testified that for many years he had been engaged in tilling the soil in the Garden of Eden. He would also dabble in landscaping. The respondent, on the other hand, spent her time doing the household chores of cooking, cleaning and child rearing. Both parties agreed that the marriage was a happy one, as far as marriages go, until the day a certain talking serpent moved into the neighborhood. Until then, there was little friction between the spouses, although as the petitioner puts it, "it was never Paradise".

The petitioner claims that once the serpent came along, the

---

* Reprinted from *Gazette of the Law Society of Upper Canada*, 1976, by permission of the *Gazette* and Marcel Strigberger.

respondent spent most of her hours gossiping with the reptile and neglecting household chores. Matters deteriorated more when the respondent started inviting the serpent frequently into the matrimonial home. The petitioner says that he would be lying in the garden, relaxing after a hard day's work when suddenly he'd be startled by a sudden hissing. He says that a serpent would frighten his family except for his son, Cain, who often had to be restrained from stoning it.

The petitioner further gave evidence that the serpent would put all sorts of crazy ideas into his wife's head and that she in turn would nag him to go along with these ideas. For many weeks, for example, the serpent suggested to the respondent that she eat the fruit of the Tree of Knowledge, assuring her that if she would do so, she would surely not die. Initially, she told the serpent that the fruit was taboo. In due course, she succumbed to the serpent's entreaty and ventured to taste a fruit. When she saw that she neither died nor became sick, she strongly urged the petitioner to try it. He adamantly refused. She then tried to trick him by sneaking some of the fruit into her baking. Fortunately, the petitioner was able to sense the difference between the forbidden fruit and his wife's usual preserves and he readily shoved the dish aside. One day, his wife told him that she would stop cooking for him altogether and that she would withhold all other matrimonial amenities unless he would try a piece of her forbidden fruit pie. The petitioner considered his dilemma and had a chat with the serpent. Upon representations by the serpent that by eating the fruit, he would not only not suffer any detriment, but on the contrary, he would increase his knowledge, he took a bite of the fruit.

The results were immediately disastrous. A great sense of embarrassment suddenly came over him causing him to hide in the bushes for several days. To make matters worse, he and his family were evicted from the Garden of Eden on short notice. As the petitioner puts it, he barely had time to get out with his fig leaf on.

He also attributes to that gourmet venture a subsequent adverse change of luck in his farming results, swearing that the farm just wasn't what it used to be. Furthermore, he has suffered additional aggravation and expense in trying to bring the talking serpent to justice. The petitioner has recently commenced an action against the serpent claiming damages for negligent misrepresentation. The action has not proceeded too far, however, as the serpent is apparently evading service.

The question to be decided now is: Has the respondent by her conduct treated the petitioner with such cruelty as to render continued habitation intolerable?

The respondent takes the position that the petitioner is oversensitive. She says that she was not aware of the consequences of eating from the Tree of Knowledge and blames the entire episode on the serpent. In her words, "the serpent beguiled me and I did eat". While it is true that the serpent was most influential in getting the respondent to eat the fruit, it is hard to believe that her ignorance of the consequences of eating from the Tree of Knowledge is as she pretends it to be. On the Tree was posted a large sign which read:

WARNING—DO NOT TAKE OR EAT THIS FRUIT OR YOU WILL BE STRICKEN.

I do not accept the evidence of the respondent that she only glanced at the sign once and felt that it read:

IF YOU SUPPORT THE FRUIT-PICKERS' STRIKE, DO NOT EAT THIS FRUIT.

Can the respondent plead as a defence to allegations of cruelty that the petitioner is over-sensitive? It is trite law that to support a petition for divorce based on cruelty, the conduct complained of must be grave and weighty, not conduct which is merely trivial or which can be characterised as tit for tat irritation, or little more than a manifestation of incompatibility of temperament. Using these clear guidelines, the test of cruelty is to be applied subjectively, the question being, whether *this* conduct by *this* woman to *this* man is cruelty.

The respondent further adds that the conduct complained of has caused the petitioner neither injury nor reasonable apprehension thereof. This argument is certainly not supported by the evidence. To this day the petitioner has a terrifying phobia of fruits. Before he bites into an apple he has one of the animals taste it while he closes his eyes and holds his ears.

In any event, injury to health or reasonable apprehension thereof is no longer a requirement to sustain a petition for divorce based upon cruelty.

The respondent then claims that the petitioner is guilty of condonation in that after their separation, the parties got together and the petitioner knew the respondent. The petitioner admits a brief resumption of co-habitation but stresses that the parties had reconciliation as its primary purpose and that accordingly the knowing fell short of condonation.

The law indeed recognizes a difference between "knowing for the purpose of reconciliation" and "mere knowing". The difference lies in the *animus*. This was a clear case of "knowing for the purpose". In any event I am of the opinion that even if there was condonation, the public interest would be best served if a decree of divorce were granted.

Let us now turn to the issue of custody of the two children of the marriage.

The older one, Cain, is 110 years old. His younger brother, Abel, is 102. Cain wants to be a tiller of the soil when he grows up. Abel has not yet made up his mind, but for the time being he keeps sheep.

The paramount consideration in determining the issue of custody is, of course, the welfare and happiness of the children. Examining the conduct of the parents, the petitioner is a tiller of the soil and he advises that he is in a position to keep a watchful eye over the boys at all times. He says that he wants to give the boys the childhood he never had. The respondent, however, has expressed her interest to travel extensively from Assyria to the Land of Goshen to deliver lectures about some new gourmet ideas she has been developing. This would certainly involve much travelling and would no doubt interfere with the education of the children.

The respondent argues that the court should follow the usual rule of thumb in granting her custody at least of Abel, who is of tender years. The petitioner, on the other hand, argues that the court must follow another rule of thumb, namely that siblings should be kept together. The boys do appear fond of one another and play together most of the time, teaching one another skills and games. Big brother Cain advises that he hopes to take little Abel to the field shortly and teach him self-defence.

The respondent argues alternatively that if the boys are to stay together, then rather than go to the petitioner, they be taken to an altar and both cut in half, with a one-half undivided share of each going to each spouse. When asked for authority for this proposition, she referred to a decision of my brother, Solomon, L. J. S. C. (as he then will be). When asked for the citation of this case, the respondent was unable to provide the court with chapter and verse, but added "so help me, it's true".

The other members of the family are not too eager about this suggestion. Cain says that he wants both to be with his brother and his father, but yet he does not want his mother to be deprived of Abel, and accordingly he suggests that Abel be cut in two and apportioned accordingly. The court will continue its long standing practice of attaching limited weight to the wishes of the children.

Custody of the children of the marriage will be granted to the petitioner with reasonable access by the respondent.

As the wife was not successful in this action, I am following another rule of thumb and am making no order as to costs.

Judgment accordingly.

All's love, yet all's law. —*Robert Browning*

Take a Letter
Attentively she sits beside him,
Writes his words in arc and hook—
Filling with her hieroglyphics
Pages of her shorthand book.

Lucky that her boss can't read them,
Lucky that he cannot tell
That she punctuates her markings
With the scrawl for ⊤＼ ℭ .

—*Anonymous*

It's no accident that all the people one truly
despises are called "in-laws." —*folk proverb*

"'And last but not least...'"

DEATH AT LAW

Ambrose Bierce
A HASTY SETTLEMENT*

"YOUR HONOR," said an Attorney, rising, "what is the present status of this case—as far as it has gone?"

"I have given a judgment for the residuary legatee under the will," said the Court, "put the costs upon the contestants, decided all questions relating to fees and other charges; and, in short, the estate in litigation has been settled, with all controversies, disputes, misunderstandings and differences of opinion thereunto appertaining."

"Ah, yes, I see," said the Attorney, thoughtfully, "we are making progress—we are getting on famously."

"Progress?" echoed the Judge—"progress? Why, sir, the matter is concluded!"

"Exactly, exactly; it had to be concluded in order to give relevancy to the motion that I am about to make. Your Honor, I move that the judgment of the Court be set aside and the case reopened."

"Upon what ground, sir?" the Judge asked in surprise.

"Upon the ground," said the Attorney, "that after paying all fees and expenses of litigation and all charges against the estate there will still be something left."

"There may have been an error," said his Honor, thoughtfully—"the Court may have underestimated the value of the estate. The motion is taken under advisement."

---

* Reprinted from Ambrose Bierce, *Fantastic Fables*, 1899.

Anonymous
OBLEWEISS WILL*

I AM WRITING OF MY WILL MINESELLUF. That dam lawyer want he should have too much money; he ask too many answers about family. first thing i want i dont want my brother Oscar get a dam ting wat i got. he is a mumser he done me out of forty dollars fourteen years since.

I want that Hilda my sister she gets the north sixtie akers where i am homing it now. i bet she dont get that loafer husband of hers to broke twenty akers next plowing time. gonoph work. she cant have it if she lets Oscar live on it. i want i should have it back if she does.

tell momma that six hundred dollars she been looking for for twenty years is berried from the backhouse behind about ten feet down. she better let little Frederick do the diggin and count it when he comes up.

pastor Lucknitz can have three hundred dollars if he kiss de book he dont preach no more dumhead talks about poloticks. he should a roof put on de medinghouse and the elders should the bills look at.

momma the rest should get but i want it that Adolph should tell her what not she should do so no more slick irishers sell her vokum cleaners. dey noise like hell and a broom dont cost so much.

i want it that mine brother Adolph should be my execter and i want it that the jedge should pleese make Adolph plenty bond put up and watch him like hell. Adolphus is a good business man but only a dumkopf would trust him with a busted pfenning.

i want it dam sure that schliemical Oscar dont nothing get. tell Adolph he can have a hundred dollars if he prove to jedge Oscar dont get nothing. dat dam sure fix Oscar.

Herman Obleweiss.

---

* This classic piece has appeared in myriad forms.

"Sorry to have kept you waiting about your will, Mr. Gilson.
Mr. Gilson?"

Cartoon by Cotham. Reprinted from *ABA Journal*, 1981.

Lord Neaves
THE JOLLY TESTATOR WHO
MAKES HIS OWN WILL*

Ye lawyers who live upon litigants' fees,
And who need a good many to live at your ease,
Grave or gay, wise or witty, whate'er your degree,
Plain stuff or Queen's Counsel, take counsel of me:
When a festive occasion your spirit unbends,
You should never forget the profession's best friends;
So we'll send round the wine, and a light bumper fill
To the jolly testator who makes his own Will.

He premises his wish and his purpose to save
All dispute among friends when he's laid in the grave;
Then he straightway proceeds more disputes to create
Than a long summer's day would give time to relate.
He writes and erases, he blunders and blots,
He produces such puzzles and Gordian knots,

* Reprinted from Lord Neaves, *Songs and Verses: Social & Scientific*, Blackwood &
Sons, 1869.

That a lawyer, intending to frame the thing ill,
Couldn't match the testator who makes his own Will.

Testators are good, but a feeling more tender
Springs up when I think of the feminine gender!
The testatrix for me, who, like Telemaque's mother,
Unweaves at one time what she wove at another;
She bequeaths, she repeats, she recalls a donation,
And ends by revoking her own revocation;
Still scribbling or scratching some new codicil,
Oh! success to the woman who makes her own Will.

'Tisn't easy to say, 'mid her varying vapors,
What scraps should be deemed testamentary papers.
'Tisn't easy from these her intention to find,
When perhaps she herself never knew her own mind.
Every step that we take, there arises fresh trouble:
Is the legacy lapsed? Is it single or double?
No customer brings so much grist to the mill
As the wealthy old woman who makes her own Will.

The law decides questions of meum and tuum,
By kindly consenting to make the thing suum;
The Aesopian fable instructively tells
What becomes of the oysters, and who gets the shells;
The legatees starve, but the lawyers are fed;
The Seniors have riches, the juniors have bread;
The available surplus of course will be nil,
From the worthy testators who make their own Will.

You had better pay toll when you take to the road,
Than attempt by a by-way to reach your abode;
You had better employ a conveyancer's hand
Than encounter the risk that your Will shouldn't stand.
From the broad beaten track when the traveler strays,
He may land in a bog or be lost in a maze;
And the law, when defied, will avenge itself still
On the man and the woman who make their own Will.

A. A. *Milne*
THE SOLICITOR*

THE OFFICE was at its busiest, for it was Friday afternoon. John Blunt leant back in his comfortable chair and toyed with the key of the safe, while he tried to realise his new position. He, John Blunt, was junior partner in the great London firm of Macnaughton, Macnaughton, Macnaughton, Macnaughton & Macnaughton.

He closed his eyes, and his thoughts wandered back to the day when he had first entered the doors of the firm as one of two hundred and seventy-eight applicants for the post of office-boy. They had been interviewed in batches, and old Mr. Sanderson, the senior partner, had taken the first batch.

"I like your face, my boy," he had said heartily to John.

"And I like yours," replied John, not to be outdone in politeness.

"Now I wonder if you can spell 'mortgage'?"

"One 'm,'" said John tentatively.

Mr. Sanderson was delighted with the lad's knowledge, and engaged him at once.

For three years John had done his duty faithfully. During this time he had saved the firm more than once by his readiness—particularly on one occasion, when he had called old Mr. Sanderson's attention to the fact that he had signed a letter to a firm of stockbrokers, "Your loving husband, Macnaughton, Macnaughton, Macnaughton, Macnaughton & Macnaughton." Mr. Sanderson, always a little absent-minded, corrected the error, and promised the boy his articles. Five years later John Blunt was a solicitor.

And now he was actually junior partner in the firm—the firm of which it was said in the City, "If a man has Macnaughton, Macnaughton, Macnaughton, Macnaughton & Macnaughton behind him he is all right." The City is always coining pithy little epigrams like this.

---

* Reprinted from A. A. Milne, *Happy Days*, 1915, by permission of Curtis Brown & John Farquharson.

There was a knock at the door of the enquiry office and a prosperous-looking gentleman came in.

"Can I see Mr. Macnaughton?" he said politely to the office-boy.

"There isn't no Mr. Macnaughton," replied the latter. "They all died years ago."

"Well, well, can I see one of the partners?"

"You can't see Mr. Sanderson, because he's having his lunch," said the boy. "Mr. Thorpe hasn't come back from lunch yet, Mr. Peters has just gone out to lunch, Mr. Williams is expected back from lunch every minute, Mr. Gourlay went out to lunch an hour ago, Mr. Beamish—"

"Tut, tut, isn't anybody in?"

"Mr. Blunt is in," said the boy, and took up the telephone. "If you wait a moment I'll see if he's awake."

Half an hour later Mr. Masters was shown into John Blunt's room.

"I'm sorry I was engaged," said John. "A most important client. Now what can I do for you, Mr.—er—Masters?"

"I wish to make my will."

"By all means," said John cordially.

"I have only one child, to whom I intend to leave all my money."

"Ha!" said John, with a frown. "This will be a lengthy and difficult business."

"But you can do it?" asked Mr. Masters anxiously. "They told me at the hairdresser's that Macnaughton, Macnaughton, Macnaughton, Macnaughton & Macnaughton was the cleverest firm in London."

"We can do it," said John simply, "But it will require all our care; and I think it would be best if I were to come and stay with you for the weekend. We could go into it properly then."

"Thank you," said Mr. Masters, clasping the other's hand. "I was just going to suggest it. My motor-car is outside. Let us go at once."

"I will follow you in a moment," said John, and, pausing only to snatch a handful of money from the safe for incidental expenses and to tell the boy that he would be back on Monday, he picked up the well-filled week-end bag which he always kept ready, and hurried after the other.

Inside the car Mr. Masters was confidential.

"My daughter," he said, "comes of age to-morrow."

"Oh, it's a daughter?" said John in surprise. "Is she pretty?"

"She is considered to be the prettiest girl in the county."

"Really?" said John. He thought a moment, and added, "Can we stop at a post-office? I must send an important business telegram." He took out a form and wrote "Macmacmacmacmac, London. Shall not be back till Wednesday. Blunt."

The car stopped and then sped on again.

"Amy has never been any trouble to me," said Mr. Masters, "But I am getting old now, and I would give a thousand pounds to see her happily married."

"To whom would you give it?" asked John, whipping out his pocket-book.

"Tut, tut, a mere figure of speech. But I would settle a hundred thousand pounds on her on the wedding-day."

"Then, after you tell them I've cut them all out of my will,
I want you to give a sort of mean, nasty cackle."

Reprinted by permission of *Punch*.

"Indeed?" said John thoughtfully. "Can we stop at another post-office?" he added, bringing out his fountain-pen again.He took out a second telegraph form and wrote:

"Macmacmacmacmac, London. Shall not be back till Friday. Blunt."

The car dashed on again, and an hour later arrived at a commodious mansion standing in its own well-timbered grounds of upwards of several acres. At the front door a graceful figure was standing.

"My solicitor, dear, Mr. Blunt," said Mr. Masters.

"It is very good of you to come all this way on my father's business," she said shyly.

"Not at all," said John. "A week or—or a fortnight—or—" he looked at her again—"or—three weeks, and the thing is done."

"Is making a will so very difficult?"

"It's a very tricky and complicated affair indeed. However, I think we shall pull it off. Er—might I send an important business telegram?"

"Macmacmacmacmac, London," wrote John. "Very knotty case. Date of return uncertain. Please send more cash for incidental expenses. Blunt."

*   *   *   *   *   *

Yes, you have guessed what happened. It is an every-day experience in a solicitor's life. John Blunt and Amy Masters were married at St. George's, Hanover Square, last May. The wedding was a quiet one owing to mourning in the bride's family—the result of a too sudden perusal of Macnaughton, Macnaughton, Macnaughton, Macnaughton & Macnaughton's bill of costs. As Mr. Masters said with his expiring breath: he didn't mind paying for our Mr. Blunt's skill; nor yet for our Mr. Blunt's valuable time—even if most of it was spent in courting Amy; nor, again, for our Mr. Blunt's tips to servants; but he did object to being charged the first-class railway fare both ways when our Mr. Blunt had come down and gone up again in the car. And perhaps I ought to add that that is the drawback to this fine profession. One is so often misunderstood.

Axiphiles
PERPETUITIES*

The law of perpetuities
Is strewn with technicalities.
Its crotchets and circuities
Exhaust the best mentalities.

It involutes inanities,
The meshes which immure it, tease
The lips to pour profanities
Upon its dark obscurities.

Its maddening profundities
Wake murderous propensities.
However sage the pundit, he's
Befuddled by its densities.

Congeries of quiddities
That tax the ingenuities—
Such are those aridities,
The rules of perpetuities.

---

* Reprinted from *Docket*, Spring 1932, by permission of West Publishing Co.

A. *Laurence Polak*
LIVES IN BEING*

INTERESTING LEGAL SPECULATIONS are aroused by a message from Hollywood, California, to the Associated Press. Lloyd's of London, it is reported, have insured the life of Rhubarb, "an orange-coloured alley-cat who will play in a new film." The message adds that "Lloyd's were insistent on the attachment, to the policy, of Rhubarb's paw-prints, front and side photographs and a sound-track of his voice."

If this kind of thing becomes general, we may expect interesting litigation and some far-reaching decisions from the courts. Such a practice will undoubtedly revolutionize the form and wording of the type of life-policy in ordinary use.

Meagre as are the details disclosed, they enable certain inferences to be drawn. Acute observers will remark particularly the concluding part of the message. What, they will ask, is the significance of annexing to the policy a recording of the voice of the assured?

At first sight this would seem to afford a reasonably certain means of identifying one particular individual in a species, several million members of which must, to the superficial human eye, closely resemble one another. The paw-prints and the photographs, it will be said, will furnish only corroborative evidence; but the vocal chords of different cats (as all light sleepers in urban areas know) are capable of producing tones of the most strikingly dissonant quality. Based upon scales of a chromatic rather than diatonic type, and exhibiting an unconventionality in the choice of musical intervals and modulations which leaves even the late Dr. Schoenberg far behind, the *leitmotif* of every cat has its own distinguishing characteristics. Identification of the individual would thus be facilitated by a careful classification of the sibilant hisses, the oboe-like wails, the plaintive cries (resembling those produced by excessive maltreatment of the E-string of the violin) and the percus-

---

* Reprinted from A. Laurence Polak, *Puffs, Balloons, and Smokeballs,* Justice of the Peace, 1952, by permission of the author.

sive expletives of the feline gamut, in all its manifold permutations and combinations.

So far, so good; but this facile explanation gives rise to obvious objections. The indications are that Rhubarb has taken out not an endowment policy but a whole-life assurance: the policy-moneys will thus become payable only on the termination of the life assured. In that case, the lawyer will argue, of what evidentiary value can the sound-track possibly be at the time when identification is most necessary—*viz.,* when the policy matures? Even the most voluble of cats is silent at the last, when death has laid its hand upon him.

Now, one of the rules relating to the construction of documents is that legal effect must, if possible, be given to every expression used. The *prima facie* presumption is that every word has its own particular significance; it is not to be lightly assumed that any expression has been inserted without meaning. Closer consideration, in this light, of the clause in question will indicate that the draftsman of the policy has exercised remarkable thought and ingenuity in formulating its terms. The sound-track proviso is not mere surplusage; the draftsman has kept in mind the proverbial cat's ninefold vitality, and has deliberately and expressly provided for all the implications.

This explanation, and this alone, renders the clause relating to aural identification intelligible and, indeed, imperative. Only thus can the original, the real Rhubarb, the cat-in-itself (may we venture to coin a phrase and say the *felis de se?*) be traced recognizably through three times three incarnations, when the elegant paws begin to fumble, the sleek fur grows grey and patchy, and the bristling whiskers curl and droop.

But ingenuity in legal matters may be overdone, and the draftsman may find himself caught in his own toils. If litigation should ensue, how are the courts likely to interpret this kind of policy? It is with extreme reluctance that we feel it our duty to remind Lloyd's legal advisers of the probable repercussions of *Thellusson* v. *Woodford* (1798) 4 Ves. 237, and the provisions of the Accumulations Act, 1800, re-enacted by s. 164 of the Law of Property Act, 1925.

Without attempting to discuss exhaustively a problem which may one day have to be resolved by the House of Lords, we venture to suggest the arguability of the thesis that this is a policy of assurance on lives rather than a life; that the postponement of the vesting date to the termination of the last of nine vital periods amounts to an accumulation for a term or terms in excess of the alternatives permitted by statute, and that this may render the entire policy void. To point to the well-recognized practice of joint life assurance is no answer to our contention. The essence of the latter arrangement is that the joint lives are both (or all) in being when the policy is taken out; but no person who has an intimate knowledge of the subject could seriously suggest that any normal cat lives all its nine lives concurrently. As regards the basic biological question itself, although there appears to be no reported case where judicial recognition has been given to the special peculiarities of feline mortality-tables, equity is familiar with the principle of "springing uses" which may, by analogy, be appropriately applied to creatures of such lithe and lively nature as those we are discussing.

In the face of a legal defect so fundamental other considerations are of slighter importance. Brief reference may, however, be usefully made to one matter, lest it may have escaped the attention of the contracting parties. We think we may, without risk of defamation proceedings, describe as promiscuous the sexual proclivities of the species to which Rhubarb belongs. Since life assurance is a contract *uberrimae fidei*, it is to be presumed that these propensities were brought to the notice of the insurers in the proposal form. Even though this duty was performed, we feel it right to warn the assured and his legal advisers that, in the event of subsequent dispute, difficulty may arise in distinguishing, among a numerous progeny, the lawful next-of-kin to whom, on an intestacy, the policy-moneys would belong, assuming always that the validity of the contract were established. We have not lost sight of the fact that the claim, on final maturity, would be made in the first instance by Rhubarb's legal personal representatives, but in the event of his death intestate it would be regrettable to find the whole arrangement void for ambiguity, or to be confronted with the insurers' plea that the fund has failed to vest during the period prescribed by the Rule against Perpetuities.

INDEX

A LEGAL HUMOR BOOK LIST

Gilbert Abbot à Becket, *The Comic Blackstone of Punch*, Detroit: Collector Publishing Co., 1897.

Gerald Abrahams, *Lunatics and Lawyers*, London: Home and Val Thal, 1951.

Sir Carleton Kemp Allen, *Law & Disorders: Legal Indiscretions*, London: Stevens & Sons, 1954.

Paul Arnold, ed., *Off the Record*, Baltimore: Legal Chatter Pubs., 1939; *For Lawyers Only*, 1939.

Thurman Arnold, *Selections from the Letters and Legal Papers*, Arnold, Fortas & Porter, 1961.

Joseph G. Baldwin, *Flush Times of Alabama and Mississippi*, NY: Appleton, 1856.

Robert Bird, *More Law Lyrics*, Edinburgh: Wm. Blackwood & Sons, 1898.

Irving Browne, ed., *Law and Lawyers in Literature*, Boston: Soule and Bugbee, 1883.

J.P.C., *Poetic Justice*, London: Stevens & Sons, 1947.

James M. Cain, *Our Government*, NY: Alfred A. Knopf, 1930.

Honoré Daumier, *Men of Justice*, 1845; *Lawyers and Litigants*, 1851; *Physiognomies of the Law Court*, 1852.

Finley Peter Dunne, *Mr. Dooley on the Choices of Law*, ed. Edward J. Bander, Charlottesville: The Michie Co., 1963.

John Marshall Gest, *The Lawyer in Literature*, Boston Book Co., 1913.

A. P. Herbert, *Uncommon Law: Being 66 Misleading Cases*, London: Methuen & Co., 1935.

Stanley Jackson, *Laughter at Law*, London: Arthur Barker Ltd, 1961.

Arnold B. Kanter, *The Secret Memoranda of Stanley J. Fairweather*, Chicago: The Swallow Press, 1981.

Geoffrey Lincoln, *No Moaning of the Bar*, London: Geoffrey Blés, 1957.

Peter V. MacDonald, Q.C., ed., *Court Jesters: Canada's Lawyers and Judges Take the Stand to Relate Their Funniest Stories*, Methuen, 1985.

Theobald O. Mathew, *Forensic Fables*, London: Butterworth & Co., 1926. Also, *Further Forensic Fables*, 1928, and *Final Forensic Fables*, 1929.

John G. May, Jr., ed., *The Lighter Side of the Law*, Charlottesville: The Michie Co, 1956.

George A. Morton and D. Macleod Mallock, *Law and Laughter*, Boston: Le Roy Phillips; London: T. N. Foulis, 1913.

Justice Michael A. Musmanno, *Verdict! The Adventures of the Young Lawyer in the Brown Suit*, NY: Doubleday, 1958.

Judge Edward Abbott Parry, *What the Judge Thought*, 1923.

A. Laurence Polak, *Legal Fictions: A Series of Cases from the Classics*, London: Stevens & Sons, 1945; *More Legal Fictions: A Series of Cases from Shakespeare*, 1946; *Final Legal Fictions: A Series of Cases from Folk-Lore and Opera*, 1948; and *Puffs, Balloons and Smokeballs*, Sussex: Justice of the Peace, 1952.

William L. Prosser, ed., *The Judicial Humorist: A Collection of Judicial Opinions and Other Frivolities*, Boston: Little, Brown, 1952.

Daniel Webster, *Wit and Humor of the American Bar*.